Urban Governance and Democracy

The issue of local governance is currently high on the institutional agenda of many local and regional authorities throughout the OECD countries. This book explores the relationship between two key issues for urban governance – leadership and community involvement – and how making these two elements more complementary to each other can lead to more effective as well as legitimate policy outcomes.

The authors collected here examine the dilemmas involved in ensuring effective governance, focussing on issues such as legitimacy, citizen participation, economic performance and social inclusion. There are chapters on the key themes, offering an overall conceptual model and providing a framework for the main arguments presented here. This model is then developed through detailed discussion of key elements such as multi-level and multi-actor governance, leadership and community involvement.

This book will be of interest to academics and practitioners concerned with questions of local governance and local democracy, in the fields of political science and urban studies and regional planning.

Michael Haus is an Assistant Professor at the Institute for Political Science at Darmstadt University of Technology, Germany. **Hubert Heinelt** is Professor of Public Administration/Public Policy and Urban Studies at the Institute for Political Science at Darmstadt University of Technology, Germany. **Murray Stewart** is Reader at the University of the West of England, UK.

Routledge studies in governance and public policy

Urban Governance and Democracy

Leadership and community involvement

Edited by Michael Haus, Hubert Heinelt and Murray Stewart

Routledge
Taylor & Francis Group

LONDON AND NEW YORK

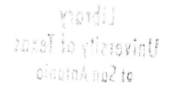

First published 2005
by Routledge
2 Park Square, Milton Park, Abingdon, Oxon OX14 4RN

Simultaneously published in the USA and Canada
by Routledge
270 Madison Ave, New York, NY 10016

Routledge is an imprint of the Taylor & Francis Group

Typeset in Baskerville by Wearset Ltd, Boldon, Tyne and Wear
Printed and bound in Great Britain by MPG Books Ltd, Bodmin

British Library Cataloguing in Publication Data
A catalogue record for this book is available from the British Library

Library of Congress Cataloging in Publication Data
Urban governance and democracy : leadership and community
involvement / edited by Michael Haus, Hubert Heinelt and Murray
Stewart.
    p. cm.
  Simultaneously published in the USA and Canada.
  Includes bibliographical references and index.
    1. Municipal government—Citizen participation. 2. Municipal
government—OECD countries. 3. Community leadership—OECD
countries. 4. Community development—OECD countries.
5. Economic development—OECD countries. 6. Public–private
sector cooperation—OECD countries. 7. Cities and towns—OECD
countries. 8. Democracy—OECD countries. I. Haus, Michael. II.
Heinelt, Hubert. III. Stewart, Murray.
  JS211.U72 2004
  352.16—dc22
                                                        2004004798

ISBN 0-415-34361-5

Contents

Contributors

Alessandro Balducci Professor for Urban Management, Head of the Department for Architecture and Planning, Politecnico di Milano.

Henry Bäck Professor at the School of Public Administration, Göteborg University.

Laurence Carmichael Research Fellow in the Cities Research Centre at the University of the West of England in Bristol.

Claudio Calvaresi Research Fellow at the Department for Architecture and Planning, Politecnico di Milano.

Bas Denters Professor of Urban Policy and Politics at the School of Business, Public Administration and Technology of the University of Twente in Enschede.

Panagiotis Getimis Professor at the Department for Regional Economy and Development and Head of the Research Institute of Urban Environment and Human Resources at the Panteion University in Athens.

Despoina Grigoriadou Research Fellow at the Research Institute of Urban Environment and Human Resources at the Panteion University in Athens.

Robin Hambleton Dean of the College of Urban Planning and Public Affairs at the University of Illinois at Chicago (UIC). Professor of Public Administration and Professor of Urban Planning and Policy at UIC. Visiting Professor of City Management at the University of the West of England, Bristol.

Michael Haus Assistant Professor at the chair for public administration/public policy and urban studies at the Institute for Political Science, Darmstadt University of Technology.

Hubert Heinelt Professor at the chair for public administration/public policy and urban studies at the Institute for Political Science, Darmstadt University of Technology.

Jan Erling Klausen Researcher at the Norwegian Institute for Urban and Regional Research (NIBR) in Oslo.

Pieter-Jan Klok Assistant Professor for Policy Analysis at the School of Business, Public Administration and Technology of the University of Twente in Enschede.

Murray Stewart Visiting Professor at the Cities Research Centre, University of the West of England, Bristol.

David Sweeting Research Fellow in the Cities Research Centre at the University of the West of England in Bristol.

Pawel Swianiewicz Professor at the faculty of Geography and Regional Studies, Warsaw University.

Acknowledgements

The editors of this book are indebted to a large number of people who made the research on which it is based possible. They include, of course, the authors of the individual chapters. Less visibly, Oliver Wolf (Darmstadt University of Technology) brought the text delivered by the authors into a form acceptable to our publisher, and Jo Howard, Laurence Carmichael and David Sweeting (University of the West of England) toiled over the language editing. We would also like to thank Annick Magnier, Vivien Lowndes and Michael Goldsmith who gave extremely helpful comments on earlier drafts of the contributions. Finally, we acknowledge the key role of the Research Directorate of the European Commission in funding the research under the 5th Framework Programme on Research and Development as well as the support by the cities involved in this project as partners: Bristol and Stoke-on-Trent in the UK, Bergen and Oslo in Norway, Stockholm and Göteborg in Sweden, Enschede and Roermond in the Netherlands, Hannover and Heidelberg in Germany, Poznan and Ostrów Wielkopolski in Poland, Cinisello Balsamo and Turin in Italy, Athens and Volos in Greece, and finally Waitakere and Christchurch in New Zealand. We benefited a lot from the comments and empirical information given by representatives of the cities. Their actual role in promoting the quality of life for citizens by leadership and community involvement will be the subject of further publications resulting from the project. The text, of course, is the responsibility of the editors, not the Commission and the involved cities.

Michael Haus
Hubert Heinelt
Murray Stewart

1   Introduction

Michael Haus, Hubert Heinelt and Murray Stewart

This book is based on the theoretical and conceptual considerations underlying a research project on 'Participation, Leadership and Urban Sustainability' (PLUS) funded by the EU 5th Framework Programme of Research and Development. The research was undertaken in nine countries in each of which two cities were taken as case studies. In each country a research team led the work; in each city the council was a partner in the research; also participating as representative bodies of groups of cities were EUROCITIES and Quartiers en Crise.[1]

The central idea of this cross-national research project was that whilst much has been written about leadership, and much has been written about community involvement, there has been little work that has attempted to link the two and establish the extent to which effective leadership can be enhanced by community involvement and empowering community involvement can be supported by leadership. The main aim of this book, therefore, is to argue for putting both urban leadership and community involvement at the centre of research on the conditions of good urban governance, and to make plausible the assumption that complementarity between both aspects is a crucial question. For the research team, this involved an attempt to document the state of research carried out so far on these subjects, to identify research desiderata, to formulate plausible hypotheses on possible 'complementarities of urban leadership and community involvement' (CULCI), to re-interpret key notions and theories of urban research in the light of the CULCI question, to link theoretical, conceptual and comparative perspectives and to reflect on the practical relevance of the discussed.

The research as a whole addressed both theoretical and applied questions. Its empirical focus was upon innovative forms of policy making targeted at fostering social inclusion and securing economic competitiveness in European cities. The main empirical findings of the project (with examples of good and bad CULCI), together with its implications for policy and practice, are documented in a report to the European Commission and in a second book. This book addresses primarily the conceptual problems which confront researchers and policy makers alike in understanding and responding to the twin issues of leadership and community involvement.

Following this introduction, there are two theoretical chapters. Michael Haus and Hubert Heinelt (Chapter 2) provide the frame of reference for the book. The chapter is divided into two parts. In the first part, general evidence is presented which supports the thesis that urban leadership and community involvement can be complementary with respect to different dimensions of legitimation. This is done by situating the CULCI argument within the context of current debates on government failures, the shift from 'government to governance' and the respective reform policies. The challenges – perhaps disadvantages – of governance, or at least the risks of 'governance failure' are highlighted, but also are the potential positive effects of a synergy between political leadership and community involvement. Such synergy may help to alleviate government, as well as governance, failure (not to forget market failure). In the second part of the chapter, the basic definitions and meanings of urban leadership and community involvement are discussed, taking into account the specific function and possible performance of each. The proposed understandings are argued to be sufficiently specific to be of relevance to the real world of urban governance but also of sufficient generality to allow for their application to different urban settings.

In the second theoretical chapter, Bas Deters and Pieter-Jan Klok discuss the possibilities of combining the specific project-related concepts developed in Chapter 2 with the Institutional Analysis and Development (IAD) concept of Ostrom *et al.* (1990). The advantage of the IAD concept, explained in the first part of the chapter, is that it offers a clear and distinctive set of rules which provide the framework within which it is possible to pursue empirical analysis. The framework points to the boundaries within which involvement or participation are undertaken, the formal positions from which actors may take decisions, and the information to be collected and distributed. Such rules are important because they determine the nature of leadership and community involvement as well as the linkages between them. How to apply this concept and in which way it can be helpful to identify forms of CULCI is demonstrated in an empirical case at the end of the chapter.

The background presented in Chapters 2 and 3 allows the development of a framework for answering the key questions of the research and of the book – *on which factors does the complementarity between urban leadership and community involvement depend?* These various factors are discussed in more detail in subsequent chapters of the book. Furthermore, these relevant factors are embedded in a common concept.

As shown in Figure 1.1, the actions of urban leaders, citizens, representatives, politicians and others can be regarded as the main *dependent variable* on the one hand (why do certain patterns of interactions occur?), and as an important *independent variable* on the other hand (what are the

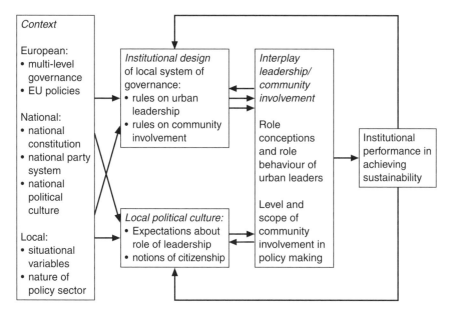

Figure 1.1 Relationship between the variables.

effects of these interactions on the policy outcomes?). The general methodological approach is that of 'actor centred institutionalism' (Mayntz and Scharpf 1995; Scharpf 1997; Scharpf 2000). This means that actions may be explained by the opportunities and constraints as well as the incentives and motivations caused by the *institutional settings* within which actors operate. By these institutions we mean the 'rules of the game' related to specific policy processes within the cities. The *personal attitudes and behaviour* of actors and the expectations raised by the cultural settings within which actors operate are only relevant when the institutional settings or rules of the game alone do not sufficiently explain behaviour. In order to explain the processes and outcomes at work in particular cities it is also important to set the analysis of variables within their specific *context*.

In order to identify the institutional *rules of the game* the IAD framework seems appropriate. The different types of rules characterising a set of policy arenas can be described in a way that makes them applicable to various urban settings. The IAD model distinguishes between the different components of an 'action arena' or 'action situation', the attributes of the participating actors, and the rules in use and characteristics of the social context which structure the action arena. It also leads to a distinction between different levels of policy choices (see Kiser and Ostrom 1982). Collective decisions made at arenas at a constitutional level (parliaments or councils for example), pre-structure decision making at the operational level (the level of action over particular initiatives where actors working individually or in groups have some say in determining outcomes).

In terms of *context* – in the sense of external, exogenous factors – global, European, national and local factors all influence the variables on which the interplay of urban leadership and community involvement is directly dependent (the institutional design of local governance, local political culture and characteristics and attributes of involved actors). Following approaches to comparative public policy (see, for example, Heidenheimer *et al.* 1990: 7–9) we conceptualise the key factors as follows:

- political-institutional aspects such as the constitutional position of local government, the competences ascribed to it, and the access of local actors to the political process,
- the party political system (nationally and locally) and the number and range of parties present together with their distinctiveness and inter-relationships,
- the national political culture.

These context variables provide an externally determined framework for the government of cities, and have an important influence upon:

- the expectations of citizens regarding the political system and the relative importance of different territorial levels of government,
- dominant assumptions about democracy in general and of local democracy in particular,
- the alternative ways of generating democratic legitimacy (the dimensions of input-, throughput- and output-legitimation discussed in Chapter 2),
- the capacities of different levels of government for efficient and effective policy implementation,
- the acquisition of a specific role for urban leadership, and
- the development of particular forms of community involvement.

Against this background, Henry Bäck (Chapter 4) further explores some aspects of context. He provides an empirically based comparative reflection on the relevance of central–local relations, on the power of local authorities (with regard to finance and function), and on the structure of local government, all with regard to the potential of urban leadership to provide complementarity between urban leadership and community involvement. Chapter 4 concludes with hypotheses about the institutional setting to be found in particular cities which are favourable (or not) for urban leadership and community involvement and a complementarity between these two aspects of urban governance. The conclusion, however, based on the initial empirical material gathered in the PLUS project, is that country-specific aspects are not of uniform importance across all cities, but that city specific effects can be the result of particular factors which are not typical of the country as a whole. (These factors are discussed further in terms of addressing space-specific or space-related aspects.)

Pawel Swianiewicz (Chapter 5) takes these common conceptual considerations further. He reflects on the particular context(s) in transition countries, that is on the specific conditions for achieving complementarity between urban leadership and community involvement under the transition from statism to democracy. His comparative analysis comes to the conclusion that the present setting of local governments in Central Eastern European countries cannot be assigned to the typology more commonly associated with Western Europe, for example, 'Northern' or 'Southern' local governments. Political imperatives, especially the call for decentralisation, seem to have had a stronger effect than considerations of size, effectiveness and democracy as traditionally discussed for Western European countries. Analysis of emergent Central Eastern European local government shows the role of leadership and community involvement in a situation of rapid institutional change and re-design. Whilst it is clear that local governments, like the countries in which they are situated are in a state of transition, it is interesting to note some – although as yet weak – interest in governance and the New Public Management and regime theory seem to be relevant for the situation and developments in these countries.

The Central Eastern Europe chapter reminds us that local and national contexts can be influenced and changed by *international* contextual variables. Such variables can influence both central–local relations (the extent of autonomy offered to cities), and the more specific ways in which individual cities are governed. In Europe this holds especially true for the relationship between the European Union and its institutions (Council, Parliament, Commission) and the member states and their sub-national bodies. Through European integration, 'Europeanisation' occurs. There is a change in actor constellations (or in opportunities) through the creation of a structure of *multi-level governance*. This new governance structure allows sub-national and local actors to be integrated into policy making in new and influential ways at the EU and national level – and also at the local level. Furthermore, EU policies, (especially the inclusion and cohesion policies supported through the structural funds), not only offer new *financial resources* for local programmes, but also influence the institutional structures, processes and routines of *domestic policies* in the member states. However, as the growing literature on Europeanisation[2] highlights, this is only one side of the coin. The other is that there are great differences between EU member states according to what has been called the 'goodness of fit' (Caporaso *et al.* 2001), i.e. the degree of institutional fit of EU policies with domestic ones. Thus within countries there are differences in the features of multi-level governance that allow sub-national and local actors to become more empowered, that permit EU funding to be used effectively to pursue policy objectives, or that bring pressures for reform from EU policies to domestic ones.

European contextual factors are addressed by Laurence Carmichael in her contribution on multi-level governance (Chapter 6). She shows how cities have become an ever more important part of the multi-level system of EU policy making and implementation. This is illustrated both by a growing emphasis on sustainability and its linkage to local empowerment, and by the application of cohesion policy with its application of the principles of partnership and focus on decentralised, area-based, horizontally integrated development strategies. The chapter also makes clear how EU policies have crucial substantive (as regards policy content), procedural and institutional impacts stipulating a required degree of community involvement. Such impacts are significant for the dimensions of input-, throughput- and output-legitimation (see Chapter 2). The relationship between the European and the municipal level, however, is influenced by national and regional levels of governance – each of which plays an important role because they mediate the flow of stimuli from the EU to the community, and in turn the extent to which stimuli from the bottom up have a chance to access the European policy arena.

While national–local systems of government establish the institutional structures across a whole country, state–society relations and especially the 'vibrancy' of civil society can differ between cities. This points to a final key contextual factor which helps to explain the differences both between cities and policies (for example inclusion or competitiveness) within any one country (John and Cole 2000). This factor can be summarised as the nature of 'place', and the influence of place on institutional capacity (Cars *et al.* 2002). It is possible to distinguish between place-specific influences and space-related factor. In terms of the specific influence of place, there are a number of considerations.

First, although national politics has a strong influence on local politics, the latter is in several ways peculiar to individual localities. The strength of different political forces within the municipality, the patterns of power in different municipal bodies, the structure of the local party system, voter turnout, the organisation and influence of local bodies (such as, trade unions or welfare organisations), are all significant. Second, there are the social, economic and environmental realities of any city (unemployment, movement, pollution, ill health) as well as the political capacity, resources and funding to address these realities. Finally, there are aspects of place-specific *political culture* which shape actor attitudes and behaviour. As the growing literature in social capital deriving from Coleman (1991) and Putnam (1993) emphasises concrete networking/relations of actors as well as the creation of trust and shared norms among them are historically determined and socially and culturally embedded in a territorial context. It is in the creation of the 'weak ties' that bind civil society to state institutions that effective community involvement and empowerment may be found (Taylor 2000). And it is through clearer understandings of the ways network governance can co-exist with hierarchy and market that place-specific institutional capacity may be built (Stewart 2002). Against the background of the globalisation of economic processes, the phrase 'glocalisation' (Swyngedouw 1997) puts emphasis on the significance of specific state–society relations and a particular 'vibrancy' or local civil society for societal and political developmental perspectives.

Besides such particular characteristics of political space, place matters also in relation to *place-related events* or *opportunities.* Such 'windows of opportunity' (Kingdon 1984) for complementarities between urban leadership and community involvement can alter political agendas and stimulate new relationships between local actors. Such 'events' cover a broad spectrum – from an event like the EXPO or the Olympic Games to 'affairs' created by an interplay between local and external political decisions. Programmes of the EU – URBAN, or Objective 1 and 2 pro-grammes – combine decisions from above with local interpretation and application. Multi-level (vertical) and multi-organisational (horizontal) capacities need to be combined to design and deliver effective outcomes.

Horizontal integration is the focus for Murray Stewart's contribution (Chapter 7). Looking at the arrangements for multi-actor governance, he unfolds the collaborative agenda in urban policy making by revisiting the literature on the initiation, maintenance and functioning of collaboration between public and private actors. Restated are the arguments about the importance of trust and social capital in overcoming the transaction cost problems in networking to make use of locally generated institutional potential for joint action. Focussing especially on public private partner-ships (and much of the recent UK experience with partnership working) he notes the preconditions, opportunities and problems of partnerships, linking conceptual issues to the more applied policy issues of competitive-ness and inclusion. In accordance with the criteria explicated in Chapter 2, problems of participation, accountability and effectiveness are discussed.

Management of both vertical (multi-level) and horizontal (multi-actor) governance requires strong leadership. Against the background of leader-ship theories, different types as well as styles of urban leaders are discussed by Panos Getimis and Despoina Grigoriadou (Chapter 8). A categorisation of leadership types can be established relating to the institutional settings within which leadership is exercised and which allow (or prevent) feasible leadership action. Leadership styles by contrast can be categorised accord-ing to the actual behaviour of leaders faced by particular situations. The discussion then addresses the question of which leadership types and styles are most likely to contribute to the achievement of a complementar-ity between urban leadership and community involvement. This is done against the background of the theoretical consideration on legitimacy and effectiveness presented in Chapter 2.

This second question is one which is also of interest to Robin Hambleton's contribution (Chapter 9). He concentrates less on the behavioural dimension of leadership and how it can be classified, but puts the emphasis instead on the styles of leadership implied by the current debates on the shift from government to governance and from public administration to the New Public Management. Additionally, he highlights the question of who the local leaders actually are, and how their respective fields of action are related to roles prescribed or determined by the organisational and institutional rules which prevail in different arenas – the political arena, the administrative arena, the public arena.

This last public arena is also explored by Jan Erling Klausen and David Sweeting (Chapter 10). This chapter examines different forms of community involvement and their relation to particular notions of democracy and legitimacy. This is done through examination of three interrelated questions – *who* should participate in policy making and implementation, by what means they can do so (*how*), and for what reasons (*why*). The normative background for answering these questions is presented through use of the dimensions of legitimation dimensions presented in Chapter 2. The 'why' question is given priority, since the authors argue it is only possible to identify the who and how of participation if it is clear what are the purposes to which the participation process is targeted. The limited decision-making power and lack of steering capacity is identified as a feature of traditional representative government which endangers its procedural legitimation via elections. Effective problem solving often requires transcending these limitations, and this is the rationale for establishing arrangements for a more participatory governance. Such arrangements, however, can give rise to fundamental problems over the realisation of access to and equality in the political process. This leads to a reflection on alternatives to territorial representation, thus addressing the 'who' question. In relation to the 'how' question, the authors stress the difference between aggregative forms of democracy, where individual preferences are weighed, and deliberative modes, where public reasoning is practised. The authors examine the implications of this distinction for different phases of the policy-making process – from problem definition and agenda setting, through decision making, to implementation. They argue that deliberative modes of participation should be concentrated on policy initiation and implementation, leaving the core of decision making to territorial representation and related forms of interest mediation embedded in local government and a leadership which is politically accountable.

Historically, in many European cities, community involvement and participation have been most evident in the specific field of town planning. In Chapter 11 Alessandro Balducci and Claudio Calvaresi place the leadership and community involvement debates in a specific context – that of planning theory. They argue that the concept of leadership was not of great interest for planning theorists until the traditional reliance on strongly formalised, legalistic and often bureaucratic systems of authorising development activity faded away. With acknowledgement of the interactive nature of planning processes came a grown interest in the practices of leadership. Citizen participation on the other hand has always been a prominent concept among planners. Active public participation, of course, has often been the vehicle through which social and political movements have mobilised support, but the reduced importance of state-centred models of legitimacy together with renewed interest in effective citizen participation has paved the way for a new openness towards questions of both citizen participation and urban leadership. The authors argue that the contingencies and complexities inherent in contemporary approaches to urban planning highlight the importance of legitimacy in arriving at planning decisions. As a consequence, the presence of a political dimension to planning has altered the conceptions of the role held by urban planners on the one hand and municipal leaders on the other. But paradoxically – as the authors argue, after decades devoted to re-building the legitimacy of planning, the core problem (the dilemma of the relationship between planning and politics) has not been solved. The new paradigms of planning theory seem to propose a reassuring, but at the end contradictory and inadequate, view of planners as leaders.

It is often the case that books which report cross-national, comparative, research disappoint. A selection of chapters, each describing a particular country, are held together by little more than a contents list setting out the countries covered. We have attempted to avoid this trap by presenting a volume which attempts to draw out a common framework for the comparative analysis of leadership and community involvement. It is certainly possible to identify the country of origin of many of the authors of chapters, but the book does not offer pictures of eighteen cities in nine countries. It attempts rather to locate the PLUS research in the conceptual framework, which in practice drove the empirical research which followed. In this sense the book is 'academic' in the best sense – intellectually driven, conceptual in its approach, innovative in its ideas but nevertheless grounded in, although developing, an established literature. We are grateful to the Commission as well as to our publishers for offering the opportunity to generate such a deliverable within the project.

If the book is 'academic' in the best sense, it might also be described as 'academic' in a less praiseworthy way – indulgent, pursuing the predilections of the researchers, irrelevant to policy and practice. 'Where are the findings?' the reader may ask. 'What are the lessons for the better running of our cities?' Our defence is twofold. In the first place, it is essential to locate urban policy analysis within a conceptual framework, and we offer no apologies for presenting as our first outputs a theoretically based product. It is the goal of the research team – and of the European Urban Research Association of which many of the team are members – to provide a rigorous and robust academic analysis of European policies and programmes. Secondly, however, there will be practical findings. In addition to a short project report giving the key messages which the Commission together with our city partners are expecting, and which will receive wide circulation (for example, through the EUROCITIES network), a second volume is already in preparation. This offers some material about the nine countries and eighteen cities of course, but more importantly draws comparative conclusions about CULCI – the complementarity of urban leadership and community involvement leadership – around which the PLUS project was built. Our hope is that whilst this first volume is free-standing and makes worthwhile reading in its own right, together the two volumes will make a significant contribution to an urban policy and practice in which leaders and citizens together forge a better quality of urban life.

Notes

1 The project and thus the group of authors involved in this book cover not only EU member states (the UK, Germany, Italy, the Netherlands, Sweden, Poland and Greece), but also Norway. Furthermore, case studies from New Zealand are included. For more information about the project see the official web page: http://www.plus-eura.org.
2 For an overview of the scholarly discussion about Europeanisation, see Héritier *et al.* 2001, Knill and Lehmkuhl 2000, Kohler-Koch 2000.

References

Caporaso, J. A., Green Cowles, M. and Risse, T. (eds) (2001) *Transforming Europe: Europeanization and Domestic Change*, Ithaca: Cornell University Press.
Cars, G., Healey, P., Madanipour, A. and Magalhães, C. de (2002) *Urban Governance, Institutional Capacity and Social Milieux*, Aldershot: Ashgate.
Coleman, J. D. (1991) 'Social Capital in the Creation of Human Capital', *American Journal of Sociology*, Vol. 94: 94–119.
Heidenheimer, A., Heclo, H. and Adams, C. (1990) *Comparative Public Policy. The Politics of Social Choice in America, Europe and Japan*, New York: St. Martins Press.
Héritier, A., Kerwer, D., Knill, Ch., Lehmkuhl, D., Teutsch, M. and Douillet, A.-C. (2001) *Differential Europe. The European Union Impact on National Policymaking*, Lanham, Boulder, CO, New York and Oxford: Rowman & Littlefield.
John, P. and Cole, A. (2000) 'When do Institutions, Policy Sectors and Cities Matter? Comparing Networks of Local Policy Makers in Britain and France', *Comparative Political Studies*, Vol. 33, No. 2: 248–268.
Kingdon, J. W. (1984) *Agendas, Alternatives, and Public Policies*, Boston, MA and Toronto: Harper Collins.
Kiser, L. L. and Ostrom, E. (1982) 'The Three Worlds of Action. A Metatheoretical Synthesis of Institutional Approaches', in: E. Ostrom (ed.) *Strategies of Political Inquiry*, Beverly Hills: Sage: 179–222.
Knill, Ch. and Lehmkuhl, D. (2000) 'Mechanismen der Europäisierung. Nationale Regulierungsmuster und Europäische Integration', *Swiss Political Science Review*, Vol. 6, No. 4: 19–50.

Kohler-Koch, B. (2000) 'Europäisierung. Plädoyer für eine Horizonterweiterung', in: M. Knodt and B. Kohler-Koch (eds) *Deutschland zwischen Europäisierung und Selbstbehauptung*, Frankfurt am Main: Campus: 11–31.

Mayntz, R. and Scharpf, F. W. (1995) 'Der Ansatz des akteurzentrierten Institutionalismus', in: R. Mayntz and F. W. Scharpf (eds) *Gesellschaftliche Selbstregelung und politische Steuerung*, Frankfurt am Main and New York: Campus: 39–72.

Ostrom, E., Gardner, R. and Walker, J. (1994) *Rules, Games and Common-pool Resources*, Ann Arbor, MI: University of Michigan Press.

Putnam, R. D. (1993) *Making Democracy Work*, Princeton, NJ: Princeton University Press.

Scharpf, F. W. (1997) *Games Real Actors Play. Actor-Centered Institutionalism in Policy Research*, Boulder, CO: Westview Press.

—— (2000) 'Institutions in Comparative Policy Research', *Comparative Political Studies*, Vol. 33, Nos. 6–7: 762–790.

Stewart, M. (2002) 'Compliance or Collaboration in Urban Governance', in: G. Cars, P. Healey, A. Madanipour and C. de Magalhaes (eds) (2002) *Urban Governance, Institutional Capacity and Social Milieux*, Aldershot: Ashgate.

Swyngedouw, E. (1997) 'Neither Global nor Local. "Glocalisation" and the Politics of Scale', in: K. Cox (ed.) *Spaces of Globalisation. Reasserting the Power of the Local*, New York: Guilford Press: 137–166.

Taylor, M. (2000) 'Communities in the Lead: Organisational Capacity and Social Capital', *Urban Studies*, Vol. 37, Nos. 5–6: 1019–1035.

2 How to achieve governability at the local level?

Theoretical and conceptual considerations on a complementarity of urban leadership and community involvement

Michael Haus and Hubert Heinelt

Introduction

The *central hypothesis* of this book is that under certain circumstances and through certain efforts a *complementarity of urban leadership and community involvement* can be achieved, making a substantial contribution to 'good' urban governance.[1] The innovative potential of this hypothesis is the combination of two strands of argumentation popular in current urban research and comparative local government: one stressing the (novelty of a) need for effective leadership in cities and the other focussing on the need to involve citizens and corporate actors in urban policy making and implementation. In this chapter, we give a theoretical account of (i) how this complementarity of urban leadership and community involvement may be understood in terms of legitimacy and (ii) its significance in the development of urban policies.

The term 'complementarity' refers to the effects of enacted urban leadership and practised community involvement in different phases of policy making and implementation. Furthermore, the term relates to direct interactions as well as to simultaneous effects. Complementarity can be understood to take two forms:

1 maximisation of opportunities through interaction with the other dimension, and
2 compensation for shortcomings or minimisation of risks related to or resulting from the other dimension – at least latently.

In order to establish how such a complementarity might come about, we first reflect on the political *functions* that can be fulfilled either by forms of political leadership or community involvement, but also the *dys*functional implications of both, *taken separately*. Second, these possible functions and dysfunctions need to be analysed in the context of deficits and failures of the political system at the local level. Strengthened urban leadership and new forms of community involvement have often been introduced by political reforms to increase participation, transparency and the effectiveness of urban politics and administration. Considering the disadvantages associated with uncontrolled leadership power on the one hand and euphoric, but euphemistic sympathy for community involvement on the other, it seems worthwhile to ask, thirdly, if a particular *co-effect*, or even *interplay* between both can lead to mutual remedy of at least some of the shortcomings. This requires an approach which sees leadership and community involvement as two factors in a complex interactive process of problem solving.

In the next section we present some general evidence for our thesis that urban leadership and community involvement can be complementary in terms of not only responding to government failure, but also to *governance* failures. This implies another question: how are urban leadership and community involvement related to new forms of urban governance which reflect changing policy challenges? In section 3 we explain our understanding of urban leadership and community involvement, considering also the specific functions and possible performances of both.

Can the interplay between urban leadership and community involvement respond to (local) government as well as to governance failures?

The question of how urban leadership and community involvement relate to changing policy challenges can be answered by:

- situating the reflection on complementarity of urban leadership and community involvement in the current debate on (urban) governance – and more precisely: on policy failures and governability,
- identifying the shortcomings of 'traditional' local government as well as of 'modern' interactive forms of governance, and
- raising the question of how the specific negative by-products, disadvantages and risks of strong leadership and widened community involvement (taken separately) could be encountered by a beneficial *interplay* of both.

Government failure can be understood to have two different dimensions.[2] First, government failure can be related to *the problematic role of representative institutions* and decision making, leading to deficits in legitimacy, efficiency and effectiveness. While a lack of legitimacy is usually related to a loss of trust in the problem-solving and interest-mediating capacity of representative institutions, a lack of effectiveness is usually seen as the actual inability of these institutions to implement either decisions taken in representative bodies or favourable policy objectives in general. Second, government failure has to be linked to the issue of coping with complexity or with the problem of coordinating societal interactions in modern society. The first dimension will be addressed (pp. 14–20), and the second will be considered on pages 21–23.

Government failure and lack of legitimacy and effectiveness

To consider government failure means that ('good') policies are measured or judged according to:

- whether political decisions and their implementation achieve the effects or objectives that are intended,
- whether they are accepted and supported by the social environment of the political system – and are not rejected, thus eventually losing their status of having binding force,
- whether political decisions make the best use of given resources (time, funding etc.) or are able to mobilise others.

The first facet addresses *effectiveness* with respect to problem-solving and target-directed control capacities. It also emphasises political self-determination, in so far as those who are involved in (and affected by) policy making are not only able to define but also to pursue their objectives. To do this effectively they have to (i) reflect specific options and constraints and take them strategically into account ('Strategiefähigkeit'/capacity to develop a suitable strategy), and (ii) be able to actually follow these strategies in their political actions ('Handlungsfähigkeit'/capacity to act). Both aspects are crucial for a sufficient 'governing capacity' of political institutions (see below).

The second dimension refers to *legitimacy*, i.e. acceptance, trust and support as well as political justifiability and enforceability, both with respect to the decision and implementation processes and to the policy objectives as such. The third dimension concerns *efficiency, i.e. the rational use of resources to reach a societal binding decision and to achieve a certain policy objective.*

These three dimensions of 'governability' may be seen as systemic imperatives which apply to any kind of political system. However, reflecting more deeply on legitimacy in *democratic* political systems, we would like to refer to three interrelated forms of democratic legitimation which cover not only the just mentioned issues of legitimacy, effectiveness and efficiency but also most of the contributions to democratic theory.[3] Together they stand for the complex requirements of a sufficient 'problem-solving capacity of democratic self-government' (Scharpf 2000: 102):[4]

- First, any democratic system needs to rest on some kind of 'authentic' participation. Authentic participation means the possibility of expressing consent or dissent with proposed policies and of influencing the decision on these policy proposals, i.e. getting one's voice heard and one's vote counted (*input-legitimation through participation*).

- Second, any democratic system has to be measured according to the degree it solves the problems that affect the fate of the community it claims to represent. This implies the acceptance by at least those actors who are crucial for the successful implementation of measures. It also implies the degree to which available information (or knowledge) is used to develop well-informed decisions (*output-legitimation through effectiveness*).

- Third, any democratic system has to be judged according to the transparency of its institutions and processes. Its social environment has to understand how measures are taken and who is responsible for them, in order to make actors accountable for what they have done and to understand the alternatives that have to be decided upon. Accountability is a precondition for the evaluation of political actors' performance, and also for efficient decisions with respect to scarce resources like time and money (*throughput-legitimation through transparency*).

Table 2.1 summarises the principles and criteria of legitimation, and the phenomena that lead to a crisis of legitimacy in relation to the three forms of democratic legitimation.[5]

The relevance of a distinction between these forms of legitimation as well as between the related criteria and phenomena of crises of democratic legitimacy can be observed in current reform discourses and policies in many countries. The guiding principles of such reforms are participation, transparency and effectiveness which should both increase consent, accountability and problem-solving capacities, and help to turn around the decline of voter turnout and trust in political institutions, 'opaque institutions' or unclear decision making and policy failure.

Although the perceived problems of representative institutions (local government in our case) do not lead to the same answers across countries and cities, there are similarities as well as particularities over time if one compares national discourses on local government reform and their impacts (see, for example, Wollman 1995 for a comparison of reform discourses in the USA and in the UK, Wollman 2000 for reforms in the UK,

Table 2.1 Different forms of democratic legitimation

	Principle	*Criteria*	*Phenomena of crisis*
Input-legitimation	Participation	Consent	Decrease of voter turnout etc.
Throughput-legitimation	Transparency	Accountability	Opaque institutions etc.
Output-legitimation	Effectiveness	Problem-solving	Policy failure etc.

France and Germany). For example, in the 1980s and 1990s questions of institutional reform were intensively debated while in recent years a new role for local government as an 'enabling' factor is widely discussed. In this context, the question of modernising public administration and its linkages with urban leadership and community involvement are also considered (for public sector reforms in a cross-country perspective see Wollman 2003).

Two main categories of reform discourses and policies can be identified: the first may be called 'from government (failure) to government (reform)', the second 'from government to governance'.

From government failure to government reform

Within comparative politics, it is well-known that different types of democracy have particular strengths and deficits with respect to the criteria of participation, transparency and effectiveness.[6] For example, the competitive Westminster democracy is especially good in accountable decision making. There is always a clear majority in parliament, and elections offer a clear political alternative of either endorsing the politics of the ruling majority or giving the opposition a chance. Participation and effectiveness are criteria that are fulfilled in a somewhat less clear manner. Elections are the preponderant way of participating, whereas participation between elections seems not to be in accordance with the logic of parliamentary sovereignty. Decisions can be reached easily and pushed through stringently, but effectiveness suffers lack of consensus and abrupt policy changes. In a consociational democracy, political decisions are often reached in an opaque way (at least for the wider public), which makes it difficult to hold certain actors accountable for the outcomes.[7] Elections do not make up for this lack of transparency. Yet, decision making is permanently involving a broad range of actors who represent different interests or strata and groups of the population. Thus participation in policy making is widened. Further, it has often been claimed that such systems generate policies that are more highly accepted, of a higher problem-solving capacity and easier to implement. These reflections point to local government institutional reforms as one approach to solve the kind of government failure measured by deficits in participation, transparency and effectiveness.

Such institutional reforms have to be understood in the light of the characteristic tension of local government within a political system: on the one hand, it is a subordinated level expected to effectively implement the objectives of the superordinate level(s) of government; on the other hand local government has to offer room for democratic choice for local actors in accordance with local preferences (Page and Goldsmith 1987). The problem of dealing with interdependence while upholding the claim of self-government which is regarded as a basic problem of national democracies today (Scharpf 2000) has thus been a long known phenomenon in local politics.

Local institutional reform within the framework of representative democracy is taking place throughout Europe: from parliamentary to presidential democracy (i.e. from the monistic rule of the councils to the dualistic distribution of competencies between councils and strong, sometimes also directly elected mayors), from consociational to competitive democracy (i.e. from proportional executives and boards to city governments relying on council majorities, from proportional representation to electoral systems providing for clear majorities) and from competitive to consociational democracy (proportionally elected executives instead of majority rule).[8]

Local government reforms also tend to emphasise one of the above-mentioned principles of legitimacy. A traditional reform path has stressed the accountability of office-holders. New Public Management modernisers have focussed on the efficiency of local politics and administration. And 'alternative modernisers' have stressed the element of direct participation or citizen involvement (see Wollman 1996; Heinelt 1997). Although certainly there are various ways of combining these strands of reform, it is also clear that different notions of local democracy come into play when one is talking about local government failure and reform perspectives: *liberal representative democracy* in the case of the traditional reform path, *managerial-administrative approaches* in the case of New Public Management modernisers, and *participatory models of local democracy* in the case of 'alternative modernisers'.

Furthermore, there is a divergence between (groups of) countries in the focus of tasks at the local level as well as of the expectations of citizens towards local government. Taking into account different types of local government (see, for example, Page and Goldsmith 1987; Hesse and Sharpe 1991) can be crucial in addressing strengths and weaknesses of legitimation – and related diagnoses of government failure. The so-called Franco type of local government (according to its Napoleonic roots) in France, Italy, Belgium, Spain, Portugal and Greece favours input-legitimation because local government is considered to cover territorially defined communities and to form structures of territorial interest mediation at the lower level of government. The mayor is expected to represent the interests of this community towards higher government levels. However, the capacity of output-legitimation is underdeveloped because of the relatively weak position of municipalities in providing public services. In the case of the so-called Anglo group – covering the United Kingdom and Ireland as well as Canada, Australia, New Zealand, and in some respects, the USA – local government has a weak legal and political status, but is important in shaping and delivering public services. Therefore, local government has a more functional than political role, leading to a potentially stronger option of output-legitimation and a weaker option of input-legitimation.

The weak formal (legal) political status of local government has to be considered in accordance with the 'supremacy of parliament' principle, i.e. the central role of national parliament in a unitary political system. This is reflected in a weak position of the mayor – as a political leader – and in the strength of 'executive officers' and councillors in respect to service provision. In the *North and Middle European* group – with the Scandinavian countries, Germany, the Netherlands, Austria as well as Switzerland – a strong emphasis is given to the shaping and delivering of public services (like in the Anglo group), but local government is equally perceived and institutionally defined (by a strong constitutional status and a relatively high financial independence) as a decentralised level of autonomous democratic policy making. As has been shown by several studies (see Wollman 2000, 2003; John 2001) the path-dependencies of different historically-rooted traditions of local government in terms of central local relationships are significant. Yet, they are transformed by new policy challenges requiring more flexible and fluid forms of problem solving.

The considerations presented in this section show that (i) different notions of democracy in general and local democracy in particular may shape the perception of government failure and good governance, and (ii) that there is a wide variety of institutional settings for re-designing the organisational structure of local government.

From government failure to governance

There is growing evidence that government reforms alone cannot address government failures. This is partly due to the fact that each institutional setting has specific advantages and disadvantages, which means that there is always a trade-off between the different criteria. But the problem of government failure goes deeper, it affects the relationship between public institutions and their social environment. In brief, there used to be (and still is in some parts of the political scene) a strong belief in replacing the coordination of societal interaction by 'the hidden hand' of the market with the intentional guidance and control of the state – or more precisely: of government based on democratic representation and a professionalised administration as its allegedly neutral instrument. However, the expectation of solving market failure with the state led to the diagnosis of state (or government) failure. This appraisal is based on a mixture of arguments: from (i) arguing that the typical (or 'traditional') instruments of the state to intervene in society, i.e. law and money, are structurally incapable of co-ordinating societal interactions effectively and efficiently to (ii) pointing out that there will inevitably be a 'governmental overload' in a democratic, i.e. in an open/inclusive political system because such a system potentially allows everyone to turn his/her problem into a political one and to shift the responsibility for problem solving to the state/government (see Rose 1980; Luhmann 1981).

From this perspective, it has been argued that a shift from government to governance should – and can – be observed, independent of the type of institutional system that has been established (but maybe supported by it). 'Governance' means a different type of coordinating societal interactions: away from the subordination and regulation of society by the state (be it a parliamentary *or* presidential, a consociational *or* competitive, a direct *or* representative democracy) towards 'horizontal' and cooperative modes of coordination.[9]

There are a lot of different roots to this debate (see Kooiman 2002: 71–73; Pierre and Peters 2000: 14–69 for an overview). However, there are some crucial elements that constitute a basic definition of 'governance'. Some of them are captured in the following definition by Schmitter:

> Governance is a method/mechanism for dealing with a broad range of problems/conflicts in which actors regularly arrive at mutually satisfactory and binding decisions by negotiating with each other and co-operating in the implementation of these decisions.
>
> (Schmitter 2002: 53)

But governance does not only cover decision making and implementation (through mutual agreements as well as regular negotiations and co-operation). It may also include, following Kooiman,

> All those interactive arrangements in which public as well as private actors participate aimed at solving societal problems [...] and the stimulation of normative debates on the principles underlying all governance activities.
>
> (Kooiman 2002: 73)

Accordingly, governance addresses both the interaction of public and private actors in policy making, and the definition of commonly agreed problems and objectives. These aspects of governance are perceived as crucial to overcome market as well as government failure.

As with the models of democracy discussed earlier, concepts of governance are shaped by certain political traditions and approaches. The question of governing beyond state and market was already addressed in the debate on *neo-corporatism,* which was preceded by the debate on competitive and consociational democracy, partly initiated by the same protagonists (see Schmitter and Lehmbruch 1979; Lehmbruch and Schmitter 1982; Lijphart 1984, see for this connected development Czada and Schmidt 1993; Steiner and Ertman 2002). The basic assumption was similar to that in the former debate about the strengths of consociational democracy: the stronger the neo-corporatist arrangements between the state and the 'social partners' and their orientation towards compromise and mutual adjustment the better the performance of the country in solving problems of inflation and unemployment (i.e. the crucial topics of the political debate in the late 1970s and 1980s). Pluralist countries characterised by weak interest groups and a dominance of party-based competitive democracy got the lowest ranking in the famous 'corporatist scales' of the time, reflecting their poor performance (see Keman *et al.* 1987; Castles *et al.* 1988). Although this assumption was fundamentally questioned not only in the scholarly debate but also in the course of the political and economic development of the 1990s, one can observe that 'the Corporatist Sisyphus is headed back up the hill' (Schmitter and Grote 1997: 1). This is not surprising because

> the 'corporatist approach' emerged as one subspecies of a much broader genus of theorizing in political economy that has been labelled 'institutionalist'. Its central claim was (and still is) that behaviour – economic, social or political – cannot be understood exclusively in terms of either the choices and preferences of private individuals or the habits and impositions of public agencies. Somewhere between markets and states there are a large number of 'self-organized' and 'semi-public' collectivities that individuals and firms relied upon to structure their expectations and each others' behaviour and to provide ready-made solutions for their recurrent conflicts.
>
> (Schmitter and Grote 1997: 1)

In a similar way the *policy network approach* arising in the early 1990s (Marin and Mayntz 1991) did not only argue that there is some hybridisation (policy networks) between market and hierarchy (see Mayntz 1993: 44). It also emphasised that a weak state on the one hand, and the growing importance of policy networks and involved strong societal actors on the other, are an expression of societal modernisation addressing the challenges of the increased complexity of modern societies (see Mayntz 1993: 41) – provided that societal actors are focussed on consensus and problem solving. In the Netherlands and Germany in particular, the policy network approach developed with close conceptual linkages to the new *governance approach*, addressing theoretical questions of 'politische Steuerung' ('political steering'). In the Anglo-Saxon world in contrast, the idea of policy networks is more often used for the empirical analysis and evaluation of specific state-society-relations (for the distinction between these two policy network approaches see Börzel (1998) and Marsh (1998)).

One has to bear in mind the roots of the idea of governance in the scholarly debate, and it is of interest that these debates were developed in and empirically based on the experiences of particular European countries. It is not only in the scholarly debate that we see different concepts of democracy emerge. *Democracy itself* and its linkages to such interactive arrangements differ across the political orders of (European) societies (see Schmidt 2002).

How to cope with market, government and governance failure?

Our analysis of policy failure does not end with market and state. As Jessop emphasises, we also have to face *governance* failure:

> market forces often fail to address the positive and negative externali-
> ties involved in situations of complex and continuing interdepen-
> dence and this leads to short-run, localised, *ad hoc* responses to
> market opportunities. Thus reliance on the invisible hand of the
> market tends to be sub-optimal and hence to generate market fail-
> ures. On the other hand, top-down command makes excessive
> demands on prior centralised knowledge or accurate anticipation of
> the likely interaction among operationally autonomous systems with
> different institutional dynamics, modes of calculation, and logics of
> appropriateness. This tends to result in the failure to achieve collect-
> ive goals because of the unintended consequences of top-down plan-
> ning or simple bureaucratic rule following.
>
> (Jessop 2002: 44)

Governance may have considerable advantages compared with the other two modes of societal coordination (see Jessop 2002: 44): it provides options for (i) simplifying models that reduce complexity without neglect-ing negative externalities, (ii) developing capacities for dynamic interac-tive learning, (iii) creating methods for coordinated actions among different interests, and over different spatial and temporal horizons, and (iv) establishing a common worldview to stabilise the orientations and expectations of involved actors, and corresponding rules of conduct. However, there is also the likelihood of governance *failure*, which is closely linked to these advantages. This failure can be summarised as 'noise' and 'talking shop' (Jessop 2002: 39, Table 2.1) as well as problems of account-ability and biased power structures (see, for example, Pierre and Peters 2000: 67–68; Getimis and Kafkalas 2002).

Jessop has two recommendations for overcoming market, state and gov-ernance failure, which may be helpful to both academics for thinking about how to achieve governability in modern society, and also to political leaders and community activists for developing their strategies:

1   '[I]f every mode of economic and political co-ordination is failure-
    prone, if not failure-laden, relative success in co-ordination over time
    depends on the capacity to switch modes of co-ordination as the limits
    of any one mode become evident' (Jessop 2002: 52). Such a 'requisite
    variety' means to be prepared to switch from market to government
    or governance or from government to market or governance – and
    back.
        'To minimise the risks of [...] failure in the face of a turbulent
    environment, one needs a repertoire of responses to retain the ability

flexibly to alter strategies and select those that are more successful. Moreover, different periods and conjunctures as well as different objects of governance require different kinds of policy mix, the balance in the repertoire will need to be varied as circumstances change' (Jessop 2002: 51–52).

2   '[S]eek to involve others in the process of policy-making, not for manipulative purposes but in order to bring about conditions for negotiated consent and self-reflexive learning. [...] Place self-organisation at the heart of governance in preference to the anarchy of the market or the top-down command of more or less unaccountable rulers. In this sense self-reflexive and participatory forms of governance are performative – [...] they [...] become a self-reflexive means of coping with the failures, contradictions, dilemmas, and paradoxes that are an inevitable feature of life. In this sense participatory governance is a crucial means of defining the objectives as well as objects of governance as well as of facilitating the co-realisation of these objectives by reinforcing motivation and mobilising capacities for self-reflection, self-regulation, and self-correction' (Jessop 2002: 55).

The context- and/or problem-related view on the appropriateness of the modes of coordination (emphasised by Jessop's first recommendation) seems important for empirical analysis, i.e. the required normative or even conceptual openness of researches for analysing a certain policy mix against the background of particular circumstances. But, more importantly, the political evaluation and selection of the modes of coordination will depend on discourses, interest intermediation and decisions about what is appropriate. Jessop (2002: 49) calls this process of re-articulating and 'calibrating' the different modes of coordination 'meta-governance'. The process of evaluating and selecting the modes of coordination depends crucially on a participatory form of self-reflection, learning and consent-building (highlighted by Jessop's second recommendation). And the self-reflexive, learning and consent-oriented character of this evaluation and selection process forms the core notion of democratic choices for cities: starting from the perspective of government as well as governance failure, democratic choices for cities can be understood as referring to three levels: urban government, urban governance and urban meta-governance. The role of urban leadership and community involvement has thus to be analysed as a component of regular politico-administrative institutions, a property of interactive ways of decision making and problem solving, and an aspect in the process of evaluating and (re-) designing governance mechanisms. Obviously, the three dimensions stand in a close relationship.

Can Jessop's two recommendations be directly related to our question of a possible complementarity of urban leadership and community involvement? – We would like to propose the hypothesis that urban leaders and active citizens/corporate actors may play a crucial part in maintaining the required 'requisite variety'. Urban leaders are crucial for securing the reliability of politics and administration regarding the results of governance and meta-governance. However, leaders are not solitary heroes in this process if Jessop is right about the required participatory, discursive character of governance and meta-governance. Reflecting on specific features of democratic government and governance as well as on the respective advantages and weaknesses of urban leaders – embedded in a system of political representation – and community involvement, we arrive at a third recommendation:

3   Find the complementarity between urban leadership and community involvement. Leadership may solve some of the problems related to community involvement through the participatory management of policy networks and by ensuring their public accountability. Community involvement on the other hand can bring dispersed knowledge and awareness of negative externalities into decision making and implementation processes and can shed public light on proceedings in representative and administrative bodies.

Using the strengths of community involvement and urban leadership and compensating their respective shortcomings

First of all, let it be emphasised that we are not talking explicitly about *combinations*, i.e. (intentional or structural) linkages between urban leadership and community involvement. We are talking about *complementarity*, because this expression leaves room to consider that both core elements are separate but work together (maybe even without the actors' intention) to bring about a certain outcome. We use the notion of complementarity also because it allows us to consider both linkages and separateness between urban leadership and community involvement. Furthermore, the term complementarity is helpful to emphasise that we are looking for 'positive sum games' regarding the power of leaders and citizens – and not for 'zero sum' ones where one part loses power in favour of the other or 'negative sum' ones where all are disempowered.

What are the contributions of urban leadership and community involvement respectively which can pave the way to a 'positive sum game'? Furthermore: what are their shortcomings which may be compensated for by the specific potentials of the other core element?

The strengths and special contributions of community involvement in achieving effective and legitimate urban governance can be clarified by looking at Dahl's (1994) 'democratic dilemma', based on 'system effectiveness versus citizen participation' (see also Dahl 1989)[10] which is a critical contribution to the on-going governance debate. This democratic dilemma lies in the fact that governability in modern societies – and thereby 'system effectiveness' – is secured (or reached) through a wide range of cooperative policy networks either at the cost of abandoning democracy in the sense of 'citizen participation' altogether, or dramatically reducing it. But does the relationship between 'system effectiveness' and 'citizen participation' really imply a contradiction in modern societies? To answer this question, one can go back to Charles Lindblom. In *The Intelligence of Democracy* (Lindblom 1965) he argued that *effective governance* is actually *generated* by participation. Taking Lindblom's argument as a starting point in looking at community involvement (participation beyond general elections), one can argue that participation is in the first place important in defining the expected outcomes of political interventions together with the policy addressees. Furthermore, participation is effective in the realisation of policy objectives because it can help to overcome problems of implementation by considering motives and fostering the willingness of policy addressees to comply as well as through the mobilisation of the knowledge of those affected.[11] Participation does not, therefore, stand in contrast to 'system effectiveness', but is actually one of its conditions. Furthermore, participation contributes to legitimacy (input-legitimation) because it includes both the option to be integrated in democratic self-determination through 'vote' and also interest articulation through 'voice' and civic engagement.

However, community involvement has also some politically unfavourable shortcomings. It may secure effective governance and increase legitimacy, but depending on its concrete forms it is more or less selective in involving citizens, and their involvement *never covers all on an equal basis of those* who may be affected by (co-)decisions taken through community involvement. Thus, Dahl's strong principle of political equality, requiring *equal opportunities* to participate in the political process (see Dahl 1989), is not fulfilled (see also Klausen and Sweeting in this book). But the lack of input-legitimation in terms of equal opportunities is not the only problem. It is also hard to answer the question: *who is accountable (for what)?* And by asking this we can identify a lack of throughput-legitimation, and are thus confronted with *a problem of legitimacy.*[12]

Here, urban leadership and its complementarity with community involvement can offer a solution. Urban leaders, selected in general elections, can bring in further legitimacy by involving active citizens concerned with the 'res publica' in policy processes. Urban leadership can complement participatory governance structures if the urban leader can be held accountable for a decision taken in these structures. But how can this be possible?

Indeed, it would be absurd to hold actors (one or several urban leaders) accountable for actions or decisions for which they have no responsibility because they have not been involved or even able to influence them. But when talking about a possible complementarity of urban leadership and community involvement it is assumed that urban leaders *have* been involved in the relevant actions or decisions – and in this respect they have been able to *influence* them. The engagement of urban leaders can take place in at least two ways, varying from a joint involvement from beginning to end (providing it is possible to determine such points in a policy process), to a partial involvement. In the latter case it is crucial that urban leaders – although 'only' incorporated for a certain phase or sequence – have the formal power to influence the outcome of actions or decisions.

Furthermore, it has to be emphasised that *accountability* depends on a clear assignment of political decisions. This is typically difficult for solutions reached by *bargaining* or *arguing* in a policy network because they require (i) compromises which are not always optimal to all (especially in the case of package deals) or (ii) a common understanding/perception of a problem and the way the problem can and shall be solved, usually through a dense and intensive process of communication between the actors involved, which is not convincing for outsiders.

Although such solutions should be justifiable and explained publicly, clear accountability will be necessary or at least helpful to legitimate decisions. This can be reached by a clear separation between (i) participatory deliberation (or negotiation), directly involving the local community or local communities on the one hand and (final) decision making in bodies of representative democracy on the other hand, as well as between (ii) decision making on the one hand and joint policy implementation on the other hand. In other words, there should be a separation as well as an interplay between

- participatory deliberation and joint policy implementation based on community involvement and
- decisions taken in representative bodies (city councils) authorised to take such decisions by general elections.[13]

Under these conditions decisions are formally legitimised. Furthermore, every citizen as *a voter* has the opportunity to react to political decisions by means of political voting. Or in other words: *vote* (of the 'ordinary' citizen) is complementing *voice* (of the active 'homo politicus').[14]

The role of urban leaders can be crucial in such constellations by mediating and acting between the spheres

- of deliberation based on community involvement and of rule/law-making bodies and
- of the public and administrative implementation of political decisions.

Furthermore, urban leadership can complement community involvement by bringing in 'common interests' or making claims on its behalf. This is a decisive function because community involvement can be – as mentioned above – quite selective in respect to involved actors, topics and interests. Urban leaders can (try to) fulfil this function by (i) influencing the agenda and (ii) setting up procedural rules for community involvement – to give actors/interests a voice who/which are suffering from problems of articulation and organisation (Lowndes and Wilson 2001: 639).

Strengthened and more legitimised urban leadership is thus often seen as a precondition for increasing *effectiveness* and *efficiency* as well as for *vitalising local democracy* (i.e. increasing legitimacy) through greater transparency and accountability. This is related to a better control of how to produce outputs (with respect to effectiveness), a higher capacity to cope with the omnipresent administrative fragmentation and a decrease of party influence (with respect to efficiency) and clearer alternatives and decisions as well as a better electoral control (regarding legitimacy).

However, urban leadership may contradict (or may not be compatible) with the requirements of cooperative policy making because it is embedded in a hierarchical organisational structure where open-minded bargaining and arguing is (often) not seen as a precondition for success. On the other hand, the deliberative characteristics of community involvement can compensate for the executive (if not technocratic) closure of narrow-minded policy making guided by administrative imperatives (see Smith and Beazley 2000: 858–860).

A further shortcoming of institutionalised strong urban leadership is that it may lead to the personalisation of politics at the expense of substantial discussion, foster paternalistic attitudes (both on the side of urban leaders and on that of citizens as well), and trigger populism. It will depend on the concrete formation and power of community involvement[15] to counteract such possible developments – by shedding light on administrative proceedings and bringing policy making into the public arena.

Urban leadership and community involvement: towards a better understanding

In the following sections we elaborate on the possible complementarity of urban leadership and community involvement by trying to clarify what we mean by 'urban leadership' and 'community involvement'. We would like to emphasise that this conceptualisation closely corresponds to the requirements of 'good governance' we have outlined above.

Urban leadership

Within urban research, leadership has been a popular topic for several decades, yet, as Stone (1995: 96) put it, 'there is no well developed theory of political leadership, perhaps not even a universally accepted definition'. Different notions of leadership refer to:

- *administrative-organisational leadership* where leadership is seen as controlling the work of organisations and administrative procedures, especially with respect to the outputs and outcomes, yet going beyond efficiency and administration by providing for creativity and responsiveness in the organisation (see the classical analysis by Selznick 1957);
- *political-executive leadership* where leadership is seen as a publicly exposed position or performance that is able to define the political goals or visions of the local community and political institutions (Elcock 2001);
- *public-charismatic leadership* which means that leadership is a personal relationship between leaders and followers with respect to certain extraordinary projects that are of major importance for cities (see the classical account of Weber 1976: 140–142; a democratised and urbanised account can be found in Stone 1995).

As will become clear, all these understandings give valuable hints for our conceptualisation of 'urban leadership'. In general terms, leadership refers to the institutionalisation of the role of leaders as well as the personal enactment of that role. By urban leaders in an *institutional* sense we mean actors who

- hold a position at the top of the city's administration or political bodies, thus being endowed (i) with organisational resources that are not available to other actors, (ii) political influence that is not available to other actors, (iii) an overall responsibility with respect to urban policies, and (iv) representative functions that are not carried out by other actors,
- are publicly visible in what they do and politically accountable for their actions by depending on some kind of consent of the citizenry or its representatives and being controlled by modes of public communication (informational rights, local media etc.).

Urban leadership thus combines some kind of organisational, administrative and political power with personal accountability. This means that urban leadership can adopt a variety of institutional forms: there are collegial and individualised forms of leadership, dualistic (separating the realms of politics and administration) and monistic (fusing them) forms, and many mixes (see the typology presented by Mouritzen and Svara 2002: 50–66, see also the contribution of Getimis and Grigoriadou to this book).

Public visibility and accountability distinguish urban leaders from other actors who might be influential with respect to key decisions in the cities, but who are not politically accountable. This *exempts* three groups of actors who are sometimes called 'urban leaders' from being labelled as such here:

- holders of merely administrative functions without political responsibility towards the citizenry (whether directly or via representative
  institutions),
- merely partisan leaders or leaders of interest groups/associations,
  although urban leaders may at the same time be e.g. a party leader
  and this may contribute to their resources of leadership (in some
  cases urban leadership is more or less deliberately linked to party
  leadership), and
- members of the business community.

This is not to neglect the existence of other kinds of 'leaders' besides what
we call urban or political leaders, e.g. 'community leaders', 'administrative
leaders' or 'leaders of the business community' (see also the chapter by
Robin Hambleton in this book). It means that this kind of leadership
rather belongs to the side of 'community involvement'. The influence of
such leaders without public legitimation may be tested by empirical analysis, whereby organisational capacities/resources or trust/the willingness of
followers etc. can be demonstrated as quite crucial for policy making. Yet,
trust and following in these cases by definition do not pertain to the local
citizenry as a whole. The entire group of influential actors may be understood as the city's 'elite', 'ruling class' or 'regime'. Urban leaders are (pre-
sumably) part of the urban elite, but not every member of the elite can be
labelled an urban leader.

As Harding makes clear, membership of an urban elite can either rest
on domination or leadership where 'leadership suggests a willingness to
follow whereas domination implies a simple inability to resist' (Harding
1995: 35). We therefore limit urban leadership to holders of positions that
can be said to be (i) institutionally linked with 'a willingness to follow' (via
elections) and (ii) endowed with the chance to mobilise further 'willingness to follow' by good performance or helpful circumstances. When it
comes to analysing how urban leadership and community involvement
can be complementary in achieving sustainable policies, it is, of course,
necessary to take into account all who share some kind of power. What we
would like to stress is that 'power' has very different roots and that different kinds of power sources can play a complementary role in good governance – leading to a constellation in which 'power over' (other actors) is
transformed into 'power to' (reach desirable collective outcomes) (see
Stone 1989: 229 and the discussion on 'urban regimes' inspired by him).

Now we turn to the question of when and how leadership is *enacted*. Not
every actor endowed with the above-mentioned powers and responsibilities will demonstrate 'urban leadership'. This question is not so much
about the performance of urban leaders (in terms of reaching desirable
outcomes). It is rather about what a measurement of performance would
refer to. Despite far-reaching disagreement on the definition of political
leadership, there is a broad consensus that leadership has something to

do with *purposes* and the mobilisation of followers for these purposes. This is well captured in Clarence Stone's explanation of the term: 'Leadership revolves around purpose, and purpose is at the heart of the leader–follower relationship' (Stone 1995: 96). Stone (ibid.: 97) summarises Burns' (1978) definition of leadership as follows: 'leadership is a purposeful activity, it operates interactively with a body of followers, and it is a form of power or causation'. Enacting urban leadership thus means to generate support for purposes relevant for the city in general:

- support of the local public and civil society,
- support of relevant municipal actors (e.g. councillors), political actors from other territorial levels and resourceful societal actors (e.g. the business community), and
- support of the local administration.

Generating support does not mean to 'give orders', but to generate or build on a willingness to follow. In fact, it is important to stress this point for at least two reasons: first, urban leadership is distinct from administering or managing, and second, this understanding of political leadership is (with respect at least to the arenas of the local public and the democratic institutions of local government) the only one compatible with democratic legitimacy as we understand it in this chapter. For, according to this understanding, democratic legitimacy is generated in interaction with relatively autonomous actors and refers to the unforced support of the political system by the citizens.

The meaning of enacted leadership is thus its capacity to establish, clarify and focus on broad purposes where this is difficult to achieve, and to accept public accountability for the realisation of these purposes. This is why enacted leadership is so important for the task of integrating different policy fields that are worked on by fragmented administrative units or the task of maintaining coherence in complex processes of policy making. Furthermore, leadership can be said to be 'a means for acting outside routine processes' (Stone 1995: 98, with reference to Selznick 1957), i.e. in the case of crisis or experiments with innovative forms of policy making.

In terms of the models of democracy discussed earlier, well-institutionalised urban leadership can be said to refer to the 'liberal' model of democracy, stressing (i) accountability of office-holders, (ii) the 'vote' as the source of political legitimacy, and (iii) institutional design as the central point of reference for reform policies. All this stands for 'responsive government'.

In terms of averting possible failures of traditional local government, urban leadership has a key function, namely that of defining, articulating and defending purposes in the context of urban politics and of pursuing an efficient and effective fulfilment of these purposes. This function is a possible reason for institutionally strengthening urban leadership and making it accountable to the citizenry. For in many countries, local government systems have been criticised for not establishing a visible, effective and accountable political leadership: councils were either said to be unable to define purposes and effectively control their implementation because of their dependence on a highly professionalised local administration; or, if a relevant strategic influence of local politicians vis-à-vis the local administration was noticed, the actual leaders in urban politics were said to be publicly invisible and to be motivated by narrow partisan considerations; or, in countries with traditionally strong mayors those were judged to be obstructed by party politics in the councils (see, for example, Elcock 2001: 166–185; Larsen 2002; John 2001: 134–153).

The enactment of leadership can thus be understood as a function of three variables:

- *institutional and organisational resources:* the power an urban leader holds within the system of local government, the connection to a political party, the position within multi-level governance etc.,
- *situational conditions:* properties of the social environment, e.g. political culture generating expectations about ways of enacting the role of leadership, the financial situation of a city and the state of a city's administrative capabilities etc.,
- *personal capabilities and attitudes:* the willingness and capacity to 'lead' by defining purposes and mobilising resources for their achievement, personal charisma and political virtues like persuasiveness, decisiveness and strategic thinking.

Community involvement

Community involvement means that actors belonging to local society take part in political decision making and implementation. Like societies in general local society can be understood as a 'social union of social unions' (Rawls 1971) or a 'community of communities' (Walzer 1998), in that the members of a local community share a common identity as citizens while at the same time enacting different roles and sharing diverse identities in a wider range of social activities (economic, scientific, religious, leisure etc.). Actors are thus involved as citizens of the local political community, and as members or (mostly) representatives of 'local communities'.

The involved actors can either be *resourceful societal actors* where resources refer to control over sector specific contributions (the business community, trade unions, welfare organisations, universities etc.) or the *local public and its associations* inhabiting a 'civic space' in the locality (associations of civil society, neighbourhoods, clubs, single citizens etc.). Many kinds of community involvement are already known in the context of 'traditional' local government, ranging from information rights, participation in council committees or planning processes (like in the case of environmental impact assessments) to local referenda where citizens have final decision authority. Within the model of local 'govern*ment*' it is always (the majority of) the citizenry as a whole or (the majority of) its representatives who have final authority. Within local 'gover*nance*' however, decisions can only be reached by some kind of self-binding of public and private actors and bargaining or public deliberation. There is a somehow *shared* responsibility for outcomes (Pierre 1998; Stoker 1998), yet the structures of this responsibility will vary according to different kinds of institutionalised interactions (see Lowndes and Skelcher 1998). However, while in most cases at least part of the outcomes must be transformed into binding decisions by representative bodies, the crucial difference between a traditional process of government and a process resting on interactive governance as well as some component of formalised government is that in the latter case the particular outcomes would not have been possible without the participation of societal actors (Haus 2003). The crucial conditions for community involvement are;

- that the involved actors are 'holders' (i) of certain *resources* necessary for solving a problem or resolving a conflict or (ii) of certain 'qualities' where qualities refer e.g. to knowledge and 'good arguments' as well as to rights and statuses to be heard which can question the legitimacy of specific solutions (see Schmitter 2002: 62–63), and
- that they are on the one hand *autonomous* (i.e. able to withdraw and to hold back needed resources or free to argue publicly), but on the other hand they are *dependent on each other* (or on some of the others) to realise their own objectives or to satisfy their preferences.

Most discussions about governance mechanisms within urban research mirror the essential features of governance in general – shared responsibility for outcomes, control of resources and mutual dependence. For example, they are focal points in the research on public–private partnerships (Stoker 1998). Yet, the deliberative side of governance relying on 'qualities' (e.g. knowledge) is not always as pronounced as the 'corporatist' side relying on sector-specific resources of organisations. As far as the involvement of the *local public* is concerned, community involvement refers to 'deliberative' models of democracy (Bohman and Rehg 1997). It gives importance to influencing office-holders by common action and public discourse (public reasoning), 'voice' is proposed as the 'instrument' of developing the 'power of the (good) argument' and legitimate demands, and political procedures are seen as points of reference insofar as particular procedures foster options of participation by *arguing* (i.e. to be heard and to be decisive).

The fact that participatory variants of governance are not as intensively discussed as governance in the form of cooperation with resourceful organisations (see Grote and Gbikpi 2002 and Heinelt *et al.* 2002), might

be due to the view that the involvement of citizens is somehow not problematic as more participation seems always to be 'good'. Yet, the
disadvantages of participatory citizen involvement are considered by
Vivian Lowndes in the normative context of democratic citizenship:

> Paradoxically, direct democracy may threaten citizens' rights as well as
> increase citizens' vote. [. . .] How can the interests of minorities be
> protected in the face of vociferous majorities? How can long-term
> strategies be developed in the face of short-term demands? How can
> the needs of the city as a whole be balanced against the interests of
> particular neighbourhoods, and the demands of one neighbourhood
> evaluated against another? How can elite manipulation of direct
> democracy devices be avoided, given the costs involved in organizing
> petitions and campaigns?
>
> (Lowndes 1995: 168–169)

Good meta-governance has to cope with these paradoxes of increased
citizen participation. However, we do have have to stop at stating that 'participation [. . .] is perhaps most valuable in the context of a strong and
vibrant representative democracy – where accountable representatives have
the authority to evaluate needs, balance demands, establish priorities, and
monitor the outcomes of the political system' (Lowndes 1995: 169). Citizen
participation can contribute to good governance if it is targeted at enhancing the deliberative quality of policy making and at activating the endogenous potential of local communities. But then, as argued above, the
linkage of deliberative arenas and decision making becomes very important – and it is the task of urban leaders to provide for good institutional
design and successful interface management. Furthermore, whereas direct
democratic decision making (through local referenda) can lead to a
'tyranny of the majority', deliberative forums are vulnerable to a 'tyranny of
the minority' by the few who are active. Biased participation in deliberative
processes (in terms of gender, class or occupational status) can be compensated by the opportunity of the citizenry to make use of their electoral veto
power. If accountability of urban leaders is well institutionalised there will
be a high incentive for them to play a communicative role in intermediat-
ing between deliberative forums and the broader public.

As for the neo-corporatist type of community involvement, i.e. *cooperation with resourceful organisations*, arguing can be important for this
kind of community involvement as well, although *bargaining* is usually
characteristic, i.e. a form of interest-mediation based on the exchange of
resources and the option to hold back certain resources (or the threat to
do so) needed by other actors (Heinelt 2002: 102–104).[16]

In the first case, public discussion generates 'communicative power'
(Habermas 1992: 435–467) by putting legitimising pressure on those
making authoritative decisions. In the second case, control over resources

generates the power to negotiate a mutually agreed solution. There are, or at least can be obvious links between these two modes of community involvement: negotiated agreements are open to public discussion and critique, in other words: have to stand the communicative power of resistance. This influences the public actors engaged in cooperation, not least because they are either directly linked to their electoral constituency or they are linked to a political arena which will publicly debate the quality of negotiated cooperation. But resourceful organisations, too, might have a vital interest in how the public perceives their cooperative efforts, as this affects their public image. On the other hand, communicative power cannot claim to represent the whole society and ignore processes of social differentiation: first, *functional differentiation* giving organisations in different societal sub-systems an autonomous space of action, second, *cultural pluralism* implying a variety of world views, and third, *social inequality* leading to different opportunities for participating in the generation of communicative power.

As well as deliberative democracy and neo-corporatism, 'communitarian' democracy is a way of conceptualising the appropriate role of communities in local democracy. In this view organisations are transformed into 'communities' when they accept responsibility not only towards their members but also towards their societal environment (Selznick 1992, 2002). Organisational leadership is seen as a crucial feature for this. Responsibility is generated within a 'moral dialogue' on the rights and duties of communities which is at the same time a dialogue on the need for communities to maintain or restore their integrity (Etzioni 1997). Communities are capable of acting in public when they can control the compliance of their members (by financial incentives, hierarchy and morality). The focus on *moral* norms and organisational *consensus* might be problematic. Yet, the logic of the 'active society' is obviously mirrored in the current debates on governance.

Final remarks

We finally return once more to the basic research question addressed in this book: how does the complementarity between leadership and community involvement relate to better, i.e. sustainable urban policies through 'good governance'? Returning to the distinction between government, governance and meta-governance (mentioned on pages 21–23), three levels of decision making can be identified at which specific choices have to be made:

- Decisions or choices are made *for* cities by national or sub-national (federal or regional) level policy makers. For them, it is of utmost importance that the most suitable institutional frameworks for facilitating a beneficial interplay of leadership and community involvement are in place, e.g. by institutionally structuring their interaction and by giving incentives for involving the local community in establishing good urban leadership.

- But such decisions or choices are also made *by* cities, i.e. by local authorities acting *within* the framework of given institutional settings. Such institutional settings offer a specific 'corridor of action' or a 'feasible set' for the choice of local actors. One of these options for democratic choices at the local level is to engage in designing more or less innovative forms of problem solving, concerning for example the involvement of certain actors, the rules for participatory governance processes, the connection of 'new' forms of governance to 'old' forms of government etc.
- Finally, decisions or choices are also made within *these* arenas, namely by actors who decide to participate or not, to adopt consensual or conflictive strategies, to trust or distrust etc.

The complementarity of urban leadership and community involvement will depend on what is the case at all three levels. A comprehensive view of generic variables and situational factors can help to make choices more informed. It is the aim of the following chapters to contribute to such a reflection.

Notes

1 Although this chapter tries to summarise discussions between the contributors to this book (i.e. partners of the PLUS project), the full responsibility for the reasoning presented here is assumed by the two authors.
2 These two dimensions can be seen as interrelated. However, they should be taken separately for analytical reasons.
3 We do not want to reflect in detail here on the differences between legitimacy and legitimation (see Sternberger 1968; Luhmann 1969; Kielmansegg 1976). However, the following short distinction may be helpful (and even necessary) for understanding our consideration. *Legitimacy* concerns the acceptance of and reliance on a political order as a status, whereas *legitimation* covers the process of acquiring such acceptance and reliance by putting forward 'arguments that justify the exercise of governing authority' (Scharpf 2000: 102). Every political order needs legitimacy. Otherwise subjugation of people under it has to be (permanently) secured/enforced by open pressure – if not violence. A democratic political order has the option to acquire its legitimacy through the mentioned forms of legitimation. Other political orders have different ones, e.g. the doctrine of divine right in the case of monarchy.
4 On the different dimensions of legitimation within a 'complex' conception of democracy see also Scharpf 1970, 1993, 1999. Scharpf himself explicitly mentions only the input and the output dimension of legitimation, yet actually also refers to the legitimatory role of throughputs. Easton's reformulation of systems theory introduced the 'withinputs' of a political system, yet more or less as a (hardly transparent) black box with no autonomous meaning for policy making (Easton 1965: 114). A distinction of input, output and throughput aspects of legitimation has also been made by Benz (2001: 5). However,

Benz connects the legitimatory principle of accountability to the feedback stage of policy making. What we want to stress here is the fact that the transformation of inputs into outputs has to be transparent in order to make actors accountable for their decisions.

5 This consideration fits nicely to the distinction (made by Almond and Verba 1963) between 'specific support' and 'general support': whereas the first refers to acceptance and support of particular policy objectives which can be achieved (solely/simply) by output-legitimation the latter refers to acceptance and support of the overall political order (of a city), thus comprising input and output as well as throughput-legitimation.

6 For different concepts of democracy in European countries (not at least for the sub-national level) see Loughlin 2001.

7 For the distinction between 'competitive' and 'consociational' democracy see Lijphart (1968, 1984). See also Lehmbruch (1967, 1969).

8 Due to the subordinate status of local government in political systems, reforms of local government also include territorial, functional and management reforms (see Caulfield and Larsen 2002 for a typology of reform strands).

9 This is not to say that organisational aspects of government and processes of governance are not inter-related: institutional reform can actually be intended to facilitate governance, e.g. by enabling local authorities to cooperate more effectively with societal actors – as it is obvious in the case of New Labour's reform strategy (Stoker 2002).

10 Dahl looked especially at supra-national relations.

11 Renate Mayntz (1987) identified these aspects as crucial problems to be resolved to achieve effective governance (*Steuerungsfähigkeit*).

12 This may be no real problem if the achieved objectives are not contested. This will give community involvement a form of governance relying on its output-legitimation; lack of political equality or unclear accountability can then be 'covered' by beneficial results.

13 For a similar concept of loosely coupling such 'arenas' with respect to the multi-level governance in the EU see Benz 1998 and Benz 2000.

14 Yet, this seems to be a too idealist perspective: it lies in the very nature of 'governance' that decisions are taken together with societal actors which may not have legally binding authority, but do in fact have high political authority because there are no alternatives to choose from. In reaction to this, it is often demanded that representative assemblies are reconstituted as the centre of political activity. This call for a re-parliamentarisation seems to forget, however, why governance came into existence in the first place. An alternative to this would be to politicise the process of designing participatory deliberation and governance arrangements and of linking the different arenas where alternatives are set and where decisions are made with the claim of public legitimation and final authority. It is one of the central theses of this book that political leaders are decisive figures with respect to this politicisation of governance.

15 However, also the functioning of other institutions can be important in counteracting against such possible features of urban leadership, not at least the councils but also upper-level (governmental) agencies.

16 For the distinction between 'bargaining' and 'arguing' see Elster 1995.

References

Almond, G. A. and Verba, S. (1963) *The Civic Culture. Political Attitudes and Democracy in Five Nations*, Princeton, NJ: University Press.

Benz, A. (1998) 'Politikverflechtung ohne Politikverflechtungsfalle. Koordination und Strukturdynamik im europäischen Mehrebenensystem', *Politische Viertel-jahresschrift*, Vol. 39, No. 3: 558–589.

—— (2000) 'Two Types of Multi-level Governance. Intergovernmental Relations in German and EU Regional Policy', *Regional and Federal Studies*, Vol. 10, No. 3: 21–44.

—— (2001) 'Restoring Accountability in Multilevel Governance', paper for the ECPR Joint Sessions workshop 'Governance and Democratic Legitimacy' in Grenoble.

Bohman, J. and Rehg, W. (1997) *Deliberative Democracy. Essays on Reason and Politics*, Cambridge, MA and London: The MIT Press.

Börzel, T. (1998) 'Organising Babylon – on the Different Conceptions of Policy Networks', *Public Administration*, Vol. 76, Summer: 253–273.

Burns, J. MacGregor (1978) *Leadership*, New York: Harper and Row.

Castles, F. G., Lehner, F. and Schmidt, M. G. (eds) (1988) *Managing Mixed Economies*, Berlin and New York: de Gruyter.

Caulfield, J. and Larsen, H. O. (2002) 'Introduction', in: J. Caulfield and H. O. Larsen (eds) *Local Government at the Millennium*, Opladen: Leske + Budrich: 9–23.

Czada, R. and Schmidt, M. G. (1993) 'Einleitung', in: R. Czada and M. G. Schmidt (eds) *Verhandlungsdemokratie, Interessenvermittlung, Regierbarkeit*, Opladen: Westdeutscher Verlag: 7–22.

Dahl, R. A. (1989) *Democracy and Its Critics*, New Haven, CT: Yale University Press.

—— (1994) 'A Democratic Dilemma: System Effectiveness Versus Citizen Participation', *Political Science Quarterly*, Vol. 1: 23–34.

Easton, D. (1965) *A Framework for Political Analysis*, Englewood Cliffs, NJ: Prentice-Hall.

Elcock, H. (2001) *Political Leadership*, Cheltenham and Northampton, MA: Edward Elgar.

Elster, J. (1995) 'Equal or Proportional? Arguing and Bargaining over the Senate at the Federal Convention', in: J. Knight and I. Sened (eds) *Explaining Social Institutions*, Ann Arbor, MI: University of Michigan Press: 145–160.

Etzioni, A. (1997) *The New Golden Rule. Community and Morality in a Democratic Society*, New York: BasicBooks.

Getimis, P. and Kafkalas, G. (2002) 'Comparative Analysis of Policy-Making and Empirical Evidence on the Pursuit of Innovation and Sustainability', in: H. Heinelt, P. Getimis, G. Kafkalas, R. Smith and E. Swyngedouw (eds) *Participatory Governance in Multi-Level Context: Concepts and Experience*, Opladen: Leske + Budrich: 155–171.

Grote, J. and Gbikpi, B. (eds) (2002): *Participatory Governance: Political and Societal Implications*. Opladen: Leske + Budrich.

Habermas, J. (1992) *Faktizität und Geltung. Beiträge zur Diskurstheorie des Rechts und des demokratischen Rechtsstaats*, Frankfurt am Main: Suhrkamp.

Harding, A. (1995) 'Elite Theory and Growth Machines', in: D. Judge (ed.) *Theories of Urban Politics*, London: Sage: 35–53.

Haus, M. (2003) 'Towards a Postparliamentary Democracy in Germany? Theoretical Considerations and Empirical Observations on Local Democracy', in: S. A. H. Denters, O. van Heffen, J. Huisman and P.-J. Klok (eds) *The Rise of Interactive Governance and Quasi-Markets*, Dordrecht: Kluwer: 213–238.

Heinelt, H. (1997) 'Neuere Debatten zur Modernisierung der Kommunalpolitik.

Ein Überblick', in: H. Heinelt and M. Mayer (eds) *Modernisierung der Kommu-nalpolitik. Neue Wege zur Ressourcenmobilisierung*, Opladen: Leske + Budrich: 12–28.

Heinelt, H. (2002) 'Civic Perspectives on a Democratic Transformation of the EU', in: J. Grote and B. Gbikpi (eds) *Participatory Governance. Political and Societal Implications*, Opladen: Leske + Budrich: 97–120.

Heinelt, H., Getimis, P., Kafkalas, G., Smith, R. and Swyngedouw, E. (eds) (2002) *Participatory Governance in Multi-Level Context: Concepts and Experience*, Opladen: Leske + Budrich.

Hesse, J. J. and Sharpe, L. J. (1991) 'Local Government in International Perspect-ive: Some Comparative Observations', in: J. J. Hesse and L. J. Sharpe (eds) *Local Government and Urban Affairs in International Perspective. Analyses of Twenty Western Industrialised Countries*, Baden-Baden: Nomos: 603–621.

Jessop, B. (2002) 'Governance and Metagovernance: On Reflexivity, Requisite Variety, and Requisite Irony', in: H. Heinelt, P. Getimis, G. Kafkalas, R. Smith and E. Swyngedouw (eds) *Participatory Governance in Multi-Level Context: Concepts and Experience*, Opladen: Leske + Budrich: 33–58.

John, P. (2001) *Local Governance in Western Europe*, London: Sage.

Keman, H., Paloheimo, H. and Whiteley, P. F. (eds) (1987) *Coping with the Eco-nomic Crisis. Alternative Responses to Economic Recession in Advanced Industrial Soci-eties*, London: Sage.

Kielmansegg, P. Graf (ed.) (1976) *Legitimationsprobleme politischer Systeme* (Politische Vierteljahresschrift, special issue 7), Wiesbaden: Westdeutscher Verlag.

Kooiman, J. (2002) 'Governance. A Social-Political Perspective', in: J. Grote and B. Gbikpi (eds) *Participatory Governance: Political and Societal Implications*, Opladen: Leske + Budrich: 71–96.

Larsen, H. O. (2002) 'Directly Elected Mayors. Democratic Renewal or Constitu-tional Confusion?', in: J. Caulfield and H. O. Larsen (eds) *Local Government at the Millennium*, Opladen: Leske + Budrich: 111–133.

Lehmbruch, G. (1967) *Proporzdemokratie*, Tübingen: Mohr.

—— (1969) 'Konkordanzdemokratie im internationalen System', in: E. O. Czem-piel (ed.) *Die anachronistische Souveränität. Studien zum Verhältnis von Innen- und Außenpolitik*, Opladen: Leske + Budrich: 147–184.

Lehmbruch, G. and Schmitter, P. C. (eds) (1982) *Patterns of Corporatist Policy-Making*, London and Beverly Hills, CA: Sage.

Lijphardt, A. (1968) *The Politics of Accommodation. Pluralism and Democracy in the Netherlands*, Berkeley, CA: University of California Press.

—— (1984) *Democracies. Patterns of Majoritarian and Consensus Government in Twenty-One Countries*, New Haven, CN and London: Yale University Press.

Lindblom, Ch. E. (1965) *The Intelligence of Democracy: Decision Making through Mutual Adjustment*, New York: The Free Press.

Loughlin, J. (2001) *Subnational Democracy in the European Union: Challenges and Opportunities*, Oxford: University Press.

Lowndes, V. (1995) 'Citizenship and Urban Politics', in: D. Judge (ed.) *Theories of Urban Politics*, London: Sage: 160–180.

Lowndes, V. and Skelcher, Ch. (1998) 'The Dynamics of Multi-Organizational Partnerships: An Analysis of Changing Modes of Governance', *Public Administra-tion*, Vol. 76, Summer: 313–333.

Lowndes, V. and Wilson, D. (2001) 'Social Capital and Local Governance. Explor-ing the Institutional Design Variable', *Political Studies*, Vol. 49: 629–647.

Luhmann, N. (1969) *Legitimation durch Verfahren*, Neuwied: Luchterhand.
—— (1981) *Politische Theorie im Wohlfahrtsstaat*, München: Olzig.
Marin, B. and Mayntz, R. (eds) (1991) *Policy Networks: Empirical Evidence and Theoretical Considerations*, Frankfurt: Campus.
Marsh, D. (1998) 'The Development of the Policy Network Approach', in: D. Marsh (ed.) *Comparing Policy Networks*, Buckingham: Open University Press.
Mayntz, R. (1987) 'Politische Steuerung und gesellschaftliche Steuerungsprobleme – Anmerkungen zu einem theoretischen Paradigma', in: *Vahrbuch zur Staats – und Verwaltungswissenschaft*, Vol. 1, Baden-Baden: Nomos: 89–110.
—— (1993) 'Policy-Netzwerke und die Logik von Verhandlungssystemen', in: A. Héritier (ed.) *Policy-Analyse. Kritik und Neuorientierung*, Opladen: Leske + Budrich: 39–56.
Mouritzen, P. E. and Svara, J. A. (2002) *Leadership at the Apex. Politicians and Administrators in Western Local Governments*, Pittsburgh, PA: University of Pittsburgh Press.
Page, E. and Goldsmith, M. (1987) *Central and Local Government Relations*, London: Sage.
Pierre, J. (ed.) (1998) *Partnerships in Urban Governance. European and American Experiences*, Basingstoke: Macmillan.
Pierre, J. and Peters, B. G. (2000) *Governance, Politics and the State*, London: Macmillan.
Rawls, J. (1971) *A Theory of Justice*, Cambridge, MA: University Press.
Rose, R. (1980) *Challenge to Governance. Studies in Overloaded Polities*, Beverly Hills, CA: Sage.
Scharpf, F. W. (1970) *Demokratie zwischen Utopie und Anpassung*, Konstanz: Universitätsverlag.
—— (1993) 'Versuch über Demokratie im Verhundelnden Staat', in: R. Czada and M. G. Schmidt (eds) *Verhandlungsdemokratie, Interessenvermittlung, Regierbarkeit. Festschrift für Gerhard Lehmbruch*, Opladen: Westdeutscher Verlag: 25–50.
—— (1999) *Governing in Europe: Effective and Democratic?*, New York: Oxford University Press.
—— (2000) 'Interdependence and Democratic Legitimation', in: S. J. Pharr and R. D. Putnam (eds) *Disaffected Democracies. What's Troubling the Trilateral Countries?*, Princeton, NJ: Princeton University Press: 101–120.
Schmidt, V. A. (2002) 'The Effects of European Integration on National Forms of Governance. Reconstructing Practices and Reconceptualizing Democracy', in: J. Grote and B. Gbikpi (eds) *Participatory Governance: Political and Societal Implications*, Opladen: Leske + Budrich: 141–176.
Schmitter, P. C. (2002) *Participatory Governance Arrangements: Is There Any Reason to Expect It Will Achieve 'Sustainable and Innovative Policies in a Multilevel Context'?*, in: J. Grote and B. Gbikpi (eds) *Participatory Governance: Political and Societal Implications*, Opladen: Leske + Budrich: 51–70.
Schmitter, P. C. and Grote, J. (1997) *The Corporatist Sisyphus. Past, Present and Future*, Florence: European University Institute.
Schmitter, P. C. and Lehmbruch, G. (eds) (1979) *Trends Toward Corporatist Intermediation*, London: Sage.
Selznick, P. (1957) *Leadership in Administration. A Sociological Interpretation*, Berkeley, CA, Los Angeles, CA and New York: Harper and Row.
—— (1992) *The Moral Commonwealth. Social Theory and the Promise of Community*, Berkeley, CA and Los Angeles, CA: University of California Press.

—— (2002) *The Communitarian Persuasion*, Washington, D.C: Woodrow Wilson Center Press.

Smith, M. and Beazley, M. (2000) 'Progressive Regimes, Partnership and the Involvement of Local Communities. A Framework for Evaluation', *Public Administration*, Vol. 78, No. 4: 855–878.

Steiner, J. and Ertman, T. (eds) (2002) *Consociationalism and Corporatism in Western Europe. Still the Politics of Accommodation?* (Acta Politica, special issue), Amsterdam: Boom.

Sternberger, D. (1968) 'Legitimacy', in: *International Encyclopaedia of Social Sciences*, Vol. 9.

Stoker, G. (1998) 'Public–Private Partnerships and Urban Governance', in: J. Pierre (ed.) *Partnerships in Urban Governance*, London: Sage: 34–51.

—— (2002) 'New Labour and Local Governance in Britain', in: J. Caulfield and H. O. Larsen (eds) *Local Government at the Millennium*, Opladen: Leske + Budrich: 27–44.

Stone, C. N. (1989) *Regime Politics. Governing Atlanta, 1946–1988*, Lawrence: University Press of Kansas.

—— (1995) 'Political Leadership in Urban Politics', in: D. Judge (ed.) *Theories of Urban Politics*, London: Sage: 96–116.

Walzer, M. (1998) 'Michael Sandel's America', in: A. L. Allen and M. C. Regan (eds) *Debating Democracy's Discontent. Essays on American Politics, Law, and Public Philosophy*, Oxford: Oxford University Press: 175–182.

Weber, M. (1976) *Wirtschaft und Gesellschaft. Grundriß der verstehenden Soziologie*, 5. revidierte Aufl., Tübingen: Mohr.

Wollman, H. (1995) 'Local Government Institutions and Democratic Governance', in: D. Judge (ed.) *Theories of Urban Politics*, London: Sage: 135–159.

—— (1996) 'Verwaltungsmodernisierung. Ausgangsbedingungen, Reformanläufe und aktuelle Modernisierungsdiskurse', in: Ch. Reichard and H. Wollman (eds) *Kommunalverwaltung im Modernisierungsschub?* Basel, Boston, MA and Berlin: Birkäuser: 1–49.

—— (2000) 'Local Government Systems: From Historic Divergence Towards Convergence? Great Britain, France, and Germany as Comparative Cases in Point', *Government and Policy*, Vol. 18: 33–55.

—— (2003) 'Policy change in public sector reforms in a cross-country perspective', in: S. Munshi and B. P. Abraham (eds) *Good Governance, Democratic Societies and Globalisation*, New Delhi and Thousand Oaks, CA: Sage: 171–192.

3 Urban leadership and community involvement

An institutional analysis

Pieter-Jan Klok and Bas Denters

Introduction

Institutional rules play a major role in the conceptual framework described in Chapter 2, both in terms of 'context variables' and the 'institutional design of local systems of governance'. It is therefore essential to develop a clear understanding of different types of rules and how they can be recognised when analysing actual governance structures and the behaviour of actors within these structures. This chapter deals with the institutional analysis of a complementarity of urban leadership and community involvement. The following section provides a short description of the 'Institutional Analysis and Development' (IAD) framework (Ostrom *et al.* 1994) (with a possible operationalisation of the key variables described in an annex). This is followed by a clarification of the links between the key forms of democratic legitimation described in Chapter 2 and the variables central to institutional analysis. On pages 47–49, the IAD framework is used to conceptualise the possible roles of leadership in enhancing effective community involvement. At this point the analysis arrives at the core question addressed in this book as a whole (and set out in Chapter 2). How can the simple co-existence of leadership and community involvement become 'complementary' in the sense that it maximises the opportunities, and minimises the risks, of interaction and increased interdependency between the two.

On pages 49–55, we will turn to an empirical example – the rebuilding of Roombeek, the neighbourhood of the city of Enschede that was destroyed by a major fireworks explosion in 2000. These sections provide a practical example of the institutional analysis of combinations of leadership and community involvement that might be seen as a *complementarity*, illustrating both the usefulness of the approach in describing such a *complementarity* and the way in which the operationalisation can be transformed into descriptions on a case level. Pages 55–61 provide an example of institutional redesign as a form of meta-governance by leaders.

Conceptual framework

The Institutional Analysis and Development framework

Analysis of the institutional arrangements and practice of a complementary urban leadership and community involvement presupposes a conceptual framework as a tool for the description of institutional arrangements and actual behaviour. Elinor Ostrom's Institutional Analysis and Development (IAD) framework represents such a tool (Ostrom 1990). The IAD framework combines actor-centred and institution-centred approaches to the analysis of policy-making processes, and also relates to the theories of actor-centred institutionalism (e.g. Mayntz and Scharpf 1995; Scharpf 1997).

This part of Chapter 3 sets out the major elements of the framework and provides some suggestions for its conceptualisation and operationalisation. The central unit of analysis in the IAD framework is the 'action arena'. Action arenas include both an 'action situation', and the actors involved in that situation.

The action situation consists of seven elements (Ostrom *et al.* 1994: 29–33):

1　The first element of an action situation includes actors who have become participants in a situation.
2　Positions are simply placeholders to associate participants with an authorised set of actions (linked to outcomes) in a process. Examples of positions include first movers, bosses, employees, monitors, voters, elected representatives.
3　The third element is the set of actions that participants in a particular position can take at different stages of a process (or, nodes in a decision tree).
4　The fourth element is the outcomes that participants can potentially affect through their actions.
5　The fifth element of an action situation is the set of functions that map participants (and/or random actions) at decision nodes into intermediate or final outcomes.
6　Closely allied to the type of information function is the sixth element – the information set available to a participant in a position at any stage in the process, recognising that the information set is often incomplete or only partially available to some actors.
7　The seventh element is the set of payoffs that assign benefits and costs to actions and outcomes.

For the explanation of the behaviour of actors – either as individuals or in groups (Scharpf 1997: 52–58), Ostrom distinguishes four attributes:

1　the preference evaluation that actors assign to potential actions and outcomes;

2   the way actors acquire, process, retain and use knowledge contingen-
    cies and information;
3   the selection criteria actors use for deciding upon a particular course
    of action; and
4   the resources that an actor brings into a situation (Ostrom *et al.* 1994:
    33–35).

The action arena is not situated in an analytical vacuum, it is part of an
institutional context. Three factors influence the nature of the arena – the
rules individuals use to order their relationships, the attributes of a physical world, and the attributes of the community (Ostrom *et al.* 1994: 37).
In Figure 3.1 this is summarised graphically.

Furthermore Ostrom provides a framework for use in describing institutional rules, distinguishing between seven types of rules, all linked to the
seven constituent elements of the action situation.

- *Position rules* establish positions, assign participants to positions and
  define who has control over tenure in a position.
- *Boundary rules* set the entry, exit and domain conditions for individual
  participants.
- *Authority rules* specify which set of actions is assigned to which position
  at each node of a decision tree.
- *Aggregation rules* specify the transformation function to be used at a
  particular node, to map actions into intermediate or final outcomes.
- *Scope rules* specify the set of outcomes that may be affected, including
  whether outcomes are intermediate or final.
- *Information rules* specify the information available to each position at a
  decision node.

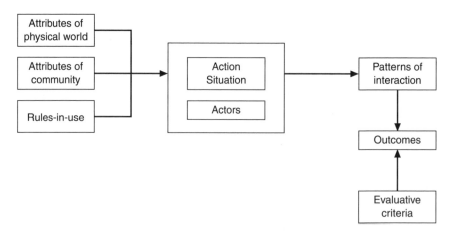

Figure 3.1 The action arena (source: Ostrom *et al.* 1994: 37).

- *Payoff rules* specify how benefits and costs are required, permitted or forbidden in relation to players, based on the full set of actions taken and outcomes reached.[1]

Discussion

Although the set of institutional rules are an important part of the conceptual framework, they are neither encompassing nor unproblematic. Rules and arenas should be clearly distinguished from the actual behaviour and interactions of actors (see Chapter 2). This draws attention to the importance of *rule compliance* and the ways in which rule compliance can be achieved. Position holders may choose to follow the rules in their actual behaviour, but they may also break them. Furthermore, it has to be recognised that rules have to be interpreted, and in this sense rules do not allow directly (that is without interpretation) for different kinds of behaviour.

This is an element missing from the IAD framework. The rules that guide authoritative interpretation of the rules (what do they mean in concrete situations and who has to decide in case of conflicting interpretations), and the rules that enable the possible use of sanctions in case of deviant behaviour, are not seen as a separate category. In an analysis focussing on leadership this is especially important, since the need to secure both authoritative interpretation and compliance is often seen as a central function of leadership. The IAD framework is indeed flexible enough to find a way out of this 'blank spot'. Both functions can be linked to a position (or a number of positions) in the arena, that has (or have) the authority to interpret the rules or to secure rule compliance.

The topic of breaking the rules by position holders draws attention to how 'deviant' behaviour might result in the adaptation of new rules. This topic of institutional change is related to the question of how the rules were set in the first place. Generally there will be two routes towards institutional change. One is formal, where new rules are explicitly decided upon; a second is informal, where actual behaviour develops gradually into a practice that is regarded as a normative standard by the position holders (and is perhaps codified into a formal rule at some point in time).

The first route is incorporated in the IAD framework in the notion of a 'collective choice arena' (Kiser and Ostrom 1982; Ostrom 1990: 50–55; Ostrom *et al.* 1994: 46). In this arena the rules – or at least initial rules – are set (or decided upon) governing the arenas at the operational level. Thus the rules for the operational arena are the output of the collective choice arena. As political leaders are often within these arenas, it is very important to notice not simply that these arenas exist, but also to identify the functions that leaders can perform through them, through the formulation and adaptation of the rules of the game.

The concept of (the development of) *informal rules* is of particular interest. The extent to which rules are formalised and laid down in written documents will vary between cases and even between arenas and rule types within cases. For example, the institutional rules of the municipal council taking a decision on a policy proposal will tend to be highly formalised and are revealed in formal documentation. However the rules for an arena where citizens are invited to discuss a problem and its possible solutions may be less formalised and/or less well articulated. A rule can be called formal if it is publicly decided by an authoritative body such as a cabinet, parliament or council. These rules will generally be found in legislation, procedures, organisational documents, policy documents etc. Informal rules are behavioural norms that are decided by actors but do not count as decisions by an authoritative body. For example, the members of a committee might decide not to have meetings on Sundays. This could be a rule that is guiding their interactions, but not a decision by the municipality (unless the council has adopted a general policy of not meeting on Sundays). These informal rules may be found in the minutes of meetings but may also only be identified by interview and observation of the behaviour of participants within the arena.

In order for the concept of informal rules to be useful, however, such rules must be clearly distinguished not only from formal rules but also from concepts as 'behaviour' and 'culture'. Therefore an informal rule should:

- have an explicit *normative* character: it indicates how actors *should* behave. This implies that other actors can hold someone accountable if he does not comply with the rule. In case the rule specifies a right, this implies that the actor holding the right can refer to the rule to legitimise his behaviour and claim that others are not allowed to interfere with his behaviour;
- have a *general* character: it indicates how actors should behave in certain situations. If a specific actor 'acts' in a certain way (behaviour), this is something that is both personal and time and space specific. (By way of example on 2 November, the Mayor of Enschede stated in a council meeting in Enschede: 'I will not resign.' A rule however would say something about the possible acts (resignation) of any actor that is Mayor of Enschede in a certain class of situations (council meetings).);
- have been *decided* upon: there should be some explicit application of the rule to the arena. The first two characteristics stated above would also apply to norms that can be seen as the cultural context of the arena. In order to distinguish between culture and (informal) rules the use of rules is restricted to those norms that have been decided to apply to the arena. This does not imply that all participants in the arena have agreed on the rule, but some actors must have decided upon it and most actors will have to agree with this decision or at least accept the rule as being applicable.

The notion of institutional change also draws attention to its conceptual counterpart institutional stability, and to the question of sustainability which is central to this book. New forms of governance, including community involvement, are very often regarded as 'experiments', which brings up the question to what extent experimental rules on participation and interaction can be transformed into a more general governance structure. The transformation of arena-specific institutional arrangements into a more general institutional structure lies at the heart of the difficult task of ensuring durable policy results through 'institution building'. Local political actors can institutionalise rules in local charters and statutes, thereby fixing the rules for future arenas. Some of the rules that are applicable to local arenas will however be a part of more general regional, state or even supra national 'legislation'. Of course, these can be changed as well, but local actors will usually play only a minor part in these processes.

The notion of the origin of the rules for local action arenas can also be used in relation to the question on whether the IAD framework will be flexible enough to cope with the large variation in local circumstances that are present in local case studies. Some of the rules might have a general character because they are part of a (supra) national or local statute. Others however might be formulated for only specific processes and thus represent specific decisions and circumstances taken into account by those who formulated them. Besides, it is important to be aware of the fact that the rules only specify a set of actions that are legitimate or illegitimate to a position holder. They do not specify exact behaviour. If formulated as rights they might even specify freedom of choice for the position holder. In the IAD framework this is reflected in the concepts of 'attributes of the physical world' and 'attributes of the community' (the other contextual factors for the action arena, see Figure 3.1) and in the concept of 'actors' and their characteristics. In other words: the same set of institutional rules might result in totally different outputs, due to variations in other contextual variables and the actual actors involved.

Legitimation and institutional analysis

In the second chapter of this book three forms of democratic legitimation were described: input-legitimation through participation, throughput-legitimation through transparency and output-legitimation through effectiveness. These forms of legitimation can be linked to specific rule types in the IAD framework.

Input-legitimation through participation is linked to position, boundary and authority rules. Together these rules guide which actors have access to the arena (and which actors are excluded), in which position they will be able to interact in the arena, and what their legitimate actions are. This implies that different models of input-legitimation will be reflected in different configurations of these rules. In an open participatory model, where all citizens can participate (boundary rule), the authority rules will reflect that they can only 'speak for themselves'. In a representative model, where a limited number of council members are chosen by elections (boundary rule), the council members will have the right to speak for the citizens that elected them. In directing empirical studies one therefore has to pay specific attention to the combinations of these rules when looking for input-legitimation. It is necessary to look not only for these rules, but also for the specific actions of actors (the practice) that evolves around them. It is one thing to have a rule that every citizen can participate, but if certain groups do not participate in practice, this has important consequences for the amount of input legitimation that is provided.

Throughput-legitimation through transparency is linked primarily to the information and aggregation rules. Transparency implies that actors in and outside of the arena know what decisions are made, how they are related to the actions and opinions of the decision makers and how these decisions are motivated. Democratic models that aim for throughput-legitimation would therefore have open access to information, and even perhaps rules that some public impetus behind collective decision making is obligatory. Likewise, clear and highly formalised aggregation rules are essential. Examples are voting rules or the rule that one actor in a certain position (e.g. the mayor) has the right to take a decision. Although in this last example there is no 'aggregation' in the sense of the involvement in decision taking by different actors, the rule specifies how the decision is reached (even if in this case the decision maker makes up her mind taking into account the opinions of other actors). Democratic models based on cooperation and corporatism would generally have less clear aggregation rules and sometimes even closed information rules. They would therefore have more problems in providing legitimation through transparency. Again this implies that the rules and practices that develop around the rules must be established empirically in order to establish the existence or otherwise of legitimacy.

In the light of the discussion above it would be tempting to link *output-legitimation through effectiveness* to scope and pay-off rules. Scope rules refer to the outcomes that can be decided upon in the arena, and pay-off rules refer to the way in which costs and benefits are divided among actors. However, legitimation through effectiveness refers, not to what is possible inside the arena, but what are the outputs and outcomes from the arena. Since effectiveness derives from the specific and actual content of the outputs, and the way in which these lead to outcomes outside the arena, effectiveness can not be linked to any specific formulations of these rules. Attempts to improve output-legitimation can be linked to all the rules of the IAD framework. For example, the need for direct participation on the part of citizens is often motivated by the expectation that through the use of their knowledge, better policy proposals will be adopted, addressing problems in a more effective way. Again, as an example, the strong position of a leader in an aggregation rule is thought to improve the quality of the policies that are decided upon. This implies that attempts to improve the output-legitimation can be present in all formations of the rules.

Problems of community involvement, functions of leadership

In the second chapter of this book a number of problematic aspects of community involvement were described. This section aims to analyse the possible *complementarity* of leadership and community involvement on a theoretical level using the IAD framework. Here we will extend this list of problematic aspects (without the assumption of being exhaustive) and analyse possible functions of leadership that could help ameliorate these problems. Although it might seem necessary to discuss the extent to which community involvement can ameliorate the problems of leadership, in practice, the IAD – with its focus on arenas of action – lends itself more easily to an analysis which builds on the impact of leadership on the problematics of community involvement rather than with the impacts of community involvement on leadership.

There is widespread recognition that there are limitations to the extent that community involvement operates effectively in practice. Among these limitations are:

*   *The selective involvement of citizens.* Arenas might be institutionally closed to some actors (as the result of boundary rules) or actors with certain characteristics are in practice not willing or able to participate.
*   *The unequal positions of actors in participation.* Actors with high levels of skills and other resources dominate actual practice in arenas.
*   *A lack of transparency in policy processes.* Due to insufficiently formulated aggregation rules it is unclear who is accountable for the outcomes of arenas. This problem might not only arise inside arenas, but could also be the result of unclear relations between subsequent sub-arenas. For example, decisions may be fixed in closed 'pre-meetings', reducing formal decision making to a 'ritual dance'.
*   *Biased outcomes towards the interests of actors that participate.* Interests that are not represented 'at the table' (for example, the long-term interests of future generations or the interests of other neighbourhoods) do not receive adequate attention.
*   *Inconclusiveness of deliberative processes.* Processes aiming at the creation of mutual understanding and consensus do not always result in these outcomes, with stalemate as a possible result.
*   *Open conflict.* Intensified interactions might result in increased understanding, but might also result in intensified conflict.

- *The increased power of public officials.* The introduction of participatory arenas alongside the traditional representative arenas might result in the 'empowerment' of other actors such as public officials, who in many cases may be the key links between arenas.

Limitations such as these may be reduced by the actions of leaders, and applying the IAD framework it is possible to discern a number of possibilities for leadership to ameliorate the problems confronting community involvement. These possibilities fall within two categories, the first that of institutional design, the second that of direct involvement in operational arenas. The following paragraphs illustrate the possibilities.

Selective involvement of citizens can be first addressed by formulating boundary rules that give actors the right to participate and by ensuring compliance of these rules (preventing actors to exclude other actors). It can also be addressed by organising sub-arenas that are specially geared to actors that are known to be lacking in common arenas. Where the perceived lack of skills or other resources is felt to contribute to the absence of actors, providing these resources (e.g. expert support) might contribute to participation.

Unequal positions of actors in participation processes can also be addressed by providing resources. It can be addressed by formulating special authority rules that empower actors in underprivileged circumstances. This can also be done by giving them a special status in the aggregation rules of the arena.

Lack of transparency in policy processes can be prevented by formulating clear aggregation rules in combination with clear boundary rules (who is to participate in producing the output). Participative, consensual and deliberative arenas are however seldom equipped with clear aggregation rules. The basic idea of deliberation is that actors gradually reach mutual understanding in the course of the debate. At what point in the process this mutual understanding is to be regarded as sufficient for an 'outcome' to be reached is in most cases hard to observe (unless under the aggregation rule of 'consensus', in which each actor has a veto possibility). As has been indicated in the first chapter of this book, transparency can also be created by designing a separate arena (with clear boundary and aggregation rules) that transforms the outcomes of deliberative arenas into formal decisions.

Biased outcomes towards the interests of actors that participate can be prevented to some extent by defining scope rules that exclude certain biased outcomes or that fix certain elements to be a necessary part of the outcome. For example, a neighbourhood may be allowed to design its own redevelopment plan, but certain facilities for minority groups have to be part of it. Biased outcomes can also be remedied by decisions of subsequent arenas that do take interests of non-participating actors into account.

Inconclusiveness of deliberative processes or even *open conflict* can be addressed by leaders (or their representatives) participating in the arena themselves. Within these arenas all kinds of actions can be taken to propose acceptable solutions or to cool down emotions in conflict (for example, propose a compromise or start bilateral negotiations). These problems can however also be addressed by changing the institutional rules of the arena, to make them more conducive to producing outcomes or consensus. Sometimes small changes in the rules might suffice, but in other instances an entire redesign of the arena might be called for (i.e. introducing new actors with different authorities).

Increased power of public officials can be prevented by formulating clear information and authority rules. Leaders have to make sure that all actors are aware of the roles that public officials should play and the actual practices that they develop in these roles. This calls for some form of 'eyes and ears' (perhaps even their own) of leaders in the participative arenas.

As has been indicated in the previous section, the task of ensuring that the actual behaviour of actors complies with the institutional rules might be a special task for leaders. This implies that leaders will have to be sure that some institutional provision is made to produce rule compliant behaviour. Of course this is equally important for the basic institutional structure of the arena as for the possible institutional solutions to the problems described above. Institutional solutions in themselves are only responses on paper, and unless backed by implementation and enforcement are mere expressions of intention.

Interactive arenas in Roombeek as an example

The section which follows provides one example of an institutional structure of leadership and community involvement. It uses the case of the rebuilding of the Roombeek area after its destruction by an enormous fireworks explosion in Enschede in May 2000.

The institutional structure of the 'citizen participation process', its links to other arenas and the role of leadership are described. The major focus is on the first phase of the decision-making process, which resulted (in the autumn of 2001) in a formal decision of the municipal council on a general plan for rebuilding the area. It should be remembered that what is discussed in this paper was only the first round of the planning process. The general plan provided the basis for more detailed plans and the subsequent realisation of these plans.

In order to facilitate 'maximum feasible participation' by the numerous victims of the explosion, the participation process was designed as a set of arenas, each geared towards the needs of different groups. These participation arenas, are described, followed by a description of the other arenas that provided the institutional framework for the first phase of the programme's development.

Participation arenas

The first phase of participation involved two stages. In February/March 2001 an open inventory of opinions on rebuilding the area was made, and in June 2001 participants were able to express their opinions on the first draft of the redevelopment programme.

The core of the *first stage* was a series of eight sessions with former residents of different areas in Roombeek and its immediate surroundings. For these sessions residence in the (former) residential location served as the criterion for inclusion in the participation process (boundary rule). Other 'arenas' were open to participants from the entire city (anyone could drop his ideas in boxes that were placed all over the city) or open to anyone connected to the Internet and able to understand Dutch (an Internet site was constructed where anyone could express his or her opinions).

In addition, special sessions were organised for functional groups. Workshops were organised for schoolchildren, and for migrants from different ethnic backgrounds, as well as for artists (who were a characteristic segment of the population of Roombeek), entrepreneurs and older people.

In terms of the institutional rules these arenas can be described as ones that gave an open access to participatory opportunity and expression of opinions. In a formal sense selection of participants (boundary rule) resulted from invitation based on location or through addresses known by organisations of ethnical or occupational groups. However, across the whole set of arenas, all relevant actors will have had an opportunity to participate.

The main *positions* in the arenas were the ones of 'participant' and 'process facilitator'. Participants had the rights to express their opinions either in an entirely open way, or related to a large number of important topics that were previously discussed with 'key-persons' from the area. The 'process facilitator' was an independent expert on participation processes who was hired by the city to organise the participation process and ensure that the outcomes would truly represent the opinions of the participants. Another key position in some of the arenas was the 'city-planner', an external expert, hired by the municipality of Enschede to prepare a first draft of the redevelopment plan (more on whose role follows in the description of the other arenas). In the eight central sessions the external city-planner was present to discuss participants' opinions and to state some general points of departure for his work. Councillors held a minor position in the sessions, fulfilling the role of 'round table host' at discussion tables, facilitating discussion and listening to the participants. They were explicitly instructed not to express their own opinions.

The role of *leadership* was very limited in this arena: leaders, be it the responsible aldermen or council members, were only present to listen.

There was however a distinctive element of leadership in the design of the positions in the different arenas. These were formulated in order to result in maximum participation by citizens from every possible background. The presence of leaders as listeners was supposed to indicate that they took the participation process very seriously. In this way leaders also made sure that they were well informed in early stages of the process.

With regards to the *scope* of the arenas, the eight central sessions were slightly 'pre-structured'. The organisers provided the participants with cues (in the form of a series of photographs and accompanying short texts) for reflection and subsequent discussion on a predetermined list of topics about the future of the redeveloped neighbourhood. The number of these topics (about eighty), however, was so high and the range of issues so wide, that the participants were able to address almost any topic they might have deemed relevant. Moreover, the notes written to reflect participant views were absolutely unconstrained, participants were able to raise topics different from those initially provided, and the entirely open ID boxes and Internet site provided further opportunities to address any issue a participant would like to raise.

Information rules were also quite open. Participants were informed of the possibility of taking part; they were informed about the general structure of the different arenas, and they were promised that a written report on the sessions would be provided to those attending. Moreover, reports were to be published on the Internet. Drafting the reports on the results per arena was a major responsibility of the process facilitator. Implicitly this also indicates the main *aggregation* rule used to 'produce' the results for each of these sessions. The opinions of participants were collected and recorded on an individual basis, subsequently serving as input to a general summary of the opinions by the facilitator. For the next steps in the process, a full report was produced by the process facilitator, summarising the output of the first stage of the participation process. This report consisted of a general summary and short summaries of all the different sessions.

Costs and benefits of redevelopment options were as yet not a topic for discussion, so at the time it was neither feasible nor necessary to specify a *pay-off* rule (all costs of the process were covered by the city).

Again, it is clear that *leadership* did not play an active role in these arenas. It did however play a role in their construction. The role of the process facilitator was specially geared towards maximum representation of the views of the participants. This was made clear in his mandate (his authority rules and his central role in the aggregation rule) as well as in his selection, being an experienced 'expert' in participation processes, with a social profile that would make him trustworthy in the eyes of participants from many backgrounds.

In June 2001 a *second stage* of the participation process was organised, very much along the lines of the first stage. However, there were fewer sub-arenas. Five central sessions were organised. The scope rules were different, however, since a draft version of the programme was available, and the discussion concentrated on the question whether this draft truly represented the opinions of the participants or not. Participants had more structured opportunities to express their opinions on issues, using coloured balls to indicate whether they agreed or disagreed with certain aspects of the plan. However, there was also an open opportunity to express any opinion a participant would like to bring to wider attention. At the end of the sessions the participants were asked (by a show of hands) whether they agreed or disagreed with the use of the plan as the basis for development of subsequent plans. This can be seen as an additional aggregation rule, which enabled a clear conclusion about the general opinion on the proposal. A printed version of the plan was distributed widely before the meetings to inform the participants. During meetings posters represented central elements of the plan.

As in the first round of the citizen participation, the direct role of *leadership* was very limited. At the start of each session, after the city planner had presented some highlights of the proposal, interviews were held with key actors representing organisations that played an important role in the process. Among these was always one political leader (an alderman or the mayor). In the interviews the key actors could present their preliminary opinion on the proposal. Subsequently participants could ask questions to these key actors or enter into debate. However, it was stressed that the objective of the meetings was to discover the opinions of the participants, with the meetings not intended to 'defend' opinions held by the key actors.

Other arenas

Alongside the participation arenas, where (former) residents played the central role, a number of other arenas were considered to provide input into the redevelopment programme. Three arenas were seen as especially important: the programme development group, the planning group and the court of mayor and aldermen.

The programme development group (PDG) can be seen as an arena where the general programme for the redevelopment of Roombeek was drafted. It was centred around three programme managers (top-level public officials). This group had to write a draft version of a document that describes which functions should be accommodated in the redeveloped neighbourhood (housing, economic activity, infrastructure, etc.) and the policies needed to achieve the programmes' goals for the area (e.g. in terms of its social structure and social cohesion).

Whilst the PDG focused on 'what' should be done, the planning group (PG) developed proposals for 'how' these functions should be incorporated in the area. This planning group was centred round the previously mentioned city-planner. The PG typically produced maps and visuals of the functions proposed for the area.[2]

When looking at the institutional design of the two arenas (PDG and PG), the *boundary rules* are clearly based on professional expertise. In the PG the external town planner was accompanied by staff members of his firm and by town planners from within the municipal administration. In the PDG, the programme managers convened with the deputy-director of the project bureau responsible for rebuilding the area and the officer in charge of the participation process. The group also included staff supplied by the external town planner's firm, who undertook the bulk of the writing and informed their colleagues in the planning group.

When looking at the *authority rules* for these position holders, two aspects are important. Elsewhere (Denters and Klok 2003), there is discussion of how authority rules might reflect the more or less binding results of preceding arenas. For the purposes of this chapter the emphasis is upon the extent to which the outputs of the participatory arenas provide constraints for the choices that position holders, in for instance the PDG, could legitimately make. The institutional design of the decision-making process was far from unambiguous in this respect. On the one hand it was clearly indicated that the output of the participation process should provide a very important input into the PDG. On the other hand, it was also stated that results of expert panels and previous council decisions should be considered as important. This implied considerable discretion for position holders in the PDG. For much the same reasons the PG members had considerable discretion.

The constellation of the position holders in the PDG is such that each of them has to consult a 'constituency'. In the case of the sectoral programme managers, they had to consult relevant segments of the standing municipal organisation and other relevant governmental, quasi-governmental and social organisations in their sector. Moreover, the programme managers had to consider the basic principles of the general municipal scenario for urban redevelopment that is the basis for Enschede's participation in the national government's urban policy initiative. Finally they had to take into account the priorities of their political principals (especially the aldermen responsible for the three 'pillars' and for the coordination of the rebuilding of the area).

The officer in charge of the participation process had special responsibilities for heeding the outputs of the participatory process. As such he formed a tandem with the 'process facilitator'. The staff members of the consultancy firm were closely linked to the planning group and were expected to represent the external planner's perspective.

On the one hand this constellation of 'linking-pins' in the PDG ensured that relevant perspectives were brought to the table. On the other hand the heterogeneity of interests in the PDG put severe pressure on the *aggregation rules* in this arena, as different perspectives suggested different outcomes in the programme. One of the characteristics of the PDG arena, however, was that no explicit aggregation rule had been formulated. The group had a collective responsibility for writing a concept version of the programme, but no mechanism was available for resolving conflicts between the different perspectives. This resulted in a situation in which on many crucially important points the draft programme merely formulated points for further discussion. Under these conditions, the results achieved in more decisive arenas, especially the preliminary planning results in the PG, were perhaps more influential in guiding the redevelopment plans than the inputs from the PDG. This is not unlikely since the heterogeneity of interests represented in the PDG stands in marked contrast to the relative homogeneity of the PG. Although the PG, just like the PDG, lacked explicit aggregation rules, this institutional weakness posed no major threat to the arena's decisiveness. The homogeneity of interests within the PG arena and the central role of the 'high profile' external city planner reduced the need for a mechanism for conflict resolution.

In order to assess whether this state of affairs could have resulted in a problematic situation, it is necessary to give attention to the *scope rules* of the arenas. The scope of the options available as output was on the one hand limited to some extent by the results of the first stage participation process. However, as already indicated this result provided ample discretion to the actors in the PG and PDG. On the other hand the scope was limited to outputs that were to be acceptable in the subsequent representative arenas, most notably the court of mayor and aldermen (CMA) and the municipal council. It was clear that the output of PG and PDG had to be approved by the CMA first, in order to be presented to the second round participation after which they were to be approved by the council.

This is a point in the process where *leadership* is directly involved for the first time (apart from its involvement in the institutional design). At different points in the process the programme managers consulted the responsible aldermen on possible options to check whether these would be acceptable or not. Towards the end of this phase there were informal meetings with the entire CMA to resolve most of the points for discussion that came out of the PDG and to discuss a first draft proposal from the PG. These informal meetings were necessary because of the tight time schedule in which the formal meeting of the CMA was embedded. This formal meeting was scheduled close to the presentation of the draft plan for the second phase of the citizen participation process. This implied that there was little room for alterations of the proposal between the formal meeting and the presentation. In order to prevent a 'do or die' scenario for this CMA meeting, it had to be consulted in good time on an informal basis. In this way the responsible aldermen and the CMA as a whole could play a role in the PDG and PG arenas without formally being part of them and alleviate some of the problems that might have resulted from flaws in the institutional design of the PDG and PG arenas.

As has been indicated above, the results of the PDG and PG arenas had to be approved by the CMA. The basic institutional rules of this arena had been established within the general institutional framework of the political system of the city (Denters and Klok 2003). Here the emphasis is on the scope rules. Normally the output of the CMA would be a formal proposal to the community council. In this process it would be a proposal that was sufficiently supported by the CMA to be sent to the second round participation process. This status was very well articulated in the second round participation, where it was not to be seen as a proposal by the CMA, but rather as a draft plan which could be changed as a result of the participation process. In this way the leadership made sure that not all options for change were removed from the second round participation (scope rule). It also created some room in its own scope rule for its meeting on the proposal that had to be sent to the council after the participation process. However, the possibilities for substantial change would be limited in case of overwhelming approval of the plan in the participation process.

The actual behaviour of the participants in the different arenas is too complex to describe here. It is however important to note two results. On the one hand there was overwhelming support for the draft plan, as indicated by many supportive (and only a few critical), reactions and by a massive show of hands in support of the plan at the end of all but one of the meetings with former residents. This severely limited the scope rules of the subsequent CMA and council arenas, as there was hardly any other option than to approve of and to proceed with the current plan. Under the time pressure of the process, and taking into account that this support could be a first step in the restoration of citizens' trust in the political and administrative actors, this was an option that was taken with a great sense of relief.

There was however one meeting where there was no massive support, but an antagonistic atmosphere between the city planner who presented the plan and residents of a special area called 'het Roomveldje'. Here the basic consensual and deliberative institutional structure of the participation arenas had not resulted in mutual understanding, but in a stalemate and a possible situation of intensified conflict. This called for the exercise of leadership which took the form of an institutional redesign that will be described in the next section.

Institutional redesign as challenge and opportunity for leadership

In May and June of 2001 the development of a possible conflict threatened to disrupt the policy design phase. Former residents of a sub-area called 'het Roomveldje' disagreed strongly with the view of the city planner to preserve and restore as many old houses as possible. Both the majority of the residents and the owner of the houses – a housing corporation – were in favour of building entirely new houses. A permit to demolish the houses that had already been approved by the city was not put into effect after strong pressure from the city planner and some members of the city council. In the first phase of the participation process the committee of residents of the sub-area presented its case with ample force. However, a significant number of other participants, mostly from other parts of Roombeek, but also some from 'het Roomveldje', supported the idea of restoration, presented with much determination by the city planner. The committee of residents and the housing corporation tried to settle the matter by conducting a written survey among all former residents asking whether they were in favour of demolition and building new houses or in favour of restoration of the old houses. A majority indicated that they were in favour of demolition. The validity of this survey was however questioned by the city planner and other actors that were in favour of restoration. The phrasing of the questions was thought to have been biased towards building new houses. When the city planner indicated that he was not convinced that demolition of the remainder of the houses was to be included in the plan he was to propose, the committee of residents publicly declared their distrust in this 'arrogant, non-responsive' expert from out of town. The city planner for his part was of the opinion that the housing corporation was 'strategically using' the residents to pursue the corporation's own interest (building new houses would be far more cost-effective). At the second round of the participation process in June, the atmosphere between the parties was hostile. In order to prevent this issue from disrupting the entire process (which had in general developed in a good atmosphere), a solution was badly needed.

After consultation between the aldermen, the office responsible for the process (the project bureau), the city planner, the housing corporation and other key position holders it was concluded that four different city planners would be invited to develop and present a plan for the area. The former residents were given the role of jury in this competition. They had the right to vote on the different plans, and the 'winning' plan would be implemented. This institutional redesign prevented an outburst of open conflict. Emotions were cooled down as a result.

This process of institutional 'redesign' had a number of important features. Residents were given one vote per household, not one per person. A rule was defined that if only a minority of 40 per cent or less of the households used their vote, additional votes (10 each) would be granted to three actors: the housing corporation that owned the buildings, the project bureau responsible for rebuilding Roombeek (also representing the city), and a review committee consisting of independent experts and representatives of the professional actors involved. This review committee was established to check whether the proposals developed by the four city planners would fit within the proposals for the entire programme (developed mainly by the central city planner) and would meet financial and other constraints. There were no more 'open sessions' between planners and residents, the planners were to develop their plans in 'solitude', present them to the residents and interested actors in two sessions, and wait for the verdict.

In terms of the institutional rules of our framework, the new 'sub-arena' on the plan for 'het Roomveldje' can be described in the following way. The following *positions* can be discerned:

- The position of 'household' of the area, being the former residents that would have the right to vote on the plans;
- The position of 'review committee', a group of experts that was to check whether proposals would meet the scope rules;
- The positions of 'project bureau' and 'housing corporation', who would have a number of votes if the participation of residents fell below certain agreed levels;
- The position of 'plan developer', a city planner that was asked to develop a plan for the area.

The *boundary* rules were, contrary to the rules for the earlier part of the process, very restrictive:

- only former residents of 'het Roomveldje' were allowed access to the position of household;
- access for the housing corporation was defined by property ownership, access to the position of project bureau was pre-decided by the public administration;
- membership of the review committee was mutually agreed between the participating organisations (for the independent chairman) and by the organisations themselves (for their own representatives);
- four city planners were asked to perform the role of plan developer. Three parties were allowed to name one each – the housing corporation, the central city planner and the project bureau. A fourth planner was picked by agreement between these three actors.

The *authority* rules were also very restrictive, but far reaching in their consequences:

- Households had the right to vote and the right to ask for information at the presentation meetings. They had the right to discuss plans with each other, but were allowed no opportunity for extensive 'organised' deliberation.
- The review committee had the right to check the four plans and remove them from the competition if they did not meet the scope

rules, and they had the right to inform the residents on what the committee thought were the pros and cons of the plans that were in competition.

- The housing corporation, the project bureau and the review committee had the right to ten votes each, if less then 40 per cent of the residents used their votes.

The *scope* rules were on the one hand restrictive, but in terms of the entire process enlarged:

- It was established that the proposals of the four city planners had to fit well within the proposal made by the central city planner for the entire programme. This included the use of part of the area for shops and apartments, the location of roads (and that they should not be used as parking space). By definition the scope was also limited to the area of 'het Roomveldje' and participants had to choose from only four alternatives (the plans in the contest).
- Plans had to meet financial and other constrains defined by the city. These included 'normal' standards for building quality, energy consumption etc. and a minimum number of houses and minimum size requirements.
- In terms of the scope related to other, subsequent, arenas in the process, it can be concluded that the scope was enlarged in a substantive way: the plan winning the contest would be implemented, irrespective of the formal right of the city council to take this decision. The right to take the decision was, although perhaps not in a formal, but certainly in a 'de facto' way, transferred from the council to the arena where the residents could vote.

The *aggregation* rules were clearly defined in advance: the plan with the most votes would win the contest. In case less then 40 per cent of the households used their votes, three actors would get 10 additional votes each.

The *information* rules implied a subsequent enlargement of the actors that would be informed by the plans:

- First, the review committee would be informed about the four plans, in order to enable the check on the scope rules.
- Then, the remaining plans were presented only to the former residents, enabling them to be informed in a quiet way, without any possible fuss from other participants in the entire participation process.
- Subsequently the plans were presented in open meetings, enabling all people that were interested to be informed.
- On the evening of the actual vote the chairman of the review commit-

tee presented the pros and cons of the plans according to the analysis by the committee.

The following *pay-off* rules can be defined:

- The housing corporation would bear the costs of the implementation of the plan.
- The households would pay a rent if and when they lived in the houses which might be built, but a rent not exceeding a fixed amount of around €350 a month. This maximum was however fixed for all corporations in the entire Roombeek area.
- The project bureau and the housing corporation would share the costs of the process (meetings, hiring experts etc.).

The institutional structure of the arena for the development of a plan for 'het Roomveldje' differs remarkably from the structure of the original process. The basically deliberative and 'open' structure (both in terms of access of actors and in terms of scope of the alternatives to be considered), was substituted by a far more closed structure based on voting as an aggregation mechanism. In practice this enabled a change in the status of the decision-making process – from the collection of opinions to be used as an input to the programme of the central city planner to a final decision on which plan was to be implemented. This extended form of community involvement can be seen as an example par excellence of 'power to the people'.

It has to be noted however that this power was given to some people (the former residents of the area) and not to others (former residents of other areas or other citizens of Enschede). It also has to be noted that the role of some other actors was restricted. The power of the central city planner was reduced, since he was not anymore in direct control of the plan that was to be accepted. The city council, and the alderman in his important position of 'gatekeeper', had to mandate their decisional power de facto to the residents. These actors however agreed that this institutional redesign could perform a vital function in the entire process – the resolution of an issue that could easily develop into an open conflict that would harm the entire process. This provides a clear example of leadership.

Moreover, the power was not given unconditionally to the people. Several institutional safeguards were built into the structure:

- the formulation of scope rules that would guarantee a plan that would fit with the overall city development plan (and thus the central concerns of the city planner);
- additional scope rules that would exclude plans with undesirable results;

- a review committee that would make sure that these rules were observed;
- information to residents from the review committee offering an 'expert' view of the positive and negative aspects of the plans;
- additional votes for three 'interested parties' should only a minority of residents exercise their right to vote on the decision to be made;
- selection of the 'plan developers' by the interested parties, including the central city planner.

This is one example of the potential for a *complementarity* of urban leadership and community involvement in two ways. First it illustrates the use of institutional redesign as an act of leadership to prevent the outburst of open conflict. Second it exemplifies an institutional design where community involvement is very strong, but is embedded in a set of rules that constrain the outcomes to the ones that are within the vital interests defined by leaders and other interested parties. But was potential reflected in actual outcome?

The first outcome of the institutional redesign was certainly a cooling down of emotions. All participants were inclined to make the competition work well, as they were all aware of the disastrous consequences of failure. The four city planners were recruited without problems and they delivered their plans according to schedule. The review committee assessed the plans and concluded that one of them did not meet the scope rules (mainly in terms of financial constraints and the size of houses). The three remaining plans were presented to the former residents at a meeting where about half the residents were present. On the evening of the vote, the chairman of the review committee held a presentation that indicated that the three remaining plans fitted well within the scope rules and were more or less evenly balanced in a matrix of different pros and cons. When the vote was conducted it appeared that the threshold of 40 per cent was missed by only a couple of votes. The 30 votes of the three interested parties were used, but did not change the outcome of the vote. The plan that won the contest was the plan that proposed to restore only four of the old houses (other plans proposed to restore considerably higher numbers of houses). The announcement of the winning plan resulted in loud cheering from a majority of the residents present, most notably from those active in the resident committee that was in favour of demolition of all the houses. The result was seen by them as a clear 'victory' over those that were striving for restoration. The housing corporation was satisfied with the result as they were also in favour of building new houses. Political and public administration actors were satisfied because the plan was well within their range of acceptable outcomes, and a possible outburst of conflict was transformed into an example of 'giving power to the people', in a careful designed way. The city planner resented the fact that most of the houses were going to be demolished, but was satisfied with the opportunity to prevent open conflict.

So at least in terms of whether a policy proposal can be translated into a decision, and in terms of the legitimacy of that decision, the Roombeek example illustrates both the complementarity of urban leadership and community involvement, and the utility of an Institutional Analysis and Development framework.

Conclusions

In conclusion the example of the institutional design and redesign of structures for rebuilding Roombeek in general, and the neighbourhood of 'het Roomveldje' in particular, show the usefulness of institutional analysis as a tool to describe and analyse combinations of leadership and community involvement. They show that the careful and balanced design of an institutional structure is an essential function of leadership. Good leadership can be seen in well-balanced institutional designs, and that the absence of good leadership can be reflected in imbalanced or insufficiently articulated institutional structures.

The examples also show that in any one arena, the exercise of leadership does not necessarily take the form of actions by the leaders themselves. Leadership may be disguised as scope rules (limiting the possible outcomes to the ones acceptable to leaders, or to the interests they represent), or they may be found in the acts of a special position holder such as the review committee (that has the authority to maintain or interpret the rules). They might also be found in the selection of actors that become holders of a certain position (for example, the city planners chosen to develop a plan).

Important within the IAD framework is the idea of configurations of rules. This implies that the choices made in relation to one particular rule or set of rules will only be appropriate if other rules are well adapted to these choices. For example the choice of a voting system (as an aggregation rule) has consequences for boundary and authority rules. The latter must make very clear which actors are allowed to vote and what will be the consequences of the result of the vote. There are also implications for the scope rules. Actors must be very clear what are the (perhaps limited) alternatives on which they are going to vote.

The concept of configuration must also be applied to the configuration of (sub)arenas. The choice of giving decision-making status to the outcome of a participation process has de facto implications for the scope of the subsequent formal decision-making arena. The options open to formal decision makers is reduced to one – accepting the decision by residents.

In this chapter we have shown that changes in the positions of relevant actors (both leaders, citizen and other actors) can be described as changes in the rules of the arena. Such changes in position can be used as a frame of reference for empirically-based description of the actual behaviour of actors in the arena. Which actors did actually participate in the process? Which alternatives came to be discussed? How were scope rules interpreted and maintained by the actors? Which information was provided by certain actors? Which proposal got the majority of the votes? In this way institutional structure can be helpfully combined with what is observed at the behavioural level as the complementarity of urban leadership and community involvement.

Annex Operationalisation of the IAD rules

Position rules prescribe which positions are to be distinguished in a particular (sub-)arena.
Examples: Councillor, mayor, chairman, citizen, neighbourhood representative, etc.
These rules define positions in the current (sub)arena. They form the starting point for other types of rules to be used to link these positions to responsibilities, formal powers, etc.
Manifestation: There is/are . . . (position).

Boundary rules prescribe how the various positions in an arena become occupied.
Examples: a councillor will be chosen through a four-annual municipal election. An alderman is chosen by and from among the councillors.
These rules determine the accessibility of various positions and thereby the openness of an arena. They specify mechanisms of exclusion (conditions under which actors cannot enter positions) and of exit (conditions under which position holders can or have to leave a position).
Manifestation: Actors become . . . (position) by . . . (condition/procedure) or;
        Only if . . . (condition), actors become . . . (position) or;
        If . . . (condition), actors have to leave . . . (position).

Authority rules prescribe the allocation of rights and obligations for every position. These rules determine the means available for a position holder to perform his duties and define the (legitimate) behavioural alternatives that are open to an actor in a position.
Examples: every participant has the right (is allowed to) to present his opinion on the subject.
The secretary has the duty (should) to make minutes of the meeting. Every participant (all position holders) should refrain from reopening the discussion once a decision has been made.
Manifestation: If . . . (condition), . . . (position holder), operator* (should, is allowed to), . . . (behaviour).
** the operator specifies whether the rule defines an **obligation** or a **right** for the position holder.*

Scope rules prescribe the possible outcomes of interaction in a particular arena. On the one hand this refers to the limits to the **content** of the outcome of the arena. I.e. a rule might specify that a redevelopment plan for an area has to include at least 200 houses in lower price regions and a common building for welfare facilities.
On the other hand the scope rules specify the status of the outcome of the (sub)arena in relation to the other (sub)arenas of the entire **process**. The

exchange of information and preliminary consultations in a committee meeting, is of a different nature than the final decisions being made in the plenary council meeting, and different again from a decision in the court of mayor and aldermen etc. These rules are also important because they provide insight in the relations between various sub-arenas: in a committee meeting preliminary positions are being taken by spokesmen for the different party groups but the final decision is preserved to the meeting of the plenary council.

Manifestation: The scope of . . . (arena) is . . . (possible outcome), or;
The outcome of the . . . (arena) has the status of . . . (status in the process).

Aggregation rules prescribe how (collective) decisions and other outcomes in an arena are being made on the basis of the contributions of different position holders.

Examples: decisions are made by unanimity, simple or qualified majority rule; through weighted voting systems.

But there may also be other 'outcomes' e.g. a committee report in which it may be prescribed that it contains either a verbatim report of the stance taken by every actor or merely a summary of the majority position.

Manifestation: . . . (outcome) is obtained by . . . (aggregation mechanism).

Information rules prescribe which information is available to the various position holders; thereby it is also prescribed how various incumbents should relate to one another in terms of providing and granting access to information. We will call these internal information rules as they specify what should be going on inside the arena.

Examples: All participants have access to all relevant information; if a council member requests for information, the mayor has to provide that information; chairpersons have access to secret documents, other position holders have no access.

These rules also pertain to the public nature of meetings and the requirement to provide explicit and written justification for decisions. We will call these external information rules as they specify the rights of actors outside the arena.

Examples: all meetings are held in public (or not); decisions shall be motivated in public.

Manifestation: as rights and obligations (like authority rules; but now pertaining to information)
. . . (position holder), operator (should, is allowed to), . . . (information), or;
as specification of information rights of actors outside the arena;
. . . (specified others), (have or have not) the right to . . . (information).

Pay-off rules contain prescriptions regarding:

- the costs and benefits generated in the arena itself (e.g. the municipality pays for the meeting costs; council members receive a reimbursement of expenses etc);
- the costs and benefits that are part of an outcome (for example: injured parties should receive adequate compensation; or the costs will be distributed on a per capita, according to everyone's ability to pay or on the basis of a benefit principle);
- the consequences of decisions (for example: councillors are or are not personally liable for the financial implications of council decisions).

Manifestation: a specification (per position or per arena) of costs and benefits or of compensations or required contributions.

Notes

1 The possibilities of operationalising the different sets of rule are set out in an annex to this chapter.
2 One of the complications of the process was that the programme development (PDG) and the planning group (PG) had to do their work simultaneously. This was a result of the understandable desire to start rebuilding the area as soon as possible. Normally one would probably decide to determine the basic goals for the redevelopment programme first and subsequently develop the plan for the neighbourhood and draw the relevant maps. The simultaneous deliberations in these arenas (PDG and PG) produced coordination problems. In some cases maps were drawn based on the planners' images of the functions needed for the area, whereas programme managers were still debating these.

References

Denters, S. A. H. and Klok, P.-J. (2003) 'Rebuilding Roombeek-West, an Institutional Analysis of Interactive Governance in the Context of a Representative Democracy', in: S. A. H. Denters, O. van Heffen, J. Huisman and P.-J. Klok (eds) *The Rise of Interactive Governance and Quasi-Markets*, Dordrecht: Kluwer: 91–110.

Kiser, L. and Ostrom, E. (1982) 'The Three Worlds of Action', in: E. Ostrom (ed.) *Strategies of Political Inquiry*, Beverly Hills, CA: Sage: 179–222.

Mayntz, R. and Scharpf, F. W. (1995) 'Der Ansatz des akteurszentrierten Institutionalismus', in: R. Mayntz and F. W. Scharpf (eds) *Gesellschaftliche Selbstregulierung und politische Steuerung*, Frankfurt and New York: Campus: 39–72.

Ostrom, E. (1990) *Governing the Commons. The Evolution of Institutions for Collective Action*, Cambridge: Cambridge University Press.

Ostrom, E., Gardner, R. and Walker, J. (1994) *Rules, Games and Common-Pool Resources*, Ann Arbor, MI: The University of Michigan Press.

Scharpf, F. W. (1997) *Games Real Actors Play: Actor-Centered Institutionalism in Policy Research*, Boulder, CO: Westview Press.

4   The institutional setting of local political leadership and community involvement

Henry Bäck

The objective of this chapter is to describe and analyse the institutional settings of the cities studied in the PLUS project, with a focus on the restrictions and opportunities for action for political leadership, and restrictions, opportunities and incentives for community involvement. An important set of restrictions of course will be the interdependencies between the local authorities on the one hand, and higher levels of government and local community actors on the other. Therefore the issue of local autonomy and local self-government will be examined in the first part of the chapter. The second part of the chapter will discuss the institutional arrangements with regard to the political executive. Finally, potential consequences of other structural differences will be discussed. The empirical data for the description is primarily provided by the academic partners of the project mentioned in Chapter 1. In principle the focus will be on *cities* rather than national systems. Cities, however, are parts of national local government systems, at the same time influencing and being influenced by national systems. Parts of the analysis therefore will be carried out with the national systems as units of analysis.[1] Nevertheless, the objective of the chapter is to say something about the particular institutional settings of the eighteen cities, and not to provide generalisations about national local government systems.

Structure of local government systems

Before entering into the discussion about the autonomy of local authorities and their relations vis-à-vis upper tiers of government, an account of the general structure of the nine local government systems in which our cities are located is given, in terms of number of tiers and the number and size of municipalities. In this case the units for comparison thus are not cities but national local government systems.

The basic rule is that local government systems are ordered in two tiers below the governmental level that according to the doctrine is regarded as the creator of local governments. This level is in central states the central government and in federal states the federated government. Of the nine countries studied the best examples of the first type are New Zealand, Norway and Sweden with upper-tier counties (*regional councils, fylkeskommuner, landstingskommuner*) and local-level municipalities (*territorial local authorities, kommuner*). The second category – the federal model – is most purely represented by Germany with states (*Länder*), counties (*Kreise*) and municipalities and cities (*Gemeinde* and *Städte*).

With devolution to Scotland and Wales in the United Kingdom and with the implementation of the constitutionally provided regions in Italy these two systems are approaching the federal model with regard to the number of governmental tiers. Britain, on the other hand, taking into account the existence of parish, town and community councils below the district level displays an even wider range of governmental tiers than federations (Scottish Parliament/Welsh National Assembly – counties – districts – towns and parishes).

Poland represents an exception to the 'general rule' displaying a three-level structure notwithstanding its character as a centralised state with regions, counties (*powiaty*) and municipalities (*gminy*). The two remaining countries with unitary government systems, Greece and the Netherlands both formally have two-tier systems of subnational government. Dutch provinces are of relatively little importance.

This brief description of the overarching structure of the local government systems in which our eighteen case study cities are located could be refined in many ways. In many of the systems there are arrangements of joint committees and other cooperative arrangements between municipalities that are recognised as public authorities with established formal institutions. Another important deviation is the merger of the two lowest levels into one-tier authorities (unitary authorities in Britain, *kreisfreie Städte* in Germany etc.). As this is an arrangement in many systems applying to large and medium-sized cities, this unitary status applies to many of the cases studied in the PLUS project. Bristol, Heidelberg, Oslo, Poznan and Stoke-on-Trent are examples. Thus, even if the county level in many of the systems has been considered a solution for providing services mainly to rural areas, there are examples of a revitalisation of the county level primarily for providing an institutional framework for growth and development policies but also for coordination of service provision also in metropolitan areas. Thus the city of Göteborg in 1999 gave up its unitary status and entered into the newly established county West Götaland Region. Another example would be the establishment of a new Hannover region county authority in 2001.

County and municipal authorities are in general formally independent of each other even if there exists in some of the systems some supervisory powers of the counties over municipalities. This formal institutional independence, however, should not overshadow the fact that there are a number of functional, economic and political dependencies between authorities in the two respective tiers.

The size of municipalities is one of the most debated themes in local government studies and is a constant concern for policy makers. This is especially the case in metropolitan regions. In the USA especially there is a political and academic controversy between the adherents of the *polycentric city* (Tiebout 1956; Ostrom *et al.* 1961; Ostrom 1972; Boyne and Cole 1998) and the advocates of *metropolitan government.*

In the well-known discussion about the importance of municipal size the democratic qualities of the small unit and the agency of the large unit have been in focus (Dahl 1967; Dahl and Tufte 1974). These propositions have been criticised by, for instance, Newton (1982).

Keating (1997) points at four matters of principle that have dominated the consolidation debate: it has been a matter of efficiency, democracy, distribution and development. The fact that central values thus have been coupled to the issue of local government structure has established a link between what Keating calls 'an apparently dry matter such as administrative reorganisation' and more basic ideological values.

In many of the countries studied there have been merger reforms, without exception attempting to achieve the coveted economies-of-scale effects. In many cases the heyday for these reforms were the 1970s that saw amalgamations of municipalities in Britain, Germany, the Netherlands and Sweden among others. That the merger reforms emphasised economic rationality and downplayed the role of community and local territorial identity seems well in line with the culmination of modernity in the second half of the twentieth century.

The resulting pattern can be described as a fourfold grouping of our nine local government systems: Britain by far displays the largest municipalities with an average population size of more than 100,000. The next cluster discernable is made up of New Zealand, the Netherlands and Sweden averaging around 20,000 to 40,000. An average municipality in Germany or Poland reaches around half that size. The smallest local authorities in our country sample, with an average size around or below 10,000 are found in Greece, Italy and Norway. As with other measures of central tendency the descriptive value of these numbers of course is reduced due to variation. It also should be noticed that in federal Germany there are regional size variations systematically following the *Länder* division.

The eighteen local authorities under observation in the PLUS project do not fully mirror this pattern. One reason of course is the focus on *cities* that implies that all the studied municipalities are larger than the national averages. The population range is from 75,000 in Cinisello Balsamo and Ostrów Wielkopolski to Turin's 900,000 inhabitants. Another reason that the cities have been chosen, is not to be representative for their respective populations of local authorities, but because they have other characteristics important in terms of the research questions of the project.

The cities studied vary in population size. The following grouping of the cities might be useful:

- under 100,000 inhabitants: Cinisello Balsamo, Ostrów Wielkopolski, Roermond and Volos,
- 100,000–300,000 inhabitants: Bergen, Enschede, Heidelberg, Stoke-on-Trent and Waitakere,
- 300,000–600,000 inhabitants: Bristol, Christchurch, Göteborg, Hannover, Oslo and Poznan,
- more than 600,000 inhabitants: Athens, Stockholm and Turin.

Athens, Oslo and Stockholm are national capitals, and Hannover is the capital city of a federated state. Many, but not all of the others function as regional capitals. At least half of the cities are core cities in larger metropolitan regions, and two (Cinisello Balsamo and Waitakere) are parts of metropolitan regions but not core cities. The others have a more independent status in the city hierarchies of their countries.

Combining the two structural dimensions number of government tiers and average size of municipalities gives an indication of the complexity of the system of subnational government in the countries considered. Britain then stands out as a deviant case with extremely large municipalities and an especially complicated structure of governmental tiers. The opposite pole of Britain would in this respect be the two European peripheries of Greece and Norway displaying small municipalities in a simple structure of governmental tiers. There are clear similarities between the three continental systems of Germany, Italy and Poland all displaying more than two governmental tiers and comparatively small municipalities. With many and often small municipalities and a more complex structure of tiers these systems stand out as the most fragmented and complex institutional settings. Their opposite parties with respect to complexity would be the Dutch, New Zealand and Swedish systems with at most two subnational tiers of government and a small number of comparatively large municipalities: 74 in New Zealand, 289 in Sweden and 548 in the Netherlands as compared to 14,800 in Germany, 8,000 in Italy and around 2,500 in Poland.

Objections of course could be levelled against these observations. One such objection would be that the meaning of a particular subnational tier varies due to constitutional status and tasks. This variation would render the pure counting of tiers meaningless. I think that although this variation is a fact, there are consequences for urban leadership following on from the number of actors in the external setting, indicated by the number of governmental tiers, and the number of other municipalities (inversely indicated by the size of municipalities) to be managed in the organisational environment. As Wollman (2004) writing about Germany puts it: 'the two-tier structure [...] is embedded in a many-layer system [...] As the local authorities carry out the lion's share of [. . .] policies [. . .] [they] [. . .] face a heavy load of *vertical* policy-coordination.'

The relevance of using the average size of municipalities in the *national* local government system as an indicator of the complexity of metropolitan areas can be illustrated by referring to the size and number of local authorities in some randomly selected metropolitan areas in some of our sample countries. The data for Manchester, Rotterdam and Turin have been extracted from the case reports in Jouve and Lefèvre (2002) while the data on Stockholm are reported by Bäck (2003) (see Table 4.1).

The ranking of the four agglomerations according to the number and average size of peripheral municipalities is exactly the same as the result of a ranking of the four national local government systems according to mean size of first-tier local authorities. The direct relation between the number of local authorities in an urban region and the magnitude of the coordination needs can be empirically illustrated by the frequency of inter-municipal cooperative arrangements in the three Swedish metropolitan regions. In the Stockholm region consisting of 22 local authorities, 69 cooperative arrangements with a total of 2,265 pair-wise cooperative relations were recorded. The Göteborg and Malmö regions with 10 and 7 municipalities respectively reported 7 and 12 cooperative arrangements. These comprised 148 and 201 pair-wise relations respectively (Bäck 2003).

Page and Goldsmith (1987) provide another discussion about the relevance of the number and size of local authorities in a country. They suggest that, for various reasons, the number and size of municipalities affect central–local relations. It has consequences for the allocation of tasks, as central governments are unwilling to allocate important tasks to a large number of small municipalities, for efficiency and for political reasons. Smaller units tend to produce administrative control of central government vis-à-vis local government. The structure of the whole national system of subnational government therefore might have consequences for the whole system – including those cities that are far bigger than the national average.

Table 4.1 Population (1,000) of core cities and peripheral municipalities in four European metropolitan regions

	Core city population	Periphery population	Number of municipalities in periphery	Mean size of peripheral municipalities
Manchester	400	2,500	9	280
Stockholm	740	900	21	42
Rotterdam	590	540	16	34
Turin	920	780	52	15

The local authority between centre and locality

Local self-government is a matter of the extent of discretion not restricted by central government that local government enjoys. One way to approach the concept of discretion is to take a starting point in the local budget decision. The budget decision can be looked upon as a choice among an infinite number of possible budgets. This number is reduced by a system of restrictions. If a higher-tier government directly has decided the restriction, we talk of restrictions on local self-government. Restrictions decided by lateral relations or relations to non-governmental actors do pose limits to local autonomy, but not to local self-government.

If the local council were a rational actor, there would be a municipal *preference function.* The budget decision then would imply the council choosing that budget out of those remaining after the impact of restrictions reaching the highest preference level (Jonsson 1972; Andersson 1979; Ysander and Nordström 1985). In the real world the preferences of the local authority are decided by the outcome of the political game. Who *participates,* and what *power resources* and power positions these participants have at their disposal will decide the outcome. Not only politicians and parties, but also bureaucrats, professions, administrations, companies, associations, citizens and citizen groups take part in this game.

There is a diversity of restrictions. The *resources* at hand constitute one restriction. If local government is free to levy taxes the aggregate income of the municipal residents will be a restriction. If local government can not freely dispose with their population's income, but is funded in some other way, other factors will decide the amount of resources available.

The *costs* of achieving various objectives also must be considered. Among other things, these depend on the *magnitude of the needs* and the *prices of production factors* that the municipality has to acquire in order to attain its goals. The size of the needs is decided by demographic conditions. The price level is in market economies only indirectly under governmental control. On the other hand there are sometimes *task specific central government grants* changing the price relations between different production factors necessary for municipal activities (see Hagen 1996).

Central government orders local government to perform *specific tasks.* Moreover, it is customary in local government systems that local authorities are entitled to undertake additional tasks. This is the meaning of the *general competence clauses* of the Local Government Acts of the Nordic countries and the German constitution. General competence clauses increase discretion. State imposed tasks imply diminishing discretion. This reduction could be compensated if central government sends money for the fulfilment of the mandatory tasks together with the order. Given that there is a particular imposition, central government furthermore can be varyingly detailed in its *instructions* for the fulfilment of the task in question.

The budget example points out a number of questions to be answered if we want to create a picture of local self-government:

- *Actors*: who decides what actors are to take the decisions of the local authority, and what power resources will be available to the actors?
- *Resources*: who decides what resources will be available to the local authority, and what will be possible using these resources?
- *Tasks*: who decides what the local authority must do and may do?

Many criteria of local self-government that can be found in the literature can be coupled with these three questions. Larsen and Offerdal (1994) use *representativity* and *task width* as criteria. Representativity refers to the extent that the local unit is representing the population in the local territory. In accordance with the Convention on Local Self-Government of the Council of Europe Nilsson and Westerståhl (1997) discuss the *decision-making organisation* of the local political unit (the criterion is that members are elected in free elections), *tasks* and *economic resources*. Page and Goldsmith (1987) discuss the dimensions *functions*, *access* and *discretion*. The concept of access is concerned with the extent to which the two governmental tiers have access to channels to influence one another. Functions is analogous with the concept of task width, while discretion is about the degree of freedom of action that the superior party allows the subordinate party within the framework of current allocation of tasks. Hagen and Sørensen (1997) who discuss the dimensions of the concept of decentralisation, focus on the allocation of tasks, central government regulation of organisation and tasks, local freedom to decide about revenues and finally the size of municipalities.

In the next sections of this chapter I will apply the first two dimensions – the political and the economic dimension – in order to locate the eighteen local authorities in the nine countries studied on the continuum between centre and locality. The task dimension will be discussed later in the chapter and will then be considered in terms of the total resources at hand for the municipality as well as the total resources related to population size as an indicator of the task width of municipal operations. The question now at hand is how do local authorities link politically and economically to their local communities and economies on the one hand, and to the national political system and the national economy on the other hand.

The political dimension

Turnout in local elections

Local administration has not always and everywhere been an expression of the self-government of local communities or even an expression for the ambitions of locally-based rulers to control localities. On the contrary, national rulers have always attempted to control their territory with the help of field administrations. Mayors and magistrates appointed by the king and regional governors and 'commissioners of the republic' are examples of such local power-holders appointed from above through history. Today, in all European states, we also find local and regional out-posts of central or federal government and central government authori-ties. It is typical that most definitions of what local government is contain the criterion that decision making either is a task for elected representa-tives of the local communities or, exceptionally, institutions of direct democracy such as general town meetings or referenda.

It is thus not surprising that in modern local government there are very few examples of central government appointees exercising decision-making functions in the municipalities. Local-level authorities ruled by central government appointees are defined out of the category of local government. The only remnants found in our sample of cities are the Dutch mayors that actually are appointed by central government. The fact that local political decision makers are locally elected should not obscure the fact that local governments in many countries fulfil tasks delegated from the centre. There are many examples of central government dele-gates 'going native', and there might be a propensity for local representa-tives partially to identify with central authorities.

With the Dutch mayoral exception and these caveats concerning the loy-alties of local representatives, there are everywhere representative assem-blies wholly elected by the local electorates. One thus could conclude that the principle that decision makers in local governments represent the local communities has prevailed over the 'magistrate' idea. On the other hand there could still be a wide variation with regard to how much local councils actually represent local populations, and to what degree they enjoy a local electoral legitimacy. In our sample there is – when looking at the latest local elections – a range in voters' participation from a low of around 30 per cent in Bristol to more than 80 per cent in the two Italian cities.

There are no steep drops in the curve when the cities are ranked according to local election turnout. A categorisation thus necessarily will be somewhat arbitrary. With a dividing line around 50 per cent the top group is made up of the north (Norway and Sweden) and the south (Greece and Italy), while the bottom group is made up of those countries geographically in between (Germany, Poland, the Netherlands and Britain) and New Zealand.

One conclusion could be that the local power-holders in Scandinavia and Southern Europe are 'more representative' of their local populations than their German, Polish, Dutch and British counterparts. Yet, represen-tativity of local governments cannot be evaluated by looking at sheer numbers of voter turnout. Therefore, this conclusion will be qualified in the next section.

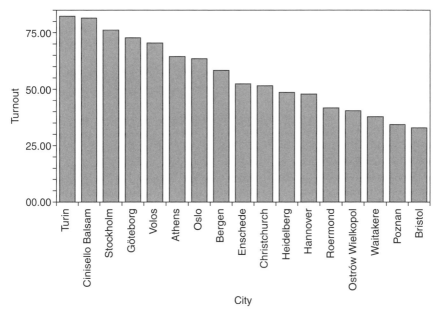

Figure 4.1 Participation in council elections in the case study cities.

Nationalisation of local elections

A common theme in descriptions of local elections is their dependence upon national party sympathies. If electoral choice in local elections primarily is an expression of national party identities and ideologies and less the result of a choice between local candidates or proposed local policies, then the relevance of the previous discussion about the importance of local turnout could be seriously questioned. Voting is for instance compulsory in Greece, and one could doubt whether local voting under such circumstances actually is an expression of support for either the local regime or for specific local policies. In Sweden local elections are held on the same day as national elections, something that without doubt contributes to the high local turnout, but at the same time as campaigning tends to be dominated by national issues. Other institutional arrangements such as not having local elections at the same day in all municipalities in the country also could be expected to have implications for the degree of nationalisation of local elections.

It is a common understanding in electoral research that there always is a strong influence from national politics on local electoral behaviour, and a strong influence from national politics on the other kind of 'second order elections' in the European context, namely the European Parliament elections (Reif and Schmitt 1997). Among factors that could produce variations in the degree of nationalisation there are the previously discussed institutional arrangements: compulsory or voluntary voting, simultaneous national and local elections and simultaneous local elections in the whole country. Another factor of course is the strength of the national party system and the degree to which the national party system has penetrated local government.

Considering the institutional arrangements concerning local elections Sweden seems to have the institutions most favourable to nationalisation of local elections and least favourable to localisation. Local elections are carried out on the same day in all municipalities and on the same day that national elections are held. The electoral method is proportional and only recently have some arrangements for allowing voters to choose between party candidates been introduced. Norway and the Netherlands have very similar systems, but with the important difference that local and national elections are separated in time. In Greece compulsory voting could favour nationalisation. The personalisation following on from the direct election of mayors, however, acts as a countervailing force. Also in Germany, Italy and Poland the direct election of mayors can be expected to counteract nationalisation. Local elections that are not simultaneous in all parts of the country in Germany and non-proportional representation in smaller Polish municipalities pull in the same direction. Britain, finally, displays with elections that are not simultaneous, the first-past-the post electoral system and the newly introduced option of direct mayoral elections, institutions that theoretically could be expected to favour localisation.

Only considering the formal institutions for local elections there is a range from the 'nationalising' systems of Northern (Sweden, Norway and the Netherlands) and Southern (Greece) Europe to the more 'localising' or perhaps one should say 'less nationalising' electoral systems of Germany, Poland and Britain.

We do not have any comparable data on the actual outcomes of these institutions. In some cases figures on the representation of national parties in local councils seem to corroborate the predictions of the institutional analysis. In Norway and Sweden around 95 per cent of local councillors represent national parties, and in the Netherlands around 80 per cent. In New Zealand on the other hand there is a very loose connection between national and local party systems, local parties are actually missing in many municipalities. In our two New Zealand case cities there is a party system for councillors, and these local parties are, however weakly, linked to national parties.

Based on the different evidence given from the case study cities I would suggest a trichotomy, where the two Scandinavian local electoral systems together with Greece stand out as those producing the most nationalised results. The opposite pole with the least nationalised local elections seems to be represented by Italy, New Zealand and Poland, with Germany and the Netherlands falling somewhere in between. The British cities in our sample would be in the same category as the German and Dutch cities.

Such a generalised classification, however, does not seem appropriate for the case of Stoke-on-Trent, where the directly elected mayor, as well as one third of the members of the council are not affiliated to any of the national parties. Generally, the introduction of directly elected mayors in a number of British local authorities is associated with a break with a tradition of party political nationalisation in British local government.[2]

Italy and Poland are interesting cases, as they seem to arrive at their outcome of relatively low levels of nationalisation of local elections from different directions. Italy used to be an example of a highly party politicised system dominated by national parties. The collapse of the party system, and the constitutional reforms following in its aftermath, have combined to produce the relatively low level of nationalisation and party politicisation of Italian local government. In Poland the case is the opposite: a modern party system has not yet fully developed after the fall of communism. If Italy could be understood in post-modern terms, Poland instead can be understood as a case of pre-modernity, if a well-developed party system is seen as an expression of modernity.

In Scandinavia institutional arrangements favouring nationalisation of local elections seem to work. In the other countries in our study, however, a comparable level of nationalisation seems to result both from institutions favouring nationalisation (as in Greece and the Netherlands) and institutions less favourable to nationalisation (as in Germany and the UK).

If both turnout in local elections and nationalisation of elections is considered, the conclusion would be that the local governments in our sample, that could be expected to best express the preferences of the local communities would be the two Italian cities displaying a relatively high level of localisation (a relatively low level of nationalisation) as well as high voter turnout. In the Scandinavian and Greek cities on the other hand participation is high, but it seems fair to perceive voting behaviour in local elections in a relatively high degree as an expression of preferences for national actors and policies rather than local conditions. The relations of the remaining cities with the national polity (Bristol, the German and Dutch cities) or the local community (the Polish and New Zealand cities and Stoke-on-Trent) are weakened by low electoral turnout.

The economic dimension

The essential aspect of local government finance with regard to central–local relations is how much of the revenues of local government can be controlled locally. In the nine local government systems studied there is a range of sources of income for local authorities. In all the systems there is some form of local taxation. Its share of total revenues, however, varies widely, as well as the discretion enjoyed by local authorities in fixing tax rates. Even if the local authority has limited power to decide on levels of taxation on income or property, local taxation constitutes a link between the local community and the local economy on the one hand and the municipality on the other hand.

Another source of income in all the systems studied, that in the same way directs a flow of economic resources from the local economy to the local authority is fees and charges for services delivered. Even if the freedom to decide on taxes, fees and charges and their levels is restricted, they link the finances of the local authority to the local economy rather than to central government fiscal developments.

There are other sources of income functioning in the opposite way – sources that are dependent only upon decisions by central government and/or the development of the national economy and central government finances. The most prominent of these of course are central government grants. In all the countries studied there are such grant systems, all with *general block grants* and *task-specific grants* in varying proportions. In federal Germany and regionalised Italy the meso level also has an important role in this context. In a number of cases there are systems installed guaranteeing local authorities shares of nationally decided and collected taxes. This is the case in for instance Germany, Poland and Britain. In Germany and Poland the local shares are proportional to the amount of taxes collected in the respective municipalities. The tax sharing systems in these two countries thus has no element of equalising the fiscal conditions of different local authorities.[3] Equalisation can be achieved either through tax sharing, through state grants as in Germany or through a system of redistribution within the local government sector as is primarily the case in Sweden.

Finally, there is in the different national systems an option of borrowing to fund primarily capital expenditure, but in some cases also current expenditure. I think, however, that borrowing could be considered a source of income only in the short term. In the long term loans sooner or later have to be repaid using one or the other of the sources of current income.

With regard to the central–local dimension and the structure of local government revenues three separate, but interrelated approaches can be applied. One could first consider *the dependence of local government funding on the local economy* or on the other hand the national economy and central government finance. Another approach would be to look into *the discretion that local authorities enjoy in spending* the different kinds of income. Take central government block grants as an example: in the first case such grants represent a nationalising and de-localising element, as they generally are granted without reference to the local economy. Applying the other approach we would classify such grants as a localising element in the whole setup of rules, as local authorities usually are free to decide on how to spend the grant. A third approach would be to consider the degree of *discretion that the local authorities have over their sources of revenue.* Does local government have the authority to set both tax rates and tax base, and who decides upon tax-sharing arrangements (Caulfield 2002)?

Here I will disregard the two latter approaches, and only try to describe local authorities in terms of their dependence on the local versus the national economy. This choice of perspective will focus on the incentives provided by the fiscal system for local leaders to engage in coalitions with local business ('regimes', see Stone 1989) and to engage in economic growth policies. Leaders of municipalities tightly linked to the local economy could be assumed to be more interested in building coalitions with local economic actors, and more interested in growth policies than leaders of municipalities primarily funded 'from above'. The alternative perspectives (spending discretion and fiscal autonomy) would focus other questions – mainly relating to intergovernmental relations.

Thus local taxes, fees and charges and the tax shares in Germany and Poland will be regarded as indicators of localism, while central government grants, other tax-sharing systems and nationally decided equalising schemes indicate centralism. It should be remembered, however, that centralism here does not necessarily imply that local actors are steered by central political actors, but that local actors are financially dependent on the national economy and central government fiscal policy.

Vetter (2002) calculated from Council of Europe data the shares of local taxes and fees of total local government revenues for 16 West European countries, including seven of our nine case study countries. In this ranking Swedish local authorities are most dependent on local income, followed by Norway, Germany, Italy, Greece, the Netherlands and finally Britain. This ranking obviously is very similar to the ranking of our case study cities reported in Figure 4.2.[4]

Given the extreme complexity of many of the national funding systems, and given the many differences in the construction of them it is hard to arrive at comparable estimates of these two components of local government revenue. Assessing figures from our case study cities the following would be a tentative grouping (numbers in parenthesis are reported 'national' shares of local government revenues):

- High levels of nationalisation: the Netherlands (73 per cent), Greece (92 per cent) and Britain.
- High levels of localisation: New Zealand (11 per cent), Sweden (15 per cent), Germany,[5] Norway (39 per cent), Poland (40 per cent) and Italy.

Political and economic dependency

We are now in the position to combine the two dimensions of central–local dependency discussed so far – political and economic dependency respectively. The ideal type of a *localised local authority* would

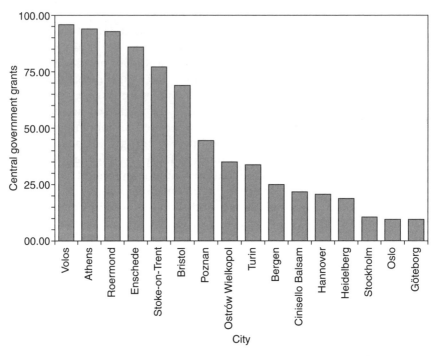

Figure 4.2 Grants from upper levels of government as shares of city budgets.

have the following characteristics: It would be politically tightly linked to the local community, which would require a low level of nationalisation of local elections, and at the same time a high level of voter participation. Campaigns would be carried out over local issues by competing local lists and independent candidates, between which a large part of the electorate would choose. At the same time the municipality would largely be funded through resources emanating from the local economy and appropriated by means of local taxes and fees and charges for municipal services delivered.

The opposite – the ideal type of *a nationalised local authority* – is primarily politically linked to the national political system via the national political parties and a high voter turnout. National issues are prominent in the election campaigns, and voters primarily are guided by ideological convictions or national party identities. The municipal activities are primarily funded with grants allocated from the higher tiers of government, and independent of the economic resources generated by the local economy.

As it seems from the previous account, there are no local government systems exactly emulating these two ideal types. The Italian, Polish and New Zealand cities could come closest to 'the localised local authority', but at least the Polish and New Zealand cities differ from the ideal type in the respect that the political link with the local community is weakened by a low electoral participation. On the other hand the Dutch and Greek cities and Bristol are those most similar to the 'nationalised local authority', but in the Dutch and British cases the political links with the centre are weakened by low participation. In the two Greek cases these links are 'artificially' strengthened by compulsory voting. Stoke-on-Trent, due to its lower degree of nationalised politics is in the category of economically, but not politically nationalised authorities.

Classifying the cities in federal Germany as 'politically nationalised' might offend a sensitive mind. It then should be remembered that nationalisation, especially in the case of economic dependency has been defined in terms of dependency on *upper tiers of government*, which in the German case includes the *Länder*. A more appropriate term then, especially in the case of Germany might have been 'a de-localised system'.

The Scandinavian cities together with the German cities stand out as interesting deviations from the ideal types. In Scandinavia there is a close link between the municipalities and their local economies, at the same time as they are politically closely linked to the centre.

The groups of local government systems thus identified display similarities with as well as differences from other categorisations in the literature on comparative local government.[6] A common trait in many of these is a North–South divide. This materialises here in the similarities between the cities in the two Scandinavian countries. South European cities are, however, in contrast with traditional categorisations, differentiated from each other.

The categorisation made here of course is a snapshot of targets that are actually moving. The most evident example of a system in transition of course is Poland, but it has also been pointed out the clear movement of the British local government system during the last decades of the twentieth century towards an increasing dependency on the national economic and financial situation, i.e. a movement from the 'Scandinavian' pole of the scheme towards 'the nationalised municipality' pole.

One might speculate whether there are any general tendencies of movement in this scheme. With regard to the political dimension there is a lot of evidence of a decreasing nationalisation of local elections. Personalities become more important at the expense of parties. Local lists and parties become more important, and local issues become more salient in local campaigns. This development is underpinned by institutional reforms, e.g. introduction of directly elected mayors, that amplifies de-party politicisation. Along the other dimension the general trend (if there is any) seems to be in the nationalising direction. Local authorities become more and more dependent on central grants or equalisation schemes, and thus less and less dependent on the economic resources generated by their own communities. If one should dare to have an opinion about the direction of change, there seems to be a rather general trend of movement away from the Scandinavian and the 'nationalised municipality' poles towards the (almost) empty lower right hand corner of Figure 4.3, where cities become politically more detached from the national polity, at the same time as they become economically more dependent on the national economy and central government.

The internal organisation of city governments

In their study of local government chief executives Mouritzen and Svara (2002) distinguish three elements that practically always are present in the municipal organisation: an elected council, a political leader (mayor) and an appointed head of the municipal administration. Each of these elements represents an organising principle: the council is an expression of the principle of 'layman rule'; the mayor stands for the principle of 'political leadership' and the chief executive the principle of 'professionalism'.

The ideal types of municipal organisation are characterised by different emphases on these three principles. *The strong mayor form* has an elected mayor that controls the majority of the council and is in charge of all executive functions. In this model where the emphasis is on the principle of political leadership we find among those systems that are studied in

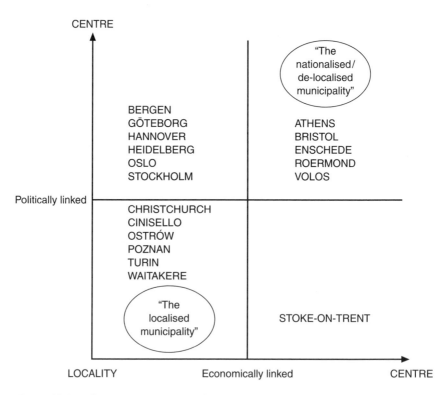

Figure 4.3 Local government systems between centre and locality.

both Mouritzen's and Svara's study and our own, the Italian system of governance.

In *the committee-leader form* one person is clearly 'the political leader' of the municipality. The leader may or may not control the council. Executive powers are shared: the political leader may have responsibility for some executive functions while others will rest with standing committees and with the chief executive. This model implies an even blending of the three principles. Of the local government systems studied in both projects the Swedish and British systems fall into this category. It should however be noted that this classification is based on the British system before the recent constitutional reforms, in which our two case study cities have chosen different options, Bristol choosing the cabinet model retaining some resemblance with the committee-leader form and Stoke-on-Trent opting for a unique model combining features of the strong mayor and council-manager forms.

In *the collective form* the decision centre is one collegiate body, the Executive Committee, responsible for all executive functions. The Executive Committee consists of locally elected politicians and the mayor presiding and implies a greater emphasis to the layman principle. The Dutch system would be an example of this model.

The council-manager form, finally, is a system where all executive functions are in the hands of the city manager appointed by the council. The council is a relatively small body headed by the mayor who formally has presiding and ceremonial functions. In this model the emphasis is on professionalism. The example given is Norway. It should however be observed that this categorisation of Norway is based on the 'Alderman model' common in Norway. Our two case study cities, however, have chosen the optional parliamentary steering model, more in line with the above-mentioned committee-leader form.

When looking at our eighteen case study cities, I first would like to make some modifications to the threefold set-up of institutions suggested by Mouritzen and Svara. In nearly all the cities, not only in those cities conforming to the committee-leader and the collective form, there is some form of collective executive political body beside the political leader or mayor. In the strong mayor systems this body is made up of the mayors' deputies, in parliamentary systems like the ones in Bristol, Bergen or Oslo the body in question would be the cabinet or 'city government'. Concerning the relation between the executive (one-man or collective) and administration it seems that the important dimension is whether the political executive actually also is the administrative executive, or if there is a political-administrative dualism in place. It seems in all our cities, except those in New Zealand and Sweden, that there is such a close link between politics and administration. The mayor or political leader also is in full charge of the municipal administration, or his deputies or the members of the cabinet function as heads of their respective departments. Only in New

Zealand and Sweden this link is missing. The mayor or the executive committee and its leader are not in charge of the administration but there is an appointed chief executive filling this function. In Stoke-on-Trent the executive is made up of the elected mayor together with the council manager.

As in all the other thirteen cities the relations between the political executive and the apex of the administrative apparatus, in principle are similar, this aspect of the internal organisation will be left out of the following analysis. This leaves us with the following constituting elements:

- the political leader (the mayor);
- the collective political executive (executive committee, deputy-mayors);
- the council.

Heinelt and Haus (in Chapter 2 of this volume) suggest that the political organisation (government as they call it) be analysed along two dimensions, that they are able to link to legitimation processes:

- consociational or majoritarian democracy (Heinelt and Haus use the term 'competitive');
- monistic or dualistic organisation.

These two dimensions are closely linked to traditional ideal types in constitutional analysis. The consociational type corresponds in its purest form to *government by assembly* while its opposite, the majoritarian form, corresponds to *parliamentary government*. The monistic form represents the principle of *parliamentary sovereignty* while the dualistic form is an expression of the principle of the *separation of powers*, which in its democratic form is represented by *presidentialism*. If the two dimensions are combined we arrive at the following typology:

- *Assembly Government* would be represented by situations where executive power is in the hands of a proportionally composed committee of the council, i.e. *monism* in combination with *consociationalism*. This is very close to what Mouritzen and Svara term 'the committee leader form'.
- *Parliamentarianism* – the combination of *monism* with *majoritarianism* – is where there is a collective executive, appointed by the council not using proportional techniques, but some variation of the majority principle. Mouritzen and Svara would probably also classify the parliamentary system as a 'committee leader form'.
- In *presidentialism* there is a separately elected mayor, appointing his own cabinet of deputies without consideration of the party-political composition of the council. In this form the *dualistic* and *majoritarian* principles are combined.

- In *semi-presidentialism* on the other hand the mayor would surround himself with a collective executive appointed by the council. Here *dualism* is combined with *consociationalism* or *majoritarianism* depending on how the collective executive is appointed by the council. I think that both this and the presidential system would be classified as 'strong mayor' forms by Mouritzen and Svara.

It thus turns out, that disregarding the relations between politics and administration, what is covered by Mouritzen and Svara's typology is what we here call the monistic-dualistic dichotomy, while the consociational-majoritarian dimension adds a new aspect, that is referring to the relationship between the council and the collective executive.

I will now continue this exercise by examining how well the constitutions of the eighteen case study cities correspond to the four ideal types sketched above.

Assembly government systems

In Swedish local government all council committees including the executive committee are elected by the council applying proportional representation. The leader of the executive committee, which is the 'political leader' or 'mayor' of the municipality, is likewise elected by the council. There was, mainly in the 1970s, a discussion where the introduction of a parliamentary system was advocated. This debate however ended up, not in parliamentarianism, but in what I have termed *quasi-parliamentarianism*. In quasi-parliamentarianism all committee leaders, including 'the mayor' are appointed by a party or a party coalition at least tolerated by the council. If the group of committee leaders headed by the leader of the executive committee is regarded as a city government, this is a parliamentary system. This analogy, however, is ambiguous. The committee leader group is not legally recognised as a collective political body, and there are no institutions for the formation or dissolution of coalitions and 'governments'. Formally, according to the Local Government Act, it is the executive committee that is the executive of the municipality. The quasi-parliamentary system was introduced in Swedish local government in the 1970s, but for some reason the two biggest cities, Stockholm and Göteborg, were laggards and did not adopt quasi-parliamentarianism until 1994 (Bäck and Johansson 2000).

The traditional system in Norway is very similar to the Swedish system in this respect. Mouritzen and Svara do place Sweden and Norway in different categories – Sweden in the committee leader group and Norway in the council-manager form. This however is due to differences in the relationship between politics and administration that have been disregarded here. Also in Norway there has been a trend, albeit not so strong as in Sweden towards quasi-parliamentarianism. In one respect, however,

Norwegian legislation has gone further, allowing local authorities to choose between a traditional 'alderman model' and a parliamentary model. This option was chosen already in 1986 (with the support of special legislation) by the capital Oslo, and in 2000 by Bergen. In those two cities, that also are our cases, there is a city government (*byråd*) elected by majority vote in the council. The members of the *byråd* are directly in charge of their respective sectors of municipal activities, much the same as cabinet ministers on the national level. This means, that our two Norwegian case study cities rather recently have moved from 'assembly government' to 'parliamentarianism' (Baldersheim and Strand 1988; Hagen *et al.* 1999).

The same applies to the British cities. The traditional British local government form of committee rule bears many similarities with the assembly government systems in the two Scandinavian countries. In the Blair regime's effort of 'modernising' the constitution of the country, reorganisation of local government political organisation has been an important element (Hambleton 2000). British local authorities have been offered three optional models:

1   a directly elected mayor with a cabinet;
2   a directly elected mayor with council manager; and
3   an indirectly elected leader with a cabinet.

Our two case study cities have chosen different routes. Bristol has decided to choose option 3 – the cabinet model, while Stoke-on-Trent is the only authority in the UK that has chosen option 2, the model where the executive is made up of the popularly elected mayor and the appointed council manager. In terms of the categories constructed here this means that Bristol has followed the same road as Bergen and Oslo, i.e. from assembly government to parliamentarianism, while Stoke-on-Trent has moved from assembly government to presidentialism.

A similar development is displayed by Polish local government. A system with directly elected mayors has replaced the previous system with an executive board, and its leader, elected by the council. Also the executive board has disappeared being replaced as a collective executive body by one to three deputies appointed by the mayor. This seems to imply that Polish local government has changed from assembly government to presidentialism.

Parliamentary systems

Apart from the cities recently or rather recently opting for this model (Bergen, Bristol and Oslo) the two Dutch cities could be situated in this category. The executive function in Dutch local government is performed by the Court of Mayor and Aldermen, the aldermen being appointed by the majority coalition in the council. The deviant part of the Dutch model is the mayor appointed by central government that has been commented upon earlier in this chapter. This renders the model a flavour of a separation-of-powers model, but not the presidential type where both parliament and president (council and mayor) derive their legitimacy from the *demos*, but in separate elections. The Dutch model rather resembles an older monarchic parliamentarianism, where parliament derived its legitimacy from the people and the monarch received his legitimacy from elsewhere (for instance from God, or in the case of Dutch local authorities from central government).

Also in the Netherlands there has been a movement for constitutional reform. The catchword for this, however, has been dualisation. A number of measures have been proposed in order to differentiate between the powers and functions of the council and the executive. Proposed measures also include the direct election of mayors, which would move Dutch local government from the parliamentary model towards semi-presidentialism. However, there is also the option that the political process will not result in semi-presidentialism, but rather in a system where the local council's recommendations will be given more weight in national government's appointment of mayors.

Semi-presidentialism

It has been pointed out above that there is in many systems a trend towards adopting directly elected mayors. This was the case in Britain and Poland, but the issue also has been on the agenda in the Netherlands. Another such trend has been surfacing in Germany. Being a federal state Germany has displayed regionally different local government systems. It has also been pointed out in the literature the importance that occupation powers after the Second World War have had in differentiating local government (Grunow 1992, Norton 1994). German local government, however, has converged (Wollman 2002, 2004). In all municipalities (except for the city-states Berlin, Bremen and Hamburg) systems with directly elected mayors have been adopted whereas deputy mayors/senior officers are appointed by the council (sometimes in agreement with the mayor). This makes German cities belong to the semi-presidential model.

The actual relations between the collective executive (deputy mayors) and the council, however, take different forms in different German cities. In both the German case study cities, however, the collective executive chaired by the directly elected mayor is proportionally elected by the city council. This implies that Hannover and Heidelberg in the terminology introduced here are to be regarded as variations of 'semi-presidentialism'. In Heidelberg, the lord/lady mayor and the deputy mayors do not form an 'executive body'. In Hannover, the deputy mayors are not elected on a proportional basis but by a coalition of Social Democrats and Greens.

There is in addition an executive committee (*Hauptverwaltungsausschuß*) in which the members, besides the deputy-mayors, are appointed on a proportional basis.

Presidentialism

As accounted for above the Polish cities in the recently introduced model with a directly elected mayor ruling together with appointed deputies represent the presidential model.

The four cities in our south European countries, Greece and Italy, also can be put in this category. In Greece and Italy there are directly elected mayors, surrounding themselves with a group of deputies representing a majority of the council. This might seem a typical semi-presidential arrangement. It should be observed, however, that this majority is not achieved independently of the mayoral election. The party or the coalition of parties winning the mayoral election is awarded a 'bonus' – a guaranteed majority in the council. This implies, that the problem of co-habitation, that is well known in national semi-presidential systems cannot occur in the Greek and Italian cities (Duverger 1997). Mayors in the Greek and Italian cities do not, as Jacques Chirac had to, have to co-exist with a cabinet representing a hostile parliamentary majority.

In the Italian case the introduction of directly elected mayors after the demise of the party system represents a move from parliamentarianism to presidentialism. Stoke-on-Trent represents with its mayor-manager form a change from assembly government to presidentialism. The Stoke-on-Trent model as well as the New Zealand cities with a more pure council-manager form are also here referred to the presidential category. Even if these three cities do not exactly fit into this group, important features are dualism and the absence of a council-appointed collective executive.

Interim results

The discussion on the internal political organisation of the cities now can be summarised.

External and internal settings

Combining the two aspects – the position of municipalities between centre and locality and the internal organisation of municipalities – logically produces sixteen different combinations. Seven of these are represented by the case study cities.

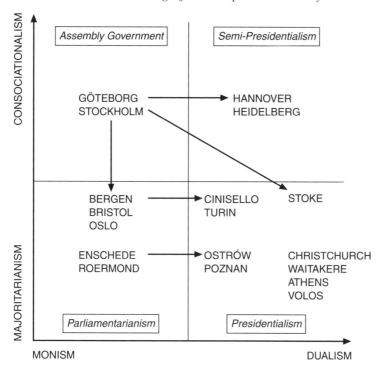

Figure 4.4 Constitutions of case study cities.

Note
Arrows denote recent changes described in text.

Table 4.2 Centre-locality and constitutional systems of case study cities

Politically localised			Politically nationalised	
Assembly government	Parliamentarianism	Semi-presidentialism	Parliamentarianism	Presidentialism
Göteborg Stockholm	Bergen Oslo	Hannover Heidelberg	Bristol Enschede Roermond	Athens Volos

Economically localised	Economically nationalised
Presidentialism	Presidentialism
Cinisello Balsamo Christchurch Ostrów Wielkopolski Poznan Turin Waitakere	Stoke-on-Trent

So what?

Institutions provide opportunities, incentives and obstacles for action. If the institutional settings sketched in this chapter should be of any relevance for considerations on partnership, leadership and certain (i.e. sustainable) outcomes in economic competitiveness and social inclusion policies the question at hand is: do we have reason to believe that there are institutional arrangements that facilitate or encourage, or the other way around, hinder or discourage community involvement, political leadership or one or the other of the two mentioned policies?

Community involvement: the degree to which the municipal organisation is linked to the national level and to the locality seems to have obvious relevance for the opportunities for community involvement. It seems that a local authority that is tightly in the hands of national political forces and/or for its survival is primarily not dependent on resources generated by the local economy would be less open to community involvement. On the other hand we would expect a more localised authority to be more appealing for actors in the local community to influence. When it comes to internal constitutional arrangements, we would primarily expect the majoritarian idea to be connected to a thin competitive conception of democracy (Schumpeter 1947). The political role of the citizenry would be holding the elite accountable by choosing between competing elites on election day. There would be no role for a more continuous civil participation in politics.

Political leadership: Mouritzen and Svara (2002) saw local government systems with a directly elected mayor as approaching the government form emphasising the principle of strong political leadership. One reason for arguing that the dualistic systems could give better opportunities for successful political leadership would be the extra political resources (i.e. an own electoral legitimation) given to the mayor. But there have also been arguments claiming that the majoritarian principle lays a better ground for leadership than the consociational principle. A politically homogenous cabinet would be a more potent decision-making body than a heterogeneous council committee, it has been suggested.

Economic competitiveness policies: a local authority that for its activities, development and very survival is dependent on the income generated by the local economy could be assumed to have more incentives to pursue policies enhancing the economic competitiveness of the local community than an authority that is funded from above and independent of the economic activities in the local territory.

Social inclusion policies: if there are any resources that socially excluded groups could contribute to the local leadership be they included, it would be votes. In settings where local political actors are more dependent on votes, there would be more incentives to pursue social inclusion policies than in settings where this dependency is less. Of the institutional dimensions discussed, political localisation (i.e. systems less tightly knit to the national political system) and majoritarianism could be assumed to have this characteristic.

This discussion would result in among others the following propositions:

• The institutions are especially unfavourable to community involvement in the British, Dutch, Greek and Norwegian cities.
• The institutional arrangement is especially favourable to strong political leadership in the Greek, Italian, New Zealand and Polish cities and in Stoke-on-Trent. The arrangements are especially unfavourable in the two Swedish cities.
• Economic dependency on the local community produces special incentives for the German, Scandinavian, Italian, New Zealand and Polish cities to carry out policies enhancing economic competitiveness.
• The degree of dependency on the local electorate is especially favourable to social inclusion policies in the Italian, New Zealand and Polish cities and in Stoke-on-Trent. The opposite could be expected in German and Swedish cities.

What if not?

Institutions do not directly produce action, but rather construct the frames within which action takes place. One obvious reason for predicted actions not to materialise then is that actors for some reason have not been able to exploit the opportunities at hand. But the argument can also be applied in the opposite direction: actors have been willing and able (clever enough) to overcome institutionally defined constraints. Another reason could be, that there are at work other structural conditions than the formal institutions analysed here, other structures that also widen or restrict the available set of opportunities. In this concluding section I will discuss some structures of potential importance not included previously:

• the general structure of the national local government systems discussed in the first section of the chapter,
• the resources and task portfolios of local government,
• the party system as an additional mechanism of coordination.

In the discussion about the overarching structure of the local government systems in the introduction to this chapter it was concluded that in terms of the number of local authorities and the number of governmental tiers there were differences between the countries studied. The most complex systems turned out to be those of Germany, Italy and Poland, and in the opposite end Dutch, Swedish and New Zealand local authorities would find themselves in the least complex governmental structures.

In Germany, Italy and Poland a city government has to manoeuvre in environments with more governmental tiers and more and smaller neighbouring authorities to relate to than is the case for Dutch, Swedish and New Zealand city governments. It seems warranted to expect that the task of political leadership in German, Italian and Polish cities thus implies a heavier burden than would be the case in the Netherlands, Sweden or New Zealand. Even if the cities under observation in Germany, Italy and Poland might be quite large, and even if some of them unite the functions of two tiers of government, they may have to operate within regions, and within national systems, with a more complex structure than our Dutch, New Zealand and Swedish cities.

The absolute size of the municipal organisation and the absolute size of the budget are political resources per se. A local political leader, a mayor, commanding an organisation collecting and using three billion euro annually (as is the case in Stockholm) has more economic power than the mayor who handles a twenty million budget (which is the case in some of the smaller cities in our sample). The mayor in charge of a city with 50,000 employees is more powerful than the head of an organisation with 500 people on the payroll.

The size of the budget of course is closely related to the size of the city. The five cities Göteborg, Hannover, Oslo, Stockholm and Turin are all reported to spend more than one billion euro a year. They all have more than 400,000 inhabitants. But the relationship is far from perfect. Large cities like Bristol (400,000) and Athens (700,000) have smaller budgets, and the correlation between population and budget size is 0.607, which means that some 37 per cent of the variation in budget size can be accounted for by population differences.

The regression equation is Expenses (1,000 euro) = 33,430 + 2,105 * Population (1,000), which could be interpreted that there is a 'fixed cost' of running a city of around thirty million euro, and that there is a marginal cost of 2,100 euro per inhabitant. This in its turn of course implies that the average cost per capita will fall with increasing size, as the 'fixed costs' will be spread on more people. Applying the regression line we can calculate an average cost of 2,440 euro per head in a city with 100,000 inhabitants and 2,150 euro in a city with 700,000 people. Using expenses per capita as an indicator of the task width, of the size of the municipal task portfolio, thus seems slightly inappropriate. The alternative would be to use the residuals from the above given regression equation, i.e. actual size of the budget minus the budget predicted from population size. If the residuals are expressed per capita, the resulting figure could be interpreted as the marginal cost in a city resulting from one new inhabitant, expressed as a deviation from the average marginal cost.[7]

The result of this exercise is reported in Figure 4.6, showing that there are some very salient positive deviations represented by the three biggest of the four Scandinavian cities (Oslo, Stockholm and Göteborg). These

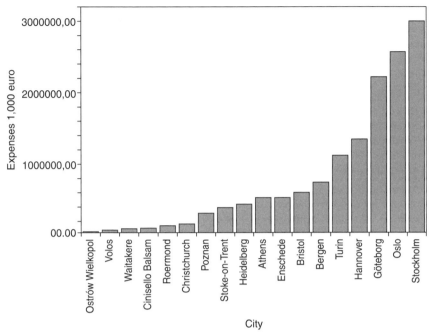

Figure 4.5 Size of city budgets (1,000 euro).

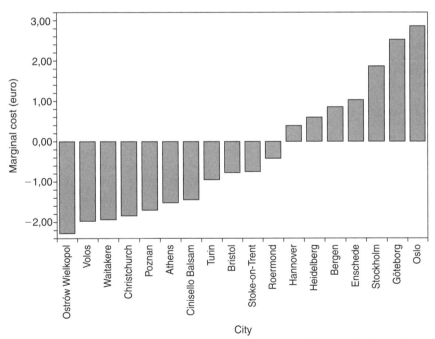

Figure 4.6 Marginal cost for one additional inhabitant (1,000 euro deviation from average marginal cost).

cities thus are suggested to be those of the selected case study cities that, relative to their populations, have the biggest and most diverse municipal activities. Their likewise obvious counterparts are the Polish and New Zealand cities, and the two smaller South European cities. Cities in Scandinavia, Germany and one of the Dutch cities all have positive residuals, while the British, Greek, Italian and Polish cities and the other Dutch city display negative residuals.

A thick task portfolio will open more opportunities for the leadership to change direction through re-prioritising than would a thin portfolio. At the same time the incentives for the local population to engage in local government affairs will be more important the more tasks the local government is responsible for. A local authority with many and resource consuming tasks will affect the lives of the ordinary citizen more than an authority with less and economically less important tasks. The task width dimension thus indicated could be expected to have implications for leadership and for community involvement.

The study of political organisations in democratic systems, and perhaps even in less democratic systems, beside the formal constitutional organisation, also must consider the parallel organisation provided by the party system (Banfield 1961). The party system is a powerful mechanism of coordination, as the internal organisation of parties usually is considerably more hierarchical than the organisation of either the state or the municipality.

We have no comparable data about variations in the strength of party coordination in the cities studied. With lack of data it seems reasonable to assume that both strength of national parties in the electoral context and the strength of party coordination within local government are expressions of the general strength of the parties. I have previously in this chapter assumed that the two Scandinavian countries form one pole of the continuum with the strongest party organisations and Italy, New Zealand and Poland the opposite end displaying the relatively weakest party system.

The structure of the party systems also could be expected to affect the challenges facing the political leadership. The more party politically fragmented the council is, the more difficult it will be for the mayor successfully to operate in the parliamentary arena. A measure of party fragmentation often used is the effective number of parties (Laakso and Tagepera 1979).

The British, Greek and New Zealand cities, and Hannover and Ostrów Wielkopolski stand out as cities with a very low degree of party fragmentation (ENP is in the range 1.90[8] to 3.46). A middle group (ENP 4.2–4.62) is represented by the two Swedish cities, and Poznan, Heidelberg and Oslo. In the Dutch and Italian cities and in Bergen party fragmentation is more extreme (ENP 5.03–6.60).

It has been concluded above, that the city governments of five of our

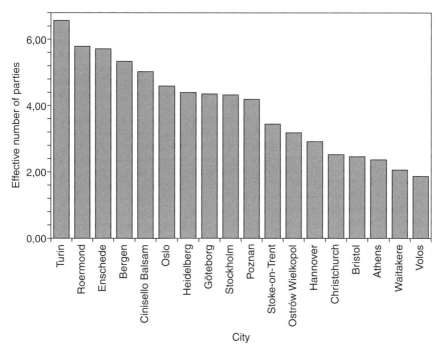

Figure 4.7 Effective number of parties in city council.

Note
The effective number of parties (ENP) constructed by Laakso and Tagepera (1979) is the inverted value of Herfindahl's index of concentration. Herfindahl's index is simply the sum of the squared market shares of companies in a particular market (here shares of seats) (Herfindahl 1950).

eighteen cities (the Dutch and the Norwegian cities and Bristol) express the majoritarian principle, i.e. the collective executive body reflects the political majority of the council, rather than the full political complexity of the council. The two Swedish cities are with the idiosyncratic quasi-parliamentary model sharing traits with the ideal parliamentary form. Furthermore electoral arrangements in the Greek and Italian cities are such that the minority in the council automatically will be excluded from the executive. It has been assumed that the majoritarian principle is an advantage to leadership in comparison with the consociational principle. If, however, ruling coalitions are very broad and include parties of very different policy positions, the dividing line between the two principles will tend to be blurred.

Taking into account (1) whether the ruling coalition commands a majority in the council or not, (2) the number of parties in the ruling coalition, and (3) the range of policy positions represented by coalition parties, the ruling coalitions in five cities seem to have the best opportunities to exert parliamentary leadership:

- Athens and Bristol have one-party majority governments;
- Göteborg, Turin and Volos have majority governments formed by relatively small numbers of parties relatively close to each other in policy space.

In three cities the composition of the city government and its backing in the council are such, that the position for the leadership seems considerably more difficult:

- Bergen and Oslo both have minority coalitions;
- the ruling coalition of Roermond is made up of no less than four parties that can be expected to have such large programmatic differenccs that it seems as if there ought to be difficulties of negotiating a common cabinet line in many issues.

Summary and hypotheses

It was hypothesised that political leadership would have problems in Sweden because of the fragmented internal structure of local government organisation. Leadership however could be enhanced by the access to large economic resources and a varied setup of activities, as well as the relatively low degree of complexity of the institutional environment. The cities collecting the most favourable factors when all the discussed dimensions are summarised are the two Greek cities, the two New Zealand cities, and Göteborg,[9] Hannover and Stoke-on-Trent. Most of these would have been predicted from their constitutional structure with presidentialism as well as majoritarianism. Göteborg on the other hand is lacking these constitutional traits, but its leadership has access to economic and political resources.

The cities at the bottom of the list have more negative than positive signs: Bergen has a fragmented council and a city government with weak parliamentary backing. Ostrów Wielkopolski and Cinisello Balsamo have small budgets, thin task portfolios and have to operate in a complicated institutional environment. The Roermond leadership finally has to deal with a fragmented council, a city government with weak parliamentary status, a small budget and relatively few tasks.

It was further hypothesised that the low degree of localisation and the incorporation of majoritarian ideas would produce an institutional environment especially unfavourable to community involvement in the British, Dutch, Greek and Norwegian cities. The consideration of other potentially important factors does not alter these predictions except perhaps for Oslo and Bergen whose large service providing responsibilities might be expected to produce special incentives for citizens to participate. The relative economic importance of local government in the Swedish and German cases also could be expected to increase motivation for participation.

Table 4.3 Summary of factors hypothesised to favour political leadership

	Presidentialism	Majoritarianism	Party consolidation	Parliamentary strength	Simplicity of local government structure	Economic size	Task portfolio
Athens	+	+	+	+			−
Christchurch	+	+	+		+	−	−
Göteborg	−	−		+	+	+	+
Hannover	+	+	+		−	+	+
Stoke	+	+	+				−
Waitakere	+	+	+	+	+		−
Volos	+	+		+	+	−	−
Bristol	−	+	+	−		−	−
Enschede	−	+	−		+		+
Oslo	−	+					+
Stockholm	−	−			+	+	+
Turin	+	+	−	+	−	+	−
Heidelberg	+	−			−		+
Ostrów W	+	+	+		−	−	−
Poznan	+	+			−		−
Bergen	−	+	−	−			+
Cinisello B	+	+	−		−	−	−
Roermond	−	+	−	−	+	−	−

Table 4.4 Summary of factors hypothesised to favour community involvement

	Political localisation	Economic localisation	Consociationalism	Task portfolio
Göteborg	−	+	+	+
Stockholm	−	+	+	+
Hannover	−	+	+	+
Heidelberg	−	+	+	+
Christchurch	+	+	−	−
Ostrów W	+	+	−	−
Poznan	+	+	−	−
Waitakere	+	+	−	−
Bergen	−	+	−	+
Cinisello B	+	+	−	−
Oslo	−	+	−	+
Turin	+	+	−	−
Enschede	−	−	−	+
Stoke	+	−	−	−
Athens	−	−	−	−
Bristol	−	−	−	−
Roermond	−	−	−	−
Volos	−	−	−	−

Considering all the different institutional features discussed and focussing on the expectations of combinations of political leadership and community involvement some cases are relatively unambiguous:

1   *Strong leadership in combination with a low degree of community involvement* is expected in Athens and in the two British cities included in the study. There are in these three cities a number of factors related to the political structure that have been expected to favour strong leadership. All three cities embrace the majoritarian rather than the consociational principle. Athens and Stoke-on-Trent are 'presidential' systems. The party systems are consolidated instead of highly fragmented. In Athens and Bristol the executive can command a majority in the council. At the same time these cities are characterised by a number of factors hypothesised to be less favourable to community involvement. The local authorities are economically and politically (perhaps with the exception of Stoke) linked more to the national level than to their localities. The other side of the coin of majoritarianism is the importance of election results, which may reduce the interest for other forms of participation. Finally the impact of current municipal operations for ordinary citizens is comparatively small due to the relatively few tasks performed by cities.

2   *Strong leadership in combination with a high degree of community involvement* is expected in Hannover and the two Swedish cities. The expectation of strong leadership in these three cities does not, as in Athens and

Britain, derive from features of the political structure, but rather the absolute and relative economic strength of the cities. The leadership of these three cities can command considerable economic resources and their cities perform many and expensive tasks. The latter fact is also expected to provide incentives for citizens to get involved with municipal business. The cities are also economically dependent on their respective local economies, which is expected to provide incentives for the political leaders to involve local communities at the same time providing incentives for actors of the local economy to become involved in city politics. Heidelberg actually is rather similar to Hannover and the two Swedish cities in the second category (the high leadership and high community involvement type). This is also the case with Oslo.

3   *Weak leadership in combination with a low degree of community involvement* is expected in only one city, namely Roermond. Both political and economic factors point in the same direction: the party system is fragmented and the parliamentary situation could be expected to make decision making difficult. The municipality is small in economic terms – absolute as well as relative. All the circumstances discussed in relation to community involvement point in the negative direction: the municipality is relatively detached politically and economically from the local community. Parliamentarianism rather than consociationalism guides the political structure and municipal activities play a relatively small role in the local economy. The three cities Bergen, Cinisello and Enschede share many features with the third category (the low leadership and low community involvement category). They all, like Roermond that was the only city in the category, run majoritarian systems under high party fragmentation. Bergen and Enschede have, just like Roermond, been classified as de-localised local authorities. Cinisello shares the absolute and relative economic smallness with Roermond.

4   *Weak leadership in combination with a high degree of community involvement.* In this analysis this category is empty.

The New Zealand and Polish cities together with Turin are more difficult to relate to the four identified groups. They have similarities with both the first and the third group. Christchurch, Ostrów and Waitakere share the low party fragmentation with the strong leadership group (Type 1) but they also share the relative economic insignificance with the weak leadership group (Type 3). With Turin and to some extent Poznan it is the other way around.

Although the conclusions are far from unambiguous three groups of cities, however, have been identified, where the institutional and structural circumstances discussed give rise to expectations about quite different combinations of leadership and involvement: strong leadership and low community involvement is expected mainly against the background of majoritarianism, consolidated party systems, de-localisation and the relatively few tasks performed by the local authorities. Strong leadership on the other hand combined with higher levels of community involvement is expected less from political-institutional arrangements but rather from economic circumstances: the cities have large budgets, perform many tasks and are fiscally dependent on their local economies. Third there is the combination of weak leadership and low levels of involvement of the local communities which is expected where cities are running highly party-fragmented majoritarian systems and most of them are politically and/or economically de-localised.

Finally it should again be underlined that these expectations are a pooled judgement of the effects of a number of institutional factors: to what extent are city governments economically and politically dependent on the locality or the centre respectively; what are the constitutional arrangements concerning the relations between citizens, councils, mayors and collective executive bodies; what is the strength and degree of fragmentation of the local party system; what is the absolute and relative size of city budgets? It is assumed that these and other institutional factors impose limitations, offer opportunities, encourage or discourage political action. Whether such action actually will occur is a matter of the willingness and ability of actors to exploit the degrees of freedom thus instituted, but also their willingness and ability to transgressing the institutional borderlines.[10]

Notes

1 In some cases we also lack data on the city level, and if there is no reason to suspect that our case study cities are deviating, such data will be used on the city level.
2 Rallings *et al.* (2002) give accounts of the eleven mayoral elections conducted until October 2002. Candidates not representing any of the three parties represented in the national parliament won four of these eleven contests, and independent candidates and non-national parties collected 7 to 64 per cent of the first votes, averaging 35 per cent. That such an outcome was anticipated, at least by the parties, is witnessed in the same issue of Local Government Studies by Cole (2002) quoting Leach and Wilson (2000): 'the fear of diminution of the power of the party group' was seen 'as the single most threatening aspect of the 1998 White Paper's proposals'.
3 Although there is actually a component of redistribution in the German tax sharing system, the shares of local authorities are in the main dependent on the incomes of the local tax-payers (Karrenberg and Münstermann 1998).
4 If we assign national figures reported by Vetter as tied ranks to our two case cities in each country, and insert the national figures given by Caulfield (2002) for Germany for the two German cities the rank correlation (Spearman) between the two series will be −0.81.
5 Karrenberg and Münstermann (1998) report for the year 1996 a total of 27.6 per cent for grants from *Länder* and federal government for West Germany and 53.8 per cent for the East German *Länder*.

6 See, for example, Bennett 1993; Bours 1993; Goldsmith 1992; Hesse and Sharpe 1991; Lidström 1996; Norton 1994; Page and Goldsmith 1987.

7 This follows from the equation: $R = Y - (A + BX)$ where R is the residual, Y is total expenses, A and B are regression estimates for fixed and marginal costs respectively and X is population. If this equation is divided with X we will get: $R/X = (Y - A)/X - B$ or in words Residual per capita = Marginal cost − Average marginal cost.

8 The lowest figure is for Volos and it is an underestimate, as it is based on the shares of the council for the majority and opposition coalitions, each consisting of two parties, and not on the shares of the seats held by the coalition parties.

9 It could be argued that leadership in the Scandinavian cities is made more difficult by the fact that all these cities have introduced systems of urban district councils with devolved power over 40–75 per cent of city budgets. It is, however, a result of evaluations that city centres have managed to secure very strong steering instruments towards districts. Most prominent of these are the appointment of district council members by the city council and the budget allocation power of the city council (Bäck *et al.* 2004).

10 See, for differences between institutionally defined leadership types and actually performed leadership functions by specific styles, the contribution by Getimis and Grigoriadou in this book.

References

Andersson, L. (1979) *Statens styrning av de kommunala budgetarnas struktur*, Göteborg: Department of Economics.

Bäck, H. (2003) 'Mellan koordination och valfrihet. Den kommunala indelningen i storstadsområdet', *Nordiskt Administrativt Tidsskrift*, No 1: 5–33.

Bäck, H. and Johansson, F. (2000) 'Reinventing the Wheel: Institutional Reforms in the City of Stockholm', EURA Workshop, University College Dublin, 13–15 April.

Back, H., Gjelstrup, G., Helgesen, M., Klausen, J. E. and Johansson, F. (2004) *Urban Political Decentralisation. Six Scandinavian Cities*, Opladen: Leske + Budrich (forthcoming).

Baldersheim, H. and Strand, T. (1988) *'Byregjering' i Oslo kommune. Hovedrapport fra et evalueringsprosjekt*, Oslo: NIBR.

Banfield, E. C. (1961) *Political influence*, Glencoe, IL: Free Press.

Bennett, R. J. (1993) 'European Local Government Systems', in: R. J. Bennett (ed.) *Local Government in the New Europe*, London and New York: Belhaven Press: 27–48.

Bours, A. (1993) 'Management, Tiers, Size and Amalgamations of Local Government', in: R. J. Bennett (ed.) *Local Government in the New Europe*, London and New York: Belhaven Press.

Boyne, G. and Cole, M. (1998) 'Revolution, Evolution and Local Government Structure: An Empirical Analysis of London', *Urban Studies*, Vol. 35, No. 4: 751–768.

Caulfield, J. (2002) 'Local Government Finance in the OECD Countries', in: J. Caulfield and H. O. Larsen (eds) *Local Government at the Millennium*, Opladen: Leske + Budrich: 153–169.

Cole, M. (2002) 'The Role(s) of County Councillors: An Evaluation', *Local Government Studies*, Vol. 28, No. 4: 22–46.

Dahl, R. A. (1967) 'The City in the Future of Democracy', *American Political Science Review*, Vol. 61: 953–970.

Dahl, R. A. and Tufte, F. R. (1974) *Size and Democracy*, London: Oxford University Press.

Duverger, M. (1997) 'A New Political System', *European Journal of Political Research*, Vol. 31, No. 1–2: 125–146.

Goldsmith, M. (1992) 'Local Government', *Urban Studies*, Vol. 29: 393–410.

Grunow, D. (1992) 'Constitutional Reform of Local Government in Germany: The Case of North-Rhine Westphalia (NRW)', *Local Government Studies*, Vol. 18, No. 1: 44–58.

Hagen, T. P. (1996) *Models of Decision-Making in Political Institutions*, Oslo: NIBR.

Hagen, T. P. and Sørensen, R. J. (1997) *Kommunal organisering. Effektivitet, styring og demokrati*, Oslo: Tano Aschehoug.

Hagen, T. P., Myrvold T. M., Opedal, S., Stigen, I. M. and Østtveiten, H. S. (1999) *Parlamentarisme eller formannskapsmodell? Det parlamentariske styringssystem i Oslo sammenliknet med formannskapsmodellene i Bergen, Trondheim og Stavanger*, Oslo: NIBR.

Hambleton, R. (2000) 'Modernising Political Management in Local Government', *Urban Studies*, Vol. 37. Nos. 5/6: 931–950.

Herfindahl, O. C, (1950) *Concentration in the US Steel Industry*, (unpublished PhD thesis), New York: Columbia University.

Hesse, J. J. and Sharpe, L. J. (1991) 'Local Government in International Perspective: Some Comparative Observations', in: J. J. Hesse (ed.) *Local Government and Urban Affairs in International Perspective*, Baden-Baden: Nomos: 603–621.

Jonsson, E. (1972) *Kommunens finanser*, Stockholm: The Economic Research Institute.

Jouve, B. and Lefèvre, C. (eds) (2002) *Local Power, Territory and Institutions in European Metropolitan Regions*, London: Frank Cass.

Karrenberg, H. and Münstermann, E. (1998) 'Kommunale Finanzen', in: H. Wollman and R. Roth (eds) *Kommunalpolitik. Politisches Handeln in den Gemeinden*, Bonn: Bundeszentrale für Politische Bildung: 437–460.

Keating, M. (1997) 'Size, Efficiency and Democracy: Consolidation, Fragmentation and Public Choice', in: D. Judge, G. Stoker and H. Wollman (eds) *Theories of Urban Politics*, London: Sage: 117–134.

Laakso, M. and Taagepera, R. (1979) 'Effective Number of Parties: A Measure with Applications to Western Europe', *Comparative Political Studies*, Vol. 12: 3–27.

Larsen, H. O. and Offerdal, A. (1994) *Demokrati og deltakelse i kommunene. Norsk lokalpolitikk i Nordisk lys*, Oslo: Kommuneforlaget.

Leach, S. and Wilson, D. (2000) *Local Political Leadership*, Bristol: Policy Press.

Lidström, A. (1996) *Kommunsystem i Europa*, Stockholm: Publica.

Mouritzen, P. E. and Svara, J. H. (2002) *Leadership at the Apex: Politicians and Administrators in Western Local Government*, Pittsburgh, PA: University of Pittsburgh Press.

Newton, K. (1982) 'Is Small Really so Beautiful? Is Big Really so Ugly? Size, Effectiveness and Democracy in Local Government', *Political Studies*, Vol. 30: 190–206.

Nilsson, L. and Westerståhl, J. (1997) 'Lokal självstyrelse i Sverige', in: S. Jönsson, L. Nilsson, S. Rubenowitz and J. Westerståhl, *Decentraliserad välfärdsstad. Demokrati, effektivitet och service*, Stockholm: SNS Förlag: 9–28.

Norton, A. (1994) *International Handbook of Local and Regional Government. A Comparative Analysis of Advanced Democracies*, Aldershot: Edward Elgar.

Ostrom, E. (1972) 'Metropolitan Reform: Propositions Derived from two Traditions', *Social Science Quarterly*, Vol. 53: 474–493.

Ostrom, V., Tiebout, C. and Warren, R. (1961) 'The Organization of Government in Metropolitan Areas: A Theoretical Inquiry', *American Political Science Review*, Vol. 55: 831–842.

Page, E. C. and Goldsmith, M. J. (1987) (eds) *Central and Local Government Relations. A Comparative Analysis of West European Unitary States*, London: Sage.

Rallings, C., Thrasher, M. and Cowling, D. (2002) 'Mayoral Referendums and Elections', *Local Government Studies*, Vol. 28, No. 4: 67–90.

Reif, K. and Schmitt, H. (1997) 'Second-order elections', *European Journal of Political Research*, Vol. 31, Nos. 1–2: 109–124.

Schumpeter, J. A. (1947) *Capitalism, Socialism, and Democracy*, New York: Harper.

Stone, C. (1989) *Regime Politics. Governing Atlanta, 1946–1988*, Lawrence: University Press of Kansas.

Tiebout, C. (1956) 'A Pure Theory of Local Expenditures', *Journal of Political Economy*, Vol. 64: 416–424.

Vetter, A. (2002) 'Lokale Politik und die Sozialisation demokratischer Einstellungen in Europa', *Politische Vierteljahresschrift*, Vol. 43, No. 4.

Wollman, H. (2002) 'Recent Democratic and Administrative Reforms in Germany's Local Government: Persistence and Change', in: J. Caulfield and H. O. Larsen (eds) *Local Government at the Millennium*, Opladen: Leske + Budrich: 63–89.

—— (2004) 'Urban Leadership in German Local Politics: The Rise, Role and Performance of the Directly Elected (Chief Executive) Mayor', *International Journal of Urban and Regional Research*, Vol. 28: No. 1: 150–165.

Ysander, B.-C. and Nordström, T. (1985) 'Local Authorities, Economic Stability and the Efficiency of Fiscal Policy', in: E. Gramlich and B.-C. Ysander (eds) *Control of Local Government*, Stockholm: Almqvist & Wiksell.

5 Cities in transition

From statism to democracy

Pawel Swianiewicz

The decade of the 1990s, which brought extremely important changes on the Central and Eastern European (CEE) political scene, was also a decade of a revival of local democracy in the region. The complementarity of urban leadership and community involvement is a key concept for this book. This chapter provides an introductory discussion of the meaning of these concepts for CEE countries. It starts with a discussion of contextual variables – institutional setting of local governments (in which special attention is placed on the position of formal local leaders – mayors), and of the nature of central–local relations. After a long period of a very centralist and undemocratic mode of governance, the devolution of power and strengthening of local government seemed to be a natural direction to many politicians. But what model of local government has appeared from these changes, and are the generalisations and theories used to describe local governments and democracy in West-European societies useful to understand processes in Central and Eastern Europe?

The chapter then turns to the nature of urban management. Can we say that Western theories of community power – such as urban regime theory – are applicable to CEE reality, or is their relevance and validity limited to the political-geographical space in which they were generated? Similarly can the widely discussed shift from traditional local government to local governance be observed in CEE countries as well? Are ideas of New Public Management vivid and recognised there, or is the validity of these ideas limited to the western parts of Europe? Clark (1993, 2000) seems to suggest a global convergence of management practices in urban governments in various countries. He uses a 'New Political Culture' label to describe new trends in different regions, including CEE cities. Is it possible to agree with the convergence proposition, or is there the emergence of a separate institutional and management model of local government in CEE countries? Finally, the chapter speculates on whether the complementarity of urban leadership and community involvement (CULCI) may have a special meaning in CEE cities.

The analysis concentrates primarily on the situation in the ten CEE countries which, at the time of writing, are official candidates for EU accession,[1] leaving aside countries of the former Yugoslavia (except for Slovenia) and the former Soviet Union (except for the Baltic states), although we draw some illustrations from those countries as well.

The institutional setting of local government

A number of different models of European local government have been identified in earlier research. However, the classifications do not cover Central or Eastern Europe, and it is important to consider how newly created local governments fit into these typologies. Do post-communist local democracies form a separate (distinctive) model, or are they (or some of them) similar to one of models already described in the West-European literature? Although there are already descriptions of new local government systems (see, for example, Coulson 1995; Baldersheim *et al.* 1996; Horvath 2000; Kandeva 2001), these are either based on very early stages in the development of new models (and therefore their conclusions are to a large extent out-dated), or they focus on description with no attempts at generalisation. In addition comparative analyses of changes in European local governments published in the 1990s usually leave aside post-communist countries.[2] This chapter contributes to filling the gap.

The new local government systems in countries of Central and Eastern Europe can be compared to two popular classifications of West-European models, developed by Page and Goldsmith (1987) and by Hesse and Sharpe (1991).[3] Both of these models were developed in the 1980s, but – as John (2001: 39) argues – their validity has been to a large extent sustained.[4] Moreover, John points out that the variations in types of local government system have implications for the transition from local government to governance.

The decentralisation of local government within modernising states

In the context of Central and Eastern Europe, any debate on local government is usually strong rooted in the historical experience of centralisation during the communist period. This is not unique to CEE countries – Hesse and Sharpe (1991) note that in Spain, Portugal, Austria or Germany there is the frequent automatic identification of centralisation with autocracy, which is absent elsewhere. This is clearly related to the earlier historical experience of these countries. In CEE countries there is a very similar frequent automatic identification of centralisation with autocracy, arising from the experience of a communist centralist state. Consequently, strong local government is often seen as a value 'by definition'. But this broad (or rather vague) commitment to decentralisation has hardly resulted in a common view of the role and position of local governments. As Peteri and Zentai (2002: 15) note 'besides [...] broad principles, rarely was any political consensus on a comprehensive model of state architecture, let alone elaborate blueprints for its establishment'. This observation relates to the lack of consensus within individual reforming countries, but even more to the lack of a common vision across different countries.

The most significant difference between countries is related to the political determination to implement the decentralisation agenda. Not everywhere have central governments been equally willing to allocate significant service functions to localities. Neither has it been common to give up strict, direct control over local authorities' policies.

Different approaches in Central and Eastern Europe to decentralisation reform may be, with some amount of simplification, clustered into the three following models (Swianiewicz 2003b):

1   *The step-by-step approach*: in this case the fundamental reforms of the 1990s had some background in earlier events. The political disintegration of 1989 and 1990 met with more or less pre-prepared suggestions for legal and economic change. Perhaps Hungary, with its economic reform started in the 1980s is the closest to this model.
2   *Jump in at the deep end:* in this case there was no time to prepare or discuss new laws in advance. Nevertheless, the reformers were determined to introduce decentralisation very quickly. Polish decentralisation reform – in both its phases implemented in 1990/1991 and 1998/1999 – shows probably the strongest features of this approach. The argument was that a 'window for reform' was usually open for a short period only, and proponents of changes had to hasten before central bureaucracy was strong enough again to block devolution (Kulesza 2002).
3   *The it's all happening too fast approach*: is related to very rapid and unexpected political change. In this approach, central state administration is very hesitant (or even reluctant) to decentralise. The main argument is that new local governments are not ready to take on new responsibilities, and real devolution of power would bring political chaos and economic turmoil. For most of the recent decade such an approach was typical for several countries of the region including Bulgaria, Romania and most of the states formed in the former Soviet Republics. Some illustrations of this approach might be found also in Slovakia and even in the Czech Republic.

Peteri and Zentai (2002) also note considerable differences between local government reforms in the region. Their classification formulates a number of models, first a quick start but long process (Poland, Hungary), second some delay followed by gradual reforms (Bulgaria, Latvia), third a late start but with later efforts to speed up reforms (Croatia, Slovakia).

What then is the present picture resulting from the most recent decentralisation reforms? First of all, it is important to stress that the institutional setting is very far from being stable. Most countries are still looking for a stable long-term model of sub-national government. Poland, the Czech Republic and Slovakia implemented new tiers of (regional) government very recently at the end of the 1990s or even at the beginning of the present decade. But they have not yet finished discussions on local financing (the current regulations are treated as temporary only). In several other countries even the basic characteristics of central–local relations are still being questioned, and are topical issues in the current political debate. The present position is thus a snap-shot in a fast changing situation.

In most CEE countries local governments enjoy a power of general competence, although in practice this is often restricted by other laws. Local governments have also a constitutional status – they are mentioned and protected by constitution (with some exceptions, such as Latvia). In Poland the constitution mentions only municipalities, while the existence of other tiers depend entirely on the decisions of Parliament. For a long time there was the opposite case in the Czech Republic, where the constitution mentions the existence of regions, even if they did not exist before 2001. There is still a similar situation in Slovenia, where the constitution mentions both a municipal and regional level of self-government, but only the former one exists in practice. The constitutional position of local government is especially strong in Hungary, where any change in an organic 'Local Government Law' requires the same majority in Parliament as it is required to change the National Constitution.

Territorial (re-)organisation

Differences between models of local government being adopted in CEE countries can be seen in their approach to territorial organisation. During the communist period the widespread belief in economies of scale, together with an authoritarian style of governance, led to reforms in terms of massive amalgamations in most countries in the region. Such territorial consolidation was introduced without real consultation with local communities. Not surprisingly, following the fall of communism, the reaction in many countries was strong bottom-up pressure for the break up of larger units.[5] This resulted in extreme fragmentation of local government in the Czech Republic, Slovakia, Hungary and – to a lesser extent – in Latvia and Estonia. In Hungary the number of municipalities was reduced from 3,021 in 1962 to 1,364 in 1988 but then increased to 3,133 in 1992. In the Czech Republic the number of municipalities was similarly reduced from 11,459 in 1950 to 4,104 in 1988, but then increased again to over 6,000 at the beginning of the 1990s. Similar changes occurred in Slovakia where the number of local governments increased by over 20 per cent (Baldersheim *et al.* 1996). Considerable territorial fragmentation took place also in Croatia (Jurlina-Alibegovic 2002), Albania (Albanian Ministry

2003) and Macedonia where the number of local governments increased from 34 to almost 150 (Maenpaa 2002).

But the pressure for fragmentation has not manifested itself with similar strength in all countries. Polish communes were amalgamated in 1973 and their number was reduced from more than 4,000 to about 2,400. Their number, however, has remained relatively stable since then (the present number of municipal governments is 2,491). In Bulgaria the number of municipalities was reduced from 2,178 in 1949 to 255 at the end of the 1980s and is still very similar (Swianiewicz 2002b). In Lithuania recent territorial reform led to considerable territorial consolidation and creation of municipal governments which are the second largest in Europe (after UK local authorities).

As a consequence, as well as many small local governments existing in some countries of the region, there are also countries with relatively consolidated territorial systems (Lithuania, Bulgaria, Poland and – to some extent – Slovenia and Romania). As is illustrated by Table 5.1, the average size of municipal local governments in Central and Eastern Europe, differs almost as much as in Western Europe.

Table 5.1 Average size of (municipal) local governments in selected European countries

Country	% of municipalities below 1,000 citizens	Average population	Average area (sq. km)
England and Wales	0.0	123,000	533
Lithuania	*0.0*	*66,000*	*1,166*
Bulgaria	*0.0*	*35,000*	*432*
Sweden	0.0	29,500	1,595
The Netherlands	0.2	20,500	60
Denmark	0.0	18,000	150
Poland	*0.0*	*16,000*	*130*
Slovenia	*3.0*	*10,300*	*106*
Finland	5.0	10,500	730
Norway	4.0	9,000	710
Romania	*2.0*	*7,600*	*81*
Italy	24.0	6,500	38
Estonia	*9.0*	*5,700*	*178*
Spain	61.0	5,000	60
Latvia	*32.0*	*4,300*	*115*
Hungary	*54.0*	*3,300*	*32*
Slovakia	*68.0*	*1,900*	*17*
The Czech Republic	*80.0*	*1,700*	*13*
France	77.0	1,300	15

Sources: Newton and Karran 1985; Baldersheim *et al.* 1996; Council of Europe 1995; Horvath 2000; Kandeva 2001.

Note
Central and Eastern European countries are highlighted in italics.

There is, however, one common characteristic of territorial organisation in CEE countries. This is the absence (or at the very least the weakness) of the meso level[6] elected government. In contrast to the tendencies in many West-European countries, where new tiers of government have been created or strengthened during the last 20–30 years (Sharpe 1993), in CEE countries the above-communal level was significantly weakened. The absence of a regional and/or county tier is perhaps natural in some small countries, such as the Baltic states or Slovenia. But the same phenomenon can be found in larger countries. In Bulgaria there is no elected sub-national government above the municipal level. In Hungary the level of 19 counties (*megye*) – plus 22 cities with county rights – has been kept, but its functions and powers have been seriously weakened compared with the previous period. In Croatia the role of 21 counties (*zupanje*) was considerably decreased a few years ago, when they lost their supervisory power over cities (*grad*) and rural communes (*obcina*). Currently, the budget of Croatian counties is more than three times lower than the budget of cities and communes. Similarly, Romanian counties (*judete*) had a very strong position till the middle of the 1990s, but they then lost many of their functions, and presently their resources are lower than those of cities (*orase*) and rural communities (*comuna*). It should be noted however, that Romanian counties still play an important role in making decisions on the allocation of grants among lower tier governments. In Poland, the Czech Republic and Slovakia the 1990 wave of reforms allowed for local self-government on a communal level only. The county or regional elected government needed to wait till 1999 (with the creation of *powiats* and *wojewodztwo* self-governments in Poland) or even 2000 or 2002 (establishment of *kraj* governments in Slovakia and the Czech Republic). Moreover, even after the establishment of meso-governments, their functions are usually very narrow, their financing heavily dependent on transfers from the central budget, and their role in coordinating (or influencing) the lower levels of governmental activity limited or minimal. Most of the vital services, as well as any revenue raising powers, have been largely reserved for a municipal (communal) level of self-government. This is illustrated in Figure 5.1, which shows that the vast majority of sub-national public spending goes through the city/communal level.

Origins of the weakness of the meso level lay in pre-1990 history. Regions or counties were exerting direct control over municipalities, and their strong position was seen as almost the synonym for the oppression of local autonomy. As a result the unwillingness to give significant powers to the meso level was to a large extent dictated by the fear of reformers and local politicians that the upper tier would still try to control municipal governments.

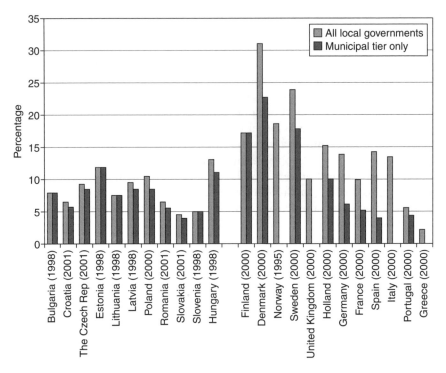

Figure 5.1 Sub-national governments' spending as percentage of GDP (source: DEXIA 2001; Caulfield 2002; Kandeva 2001; Horvath 2000).

Central–local relations

Figure 5.1, also suggests that in terms of the allocation of functions CEE countries remain more centralised than most countries in the Northern part of Western Europe. The share of sub-national government spending in GDP[7] varies between about 5 per cent in Slovakia and Slovenia to slightly over 10 per cent in Estonia, Hungary and Poland. By comparison the same figure in North-Western Europe is often above 15 per cent (in the Netherlands, Finland and Norway), or even above 20 per cent (in Sweden and Denmark).

These trends have not been uniform across the region. The ratio of sub-national budgets to GDP has been increasing during the last decade in Estonia and Poland, but decreasing in Bulgaria, Lithuania and Hungary. In the Czech Republic there had been a gradual decrease, but more recently an increase related to the fresh push of decentralisation reforms. The trend was unclear or showed stability in the remaining countries of the region.

In contrast to Page and Goldsmith (1987) on Western Europe, there is no strong correlation between the size of municipal budgets and their average population size in the CEE region. There are countries in which small size corresponds to the low share of municipal spending in GDP (Slovakia), and countries where larger municipalities have a relatively high share in GDP (Poland). But as the Hungarian and Estonian cases show, there can be small local governments spending relatively large amounts of money, as well as large local governments having relatively small budgets (Lithuania, Bulgaria). It seems that the general determination to decentralise has been more important than the size structure.

As mentioned above, on the one hand the tendency towards greater local autonomy seems to many reformers an intuitive direction after years of an extremely centralised communist system. But there is also opposition to the devolution of power, which in Central and Eastern Europe typically comes from two directions. First this opposition is related to the fear that too much autonomy for local (and especially regional) governments may lead to disintegration of the 'national' identity. After a period of 'sleeping' nationalism and the formal absence of any other centrifugal forces, this fear is easy to understand. A good example is provided by Slovakia, where some political parties are very much afraid of autonomy for the Hungarian minority. Similar observations can be made in Romania, Latvia and the states formed from the former Yugoslav Republics. In the Ukraine there is some fear of a split between the Ukrainian-speaking west and the Russian-speaking eastern part of the country. But less logically, similar fears have been sometimes formulated in more homogenous (from the ethnic point of view) countries, such as Poland.

The second source of fear about decentralisation is rooted in the traditionally strong position of a central level bureaucracy, which (successfully) tries to protect this position of strength. A highly politicised central administration provides additional strength for centralist tendencies. It can be suggested, perhaps with the danger of over-simplification, that an achieved degree of functional decentralisation may be treated as an outcome of a political struggle between pro-decentralisation reformers on the one hand, and conservative bureaucracy reinforced by nationalist fears of devolution on the other.

Two other dimensions considered by Page and Goldsmith (1987) – the *discretion* of local governments to make decisions independent of central policies and the *access* of local governments to formulation of central policies are beyond the scope of this chapter to discuss in detail. Nevertheless a few general observations can be made. As in Western Europe discretion varies considerably from one function to another, perhaps more than between countries. However some countries – such as the Czech Republic, Hungary, Poland or Slovakia – are closer to 'the relative autonomy' model (as defined in Stoker 1991), while some others – such as Romania or Bulgaria – are closer to the agency model with the direct, administrative intervention of upper tiers in local government activities.

In the latter group (for example: Romania, Bulgaria) sometimes these interventions have an informal character, but even then many local leaders are not strong enough to resist. Lack of objective criteria for resource allocation (and/or very frequent changes of these criteria) also help the exercise of strict control over local governments. Such allocation, often based on subjective decisions made by the state administration, is often an element of the wider central/local bargaining process. In the former of the two groups of countries, however (for example in the Czech Republic, Hungary, Poland and Slovakia), direct limitation of local discretion is a phenomenon of a considerable importance. This is achieved mostly through specific grants which are distributed according to criteria which are not always transparent. In Poland, specific grants constitute a relatively modest part of the municipal budget (about 18 per cent), but on a county and regional level they constitute almost half of total revenues.

Access to central policies shows more similarities to the model which Page and Goldsmith (1987) identify with Southern Europe. Similarities with the French *cumul des mandats* system is not an exception in Central and Eastern Europe, and in Poland has only recently been abolished. In the 1997 Parliamentary election about 100 mayors and councillors were elected to the Parliament accounting for almost 25 per cent of all MPs elected that year. Most kept their positions in local governments in parallel with their new functions in the central legislature. But even after the abolition of the *cumul des mandats* the practice of local MPs lobbying for individual decisions concerning their home local governments is almost the rule. Holding a mandate of a mayor and member of the parliament at the same time is still quite common in Hungary and Slovakia, although in the latter case it is highly criticised and there are discussions about forbidding such an accumulation of positions. In Romania *cumul des mandats* is not allowed, but many Romanian mayors are powerful political figures and they have considerable influence on decision making on a central level.

This does not mean that negotiation as a style of access to central policy making is totally absent. Associations of towns and communes in the Czech Republic (SMOR), Slovakia (ZMOS), and Bulgaria (NAMRB) as well as more numerous associations in Poland and Hungary play an important role in negotiations with central government. In Poland, where separate associations have been created by rural communes, small towns, cities, metropolitan cities and countries there is a Joint Central–Local Government Commission officially recognised in the national legislation in which all major associations are represented. Theoretically, no new legislation having an impact on local governments can be submitted to Parliament before it is discussed by the Commission. But low recognition of the Commission in the everyday activity of central government, together with some difficulties in its functioning, strengthens the impression that direct but unofficial access is more characteristic of local political culture.

Hesse and Sharpe (1991) note variations in attitudes towards the basic values of local government. By contrast with the North European model, in Napoleonic states local identity seems to be more important than that related to efficient service delivery. There is a similar variation in attitudes of Central European mayors. It was discovered, in a survey of mayors in Poland, the Czech Republic and Slovakia that Polish mayors, in their thinking on the most important role of local governments, were more often focused on effectiveness in service delivery, while Czech and especially Slovak mayors stressed local autonomy first and then democratic values (Swianiewicz 2003a).

Mayors as city leaders

Since the position of urban leaders is crucial to the complementarity between urban leadership and community involvement, the following section is dedicated to that issue. Even for those who define styles of leadership first and foremost by political culture (for example Leach and Wilson 2000: 13), the formal position of leader is recognised to be important.

In traditional local government systems, a strong role for the individual as leader (even if until recently rarely strengthened by direct, popular election of executive mayors) was treated as more typical for Southern than for Northern Europe. In the latter, more collective forms of leadership were more often found. However this traditional distinction between individual and collective has become blurred. Larsen (2002) quotes examples of several European countries which have decided on reforms leading to direct elections of mayors. Not long ago the direct election of mayors was introduced in all German *Länder*, while the 2000 election of the mayor of London initiated similar reforms in the United Kingdom. Italy started reform in 1993, Ireland plans similar change for 2004, and twenty Norwegian municipalities experimented with direct elections of mayor in 1999.

The same trend may be noticed in Central and Eastern Europe. The direct elections of the mayor was introduced at the beginning of the 1990s in Slovakia, Bulgaria, Romania and Slovenia, in 1994 in Hungary,[8] and quite recently (in 2002) in Poland. So only three Baltic states and the Czech Republic still rely on the system in which the mayor is elected by the council, or more collective forms of leadership are exercised.[9]

However, the position of the directly elected mayor varies from one country to another. Table 5.2 briefly summarises these differences. The first observation is that, as opposed to most of the recent reforms in Southern Europe, the CEE mayor does not always have a majority in the council. This may lead, and often in practice does lead, to serious management problems when the mayor faces an opposition which holds the majority in the council. Given the low stability and high fragmentation of political parties in CEE countries, there are likely to be numerous cases in

Table 5.2 Directly elected mayors in selected countries of Central and Eastern Europe

	Guaranteed majority in the council for mayors' group?	Chief executive position	Discretion in appointment decisions, organisational structure of administration	Budget decisions
Bulgaria	No	Yes	Moderate – mayor decides on most of appointments, but organisational structure and deputy mayors have to be approved by the council	Mayor submits a proposal, which can be changed by the council
Hungary	No, election of mayor does not need to be on the same day as for the council	No, mayor acts through CAO who is appointed by the council	Weak, CAO appoints officers	Mayor submits a proposal, which can be changed by the council – in practice asymmetry between full-time mayor and 'amateur' councillors
Poland	No	Yes	Moderate – mayor decides organisational details and appoints most of key administrators, but appointment of the treasurer and city secretary requires approval of the council	Mayor submits a proposal, which can be changed by the council. But council must not increase amount of borrowing
Romania	No	Yes	Strong	Mayor submits a proposal, which can be changed by the council
Slovakia	No	Yes	Strong	Mayor submits a proposal, which can be changed by the council
Albania	No, 3/5 majority in the council required for many important decisions	Yes	Moderate – mayor decides on most of appointments, but organisational structure is decided by the council	Mayor submits a proposal, which can be changed by the council

which effective decision making may be difficult. Among 42 Polish cities with a population over 100,000, only seven mayors have a clear support of the majority of councillors. In most of the remaining cases he/she needs to rely on more or less stable coalitions. In five cities the situation is even more complicated – the majority in the council is held by the group which is definitely in opposition to the mayor (Swianiewicz and Klimska 2003). Similar problems are reported in other countries, and sometimes in major cities, such as the Romanian capital – Bucureşti, or the Albanian capital – Tiranë.

One major difference is between the position of a mayor in Hungary and that in the remaining countries. A Hungarian mayor, although elected directly by citizens, does not have an executive function and his/her position is more similar to the position of Norwegian mayors in those cities which have recently experimented with direct elections. In the remaining countries the mayor has full executive power, although the level of discretion in making important personal and organisational decisions varies. In all of the countries under analysis it is the responsibility of the mayor to submit a budget proposal to the council. Councillors may introduce changes to the proposal, which in turn cannot be vetoed by the mayor (with some exceptions, such as in Poland, where the mayor can disagree with the suggestion to increase borrowing by the city).

Mouritzen and Svara (2002) define four ideal types of leadership: strong mayor, committee leader, collective and council manager. To some extent similar situations can be recognised in countries of CEE. In the Czech Republic, where executive functions are exercised by the board, the situation is the closest to the collective form of leadership (a situation almost identical to that of Poland before 2002). Baltic states, where the mayor is appointed by the council are not very far from this model either. Hungary with a strong role for the council, and most executive functions lying with chief administrative officers (CAO) is not far from the council-manager form, although the direct election of a mayor and a more than ceremonial role for him/her is a departure from the ideal model. The situation in Bulgaria, Poland, Slovakia and Romania is more difficult to classify. They are definitely close to the strong-mayor system, but lack of control of the majority of the council is an important difference from the ideal type of Mouritzen and Svara. The same refers to the limitation in hiring or firing key-persons in the administration (such as city treasurer in Poland or deputy mayor in Bulgaria). Perhaps this form could be called 'strong mayor with a strong control by the council' – closer to the 'shared leadership' form used by Getimis and Grigoriadou in Chapter 8.

Institutional setting: a summary

Table 5.3 briefly summarises the features most characteristic of local government systems in Central and Eastern Europe. From that table and

Table 5.3 The most important characteristics of the local government system

	Constitutional position	No. of tiers of elected local governments	Territorial fragmentation on a municipal level	Directly elected executive mayor	Scope of functional decentralisation[a]	Dominant mode of control over local governments
Estonia	Yes	1	Yes	No	Wide	
Latvia	No	1[b]	Yes	No	Narrow	
Lithuania	Yes	1	No	No	Narrow	
Poland	Yes	3	No	Yes	Wide	
The Czech Rep.	Yes	2	Yes	No	Narrow	
Slovakia	Yes	2	Yes	Yes	Narrow	
Hungary	Yes[c]	2	Yes	Yes[d]	Wide	
Romania	Yes	2	Yes	Yes	Narrow	Admin.
Bulgaria	Yes	1	No	Yes	Narrow	Admin.
Slovenia	Yes	1	No	Yes	Narrow	

Notes
a 'Wide' defined as over 10% of GDP spent by local governments.
b Plus upper tier with indirectly elected council.
c Constitutional majority required to change Local Government Law.
d The Hungarian mayor is directly elected but has no executive powers, which are held by the CAO appointed by the council.

from the preceding analysis some summary conclusions may be drawn about institutional settings.

First and foremost the system is in flux. Therefore it is unclear what may be the position in future years. Second there is not one model of local government common to all (or at least most) countries of the CEE region. Across all countries there is a high level of variation as regards territorial organisation, allocation of functions, and the extent of local discretion and values which are associated with local government.

Nevertheless there are some features characteristic for most of the countries of the region. These include a weak or non-existent meso level of elected governments, and frequent clientelist contacts between central and local governments. There is also a growing tendency to adopt models of local governments based on a direct, popular election of a mayor (although as yet not in the Baltic states nor the Czech Republic). In most cases the directly elected mayor is a chief executive, Hungary providing the only exception to this rule.

Some countries of Central and Eastern Europe show more similarities to North European models of local governments (Estonia, Poland), while in some others the situation is more similar to the Southern (Napoleonic) model (Slovakia, perhaps Bulgaria and Romania). But in none of the CEE countries can the position of local government be simply identified with the types hitherto described in analyses deriving from Western Europe.

From local government to local governance?

Given the considerable activity of foreign local government experts (financed either by EU or by bilateral programmes such as USAID or the British Know How Fund), it is reasonable to hypothesise that the changes in political and administrative management styles widely noted in West-European local government have also been reflected in Central and Eastern Europe.[10] Although the impact of foreign consultants on the institutional setting of new local government systems in CEE has been very limited,[11] their influence on the management styles of local leaders has been more visible.

The widely observed trends in several West-European countries are frequently summarised as a shift from local government to the wider concept of local governance and the introduction of new public management. Hambleton (1998, 2001) defines the change to local governance as a shift from the perspective which sees local government simply as a vehicle for providing a range of important public services to a new emphasis on community leadership. Governance involves processes of influencing and negotiating with a wide range of public and private sector agencies to achieve desired outcomes. John (2001: 9) defines governance as 'a flexible pattern of public decision making based on loose networks of individuals'. This includes cooperation with a variety of actors, including NGOs and business organisations as well as combining private and public resources in development programmes. John enumerates a number of factors which in practice have catalysed change from government to governance, such as the internationalisation of sub-national governments, privatisation, the contracting-out of services, and the adaptation of management techniques labelled as New Public Management.

Have these tendencies been observable in local government in CEE countries? In Poland in 1990, 78 per cent of councillors and over 90 per cent of mayors were newcomers – with no earlier experience in local politics and administration (Swianiewicz 2003c). The numbers in other countries of the region were somewhat lower, but also significantly high – in Slovakia the councillors with no earlier experience constituted in 1990 as many as 74 per cent of all elected local representatives, in the Czech Republic the relevant number was 71 per cent and in Hungary 60 per cent (Baldersheim *et al.* 1996). The economic environment in which they needed to operate was also to a large extent new. Not surprisingly new politicians and administrators needed to look for new inspirations and solutions, with the consequence that ideas brought by Western advisers coming to Central and Eastern Europe often found fertile ground to be cultivated.[12] Thus numerous elements from the Hambleton or John definitions of governance – as well as the factors identified as being conducive to and facilitating governance – can be found in the practice of CEE local urban management.

Local government and local economic development

The interests of local mayors and councillors in CEE countries are by no means limited to a narrow set of mandatory municipal functions. Most local governments do not see their role only as service providers but feel responsible for the overall welfare of the governed communities. In a survey conducted in 1991 in the Czech Republic, Hungary, Poland and Slovakia both local mayors and councillors mentioned 'economic development', 'creating new jobs' and 'coping with unemployment' among the most important tasks for local authorities. That was especially true for respondents from Hungary and Slovakia but least noticeable in case of Czech local politicians (Baldersheim *et al.* 1996: 169–170). These hierarchies have been confirmed by subsequent surveys of Polish candidates in 1994 local elections, and 1997 survey of mayors in the Czech Republic, Poland and Slovakia.[13] Table 5.4 shows that long-term economic development is seen as being among the most important priorities by Czech and Polish mayors. Polish and – to lesser extent – Czech and Slovak local leaders believe that day-to-day contact with local businessmen is very important in their everyday work. However, Polish leaders (somewhat contrary to their Czech and Slovak colleagues) do not think they need more formal competencies related to economic development, but believe they can rely on network cooperation rather than on formal authority. Mayors

Table 5.4 Mayors' opinions on the importance of economic development issues in local governments' activity

	Poland		Czech Republic		Slovakia	
	All local governments	*Cities over 30,000*	*All local governments*	*Cities over 30,000*	*All local governments*	*Cities over 30,000*
To concentrate on long-term development issues is the most important task for mayor (% selections from among 15 options)	16% (3rd selected option)	32% (1st selected option)	25% (1st selected option)	36% (1st selected option)	7% (4th selected option)	8% (3rd selected option)
In performance of mayor function it is important to work closely with local businessmen (% answers 'important' + 'very important')	58%	69%	48%	55%	42%	46%
Too little authority in economic development is a serious problem for my municipality (% answers 'important' + 'very important')	35%	46%	61%	54%	65%	46%

Source: LDI project survey in 1997.

of the larger local governments more often give most attention to economic development than do their colleagues from small communities.[14]

Given the existence of such linkages with local business, can local economic policies in post-communist Europe be interpreted in light of regime theory (see Stewart, Chapter 7 in this book)? Such an attempt has been recently undertaken by Sagan (2000) who analyses 'regimes' in a number of Polish cities. She starts with the observation that cities are in transition, with various actors trying to find their place in newly forming regimes. Local entrepreneurs are very often dominant actors. Sagan gives special attention to foreign capital. Most cities are dramatically hungry for new investment, and this situation allows foreign companies to play an important role in newly formed regimes. In addition to Sagan's observations about the role of inward investors, other, more local, actors play an important role in the politics of many Polish cities. These include small retail trade owners (and their associations) on the one hand, and managers of construction companies (often privatised, formerly communal enterprises) which are bidding for implementation of the largest infrastructure development projects on the other. These businesses and companies are not only interested in winning contracts (and frequently use informal contacts to improve their chances in public tender), but are also active in influencing city policies in a way that increases the actual number of projects to be won.

Sagan claims that the position of local government in contemporary growth coalitions is relatively weak. This is due to the financial weakness of city governments and due to their dramatic demand for more resources, both contributing to the dominant position of business. This claim needs to be weighed against the evidence from reputational community-power studies. In a 1991 survey, none of the interviewed group of actors[15] mentioned business or local companies among the most influential groups in local decision making (Baldersheim *et al.* 1996). The same conclusion remained even when small towns and rural communities (below 30,000 population) were left out. The picture remained unchanged in a second survey (this time limited to local mayors only) which was conducted in 1997. At the same time the respondents to these surveys were predominantly local government politicians, whose responses might be expected to overestimate their own influence, and – somewhat naively (or cynically) – to underestimate the impact of external pressure groups (including businesses) on their behaviour.

Sagan notices also a specific feature of regime policies pursued in several mid-size and small cities, with cultural events often being treated as important vehicles (engines) of the local growth machine – Zakopane in the mountains and Mrągowo in the Lake District for example. Elsewhere the city of Cieszyn (located on the Polish–Czech border) built its development strategy around cultural events (Bończak-Kucharczyk *et al.* 1996). That several towns with an important tourist/recreational function are among those Polish towns which are the most attractive for external investors (Swianiewicz 2002a), confirms the conclusion that the recent concept of the 'city as an entertainment machine' (Clark 2003) finds some support in the policies of Polish urban regimes.

Clark (1993, 2000) suggests that the traditional 'growth machine' type of urban regime is no longer dominant, and that more attention should be placed on urban anti-growth movements. Sagan suggests that it would be very unlikely that any anti-growth coalitions could be found in Polish cities. If her observation seems correct in terms of the lack of stable and influential coalitions, one can also refer to spontaneous (although some-times effective) anti-growth initiatives slowing down or even stopping planned growth projects. For example there have been initiatives by local shop-owners to stop the development of hyper-markets pursued by inter-national networks, and by ecological movement protesters against the con-struction of commercial buildings or roads construction which would result in cutting down trees.[16] These cases suggest that effective anti-growth coalitions are possible in CEE cities as well, even if Sagan is correct in observing that growth-machine coalitions are dominant among urban regimes in Polish cities.

Privatisation and the contracting-out of local services

Horvath and Peteri (2001) provide several examples of contracting-out and privatisation of services by local governments in the Czech Republic, Hungary, Poland and Slovakia.[17] In Hungary, for example 11 per cent of organisations dealing with solid waste disposal are now in private owner-ship. In Poland in some sectors of local services – such as maintenance of green space, street cleaning and street maintenance – over half of providers are now private (Aziewicz 1998). It should be stressed that these market-oriented changes were not imposed by legal regulations, but were an independent policy choice of individual local governments.

In addition the majority of local mayors agree with the statement that 'the municipality ought to a larger degree purchase services from the private sector, rather than producing them on its own' (see Table 5.5), an opinion more frequently held by officials from large towns than from small communities.

Table 5.5 Per cent of mayors agreeing with the statement: 'the municipality ought to a larger degree purchase services from the private sector, rather than producing them'

	Poland	Czech Republic	Slovakia
All local governments	57%	52%	46%
Cities over 30,000 population	63%	63%	61%

Source: LDI project survey of mayors, 1997.

Networking through the cooperation with NGOs

Before 1990 there were few NGO active in CEE countries, but since then the number has grown. The total number of NGO-type organisations registered at the end of 1990s reached almost 48,000 in Hungary, well over 40,000 in Poland, 5,000 in Latvia and a somewhat lower number in Romania (Soos *et al.* 2002; Siedlecka 2002).

Many local governments are more and more aware that to achieve their goals they need to work in partnership with other actors. In principle this is probably accepted by the vast majority of local politicians and administrators, but in practice the policies required by such an approach are still rare rather than the norm. Nevertheless, such innovative attitudes do exist and may mark the beginning of a wider trend for the future.

The cooperation with NGOs in providing many vital services (mostly in the area of social services) requires special attention. In Poland, the first complex programme of cooperation was launched in Gdynia in 1995. Between 1993 and 1996, the proportion of NGOs receiving support from local government increased from 16 per cent to 29 per cent (Regulski 2000). Also in relation to building partnerships between NGOs and local governments, the incentives provided by foreign programmes (in this case mostly the PHARE programmes financed by the European Union) played an important role (Brud 2002). The relationship between the statutory local government sector and the non-governmental sector is far from ideal. Survey results, however, suggest (Brud 2002) that local politicians are often afraid of cooperation because:

- they see some NGOs in competition with the traditional service delivery role of public organisations;
- they doubt the competence of NGOs volunteers and employees;
- they are afraid of complications resulting from the unstable financial situation of many NGOs.

On the other hand NGO activists perceive local government staff as bureaucratised, not interested in real partnership, and not understanding the specific problems of NGOs.

Despite the frequent lack of mutual trust, there are nevertheless increasingly frequent examples of cooperation. An increasing number of local managers agree with the claim that cooperation with NGOs in service delivery often brings more substantial savings than contractual arrangements with the private sector. Currently, about 44 per cent of Polish local governments contract NGOs to provide some local services. This is even more evident in Hungary, where 88 per cent of local governments declare contracts with NGOs, while 37 per cent of Hungarian municipalities also engage in consultation with NGOs during local decision making. But neither the network of NGOs nor the frequency of their cooperation are equally spread across the region. In Latvia contracting NGOs is much more rare. In Romania it is even more seldom for the simple reason that in 82 per cent of all local government units no NGO exists, while in 8 per cent of the municipalities there is only one NGO registered (Soos *et al.* 2002).

Management techniques

Several local governments in CEE countries have recently experimented with new management techniques of which management of local finance and quality control techniques offer helpful examples.

In Poland an increasing number of local governments are introducing methods of task-oriented budgeting, consolidated city accounts, using sophisticated credit instruments in multi-year financial programmes etc. (Pakoński 2001). Similar innovations have also been applied in other countries such as the Czech Republic and Hungary (Pigey 1999).

Soos (2003) informs us that some Hungarian municipalities have already introduced quality management systems related to ISO certificates, a process already started in Poland in earlier years. By the middle of 2002 there were 23 Polish municipalities, five counties and one region which had by that date received ISO 9000 or 9002 certificates, and 70 local governments have already started the procedure to receive similar ones (Winder 2002). Wysocki and Buchacz (2003) point to the fact that at the end of 2002 three regions (19 per cent of all Polish regions), eight counties (3 per cent out of all), thirteen cities over 100,000 citizens (31 per cent) and 30 smaller municipalities (1.5 per cent) had obtained already formal certificates.

Towards local governance?

In conclusion there is no doubt that New Public Management, as well as a shift from local government to the wider concept of local governance, has attracted a lot of attention at the local level in some of the CEE countries. However, at the same time most of those who will take forward these innovations do not use (or even do not know) the names of these fashionable concepts. A good illustration is a fact that the term 'local governance' does not have its Polish equivalent. Nevertheless, since traditionally (during the communist period) local authorities played a formal role not only in service delivery but also in overall social and economic planning, acceptance of the new role of being responsible for the overall wealth and welfare of the local community, rather than just for delivery of compulsory local functions, came easily to local councillors in CEE countries.[18]

But any generalisation would be an oversimplification. The single and most characteristic feature of the new situation has been the great variation among local governments – both between CEE countries and within individual countries. The region should not be regarded as a single homogenous block. Most of the innovative examples mentioned above have been taken from Hungary, Poland and the Czech Republic. Elsewhere, for example, in Bulgaria or Romania (and leaving aside the former Yugoslav republics, Albania or CIS states) examples of similar changes are much more difficult to find.

But there is also great variation from one city to another. On the one hand there have been open-minded and innovative leaders who have adopted modern management techniques. On the other hand there remains a majority of local governments with no access to, and/or no interest in innovation, and with traditional approaches to management. The innovative approach is more common among larger cities, but it would be an oversimplification to explain variation in management approach and performance by reference to variations in the size of local government. There are examples of very innovative small towns or even rural local governments as well as examples of very traditional big cities.

What should be stressed is the role of leadership. Strong and open-minded leaders (most often mayors) have usually been the engines of innovations in local government management. This has been a strength but also a weakness of much local reform. Many changes were driven by the leader him/herself, without sufficient support (or often even without sufficient understanding) of the rest of local politicians and staff. Therefore, a change of mayor may in some cases mean the end of innovation and a return to traditional methods of management. Such a situation has been especially frequent in small local governments, where the number of sufficiently skilled staff has been very limited.

Some scepticism about the trend to governance in CEE local governments is also supported by Gaspar and Wright's study of organisational culture in four mid-size Hungarian cities (1996). They noted a large gap between the use of 'fashionable labels' and the real implementation of policies, and between the declared and real values of local actors. They call this phenomenon 'window dressing', a practice which may bring an observer to 'cultural illusion'.

The development of New Public Management related innovations is not universally praised. Verheijen (2000), concentrating on central level administrative reform, suggests that NPM managerial techniques may have a negative effect in CEE countries. He identifies NPM with the creation of semi-independent agencies and indicates accountability problems. These can usually be solved in the Western European context, but only with much more difficulty in Central and Eastern Europe. In the CEE region the creation of semi-independent agencies is much more a central than a local level phenomenon, although there are some examples supporting Verheijen's claim in the context of a developing sphere of local governance. It seems clear, however, that the progress of European integration will strengthen tendencies towards new management techniques and governance structures at the local level.

The concept of CULCI for countries of Central and Eastern Europe

Many of the CEE countries have common historical roots, but the emergence of local democracy, the institutionalisation of local government and the decentralisation of structures in Central and Eastern Europe do not point in any uniform direction. There is definitely no distinct CEE model of local government common to the countries of the region. The system is still being formed, but it looks as if some countries are evolving in the direction of the model described in the literature as North European or North and Middle European (Poland, Estonia), while some others seem to be closer to the South European (Napoleonic) model (Slovakia, Romania, perhaps Bulgaria). This does not mean there are no specific features of the local government system in CEE countries which make them distinct from local democracies in Western Europe. But these specific characteristics do not allow the identification of a separate type, nor the rejection of the hypothesis of a gradual convergence with the two models identified in Western Europe.

It is also clear that local politicians in at least some of the CEE countries (Poland, Hungary, the Czech Republic) have been attracted by the idea of the shift from traditional government to the wider concept of governance, and by management styles identified often with the New Public Management. The presence and role of international contacts and foreign advisers in CEE cities during the 1990s has had a significant impact on such developments. At the same time most of these leaders do not use (or even do not know) the labels of 'NPM' or 'local governance'. The social and economic reality of the region means that the conditions for practical implementation of 'local governance' policies are different to those in Western Europe. There are, for example, limited resources in the hands of local businessmen, the relative weakness of NGOs, and a limited market of suppliers of contracted out services. The processes of European integration will strengthen, together with tendencies towards adaptation and convergence in the region.

Whether a complementarity between leadership and community involvement (CULCI) is especially important for local governments in post-communist Europe and whether there is already good practice in CULCI to be found is a hard question. Obviously, among several thousands of local governments one may find some positive examples. But in general, practical experience in 'community involvement' is extremely limited. As suggested in a recent study on citizen's relation to local government

> most local politicians [in Central and Eastern Europe] thinking about better communication with citizens, think first and foremost about how to inform the public about the plans and achievements of local

authorities, rather than about how councillors and local administrators can better learn about citizens' preferences. Moreover, techniques of learning about citizens' preferences, such as surveys, are sometimes used not to learn how to change local policies in order to make them closer to popular expectations, but to maximize political gains for the mayor and the ruling party.

(Swianiewicz 2001: 32)

This description is very far from the vision of 'community involvement'. And even relatively rare 'innovators' have usually limited experience and limited knowledge about useful methods for including communities in local decision-making processes.

The 'leadership' component is not much easier to identify. Traditional organisational culture is sometimes expressed in terms such as risk aversion, inertia, hierarchy and sometimes political clientelism (see, for example, Gaspar and Wright 1996). Leadership styles associated with this kind of political culture are far removed from the values and expectations which might be linked to an effective complementarity between leadership and community involvement.

Any negative picture, however, should not overshadow the more positive evolution of local governance. This chapter suggests that there are indeed local politicians who are looking for innovative ideas to govern their cities. Perhaps one may risk a claim that most of them have more success in looking for technical innovations in the way that local service can be delivered than in improving their relationship with the public. All this suggests that with respect to CEE countries, pursuit of a complementarity between leadership and community involvement is timely and attractive.

Notes

1 Bulgaria, the Czech Republic, Estonia, Hungary, Latvia, Lithuania, Poland, Romania, Slovakia, Slovenia.
2 For example Stoker (1991: 1) notices that *establishment of viable local government in Eastern Europe is seen as central to the establishment and maintenance of a democratic process*, but his book does not include any deeper analysis of any countries other than EU members.
3 For these models also the chapters of Haus and Heinelt and Bäck in this book.
4 In his analysis John concentrates on the Page and Goldsmith model, but Hesse and Sharpe show many similarities and provide useful, complementary observations.
5 For more about changes in territorial organisation and current debates in CEE countries, see Swianiewicz (2002b).
6 Following Sharpe (1993: 1) terminology I use the term 'meso level' to describe 'intermediate level of government between the centre and the basic municipal or communal level'. It may take the form of regional or county-type level of government.
7 The best measure of functional decentralisation seems to be the share of subnational self-governments in total public spending, but this measure creates

several methodological and data problems due to the existence of various extra-budgetary public funds in several countries. Instead a less perfect but clearer indicator is used – namely the share of sub-municipal spending in GDP.

 8 Before 1994 Hungarian mayors of small towns (below 10,000) were elected by citizens, while in larger cities they were appointed by the council.

 9 Direct election of mayors is also popular in several other countries of the CEE region (which are not covered by this chapter) such as: Albania, Ukraine, Russia etc.

10 Comments in this and next sections are to a large extent based on Polish experience and to a lesser extent on examples drawn from the Czech Republic, Hungary and Slovakia.

11 Illner (2003) and Soos (2003) formulate a similar opinion on the basis of Czech and Hungarian experiences.

12 For example, ideas of New Public Management have been quite widely discussed by Polish local politicians and top executive staff. It is very telling that the famous Osborne and Gabler book *Reinventing Government* was translated into Polish by one of the former top executives in the city of Gdańsk. It is also very characteristic that one of the well-known progressive local politicians – former vice executive mayor of the city of Krakow – has been promoting in his lectures across Poland the idea that managing a city is identical to managing a big company. Finally, it is worth mentioning that the term 'New Public Management' is directly referred to the current programme of training for local administration, which is sponsored by the World Bank and implemented through the Polish Ministry responsible for public administration (Potkański 2002).

13 The survey was part of an international research project 'Local Democracy and Innovation' (LDI) coordinated by the University of Bergen and sponsored by the Norwegian governments.

14 However, it should be added that despite policy preferences expressed by local politicians, there is a huge gap between local officials' and local businessmen's perception of the impact which local authorities have on economic development. Only 4 per cent of local businessmen in Poland see positive results of local economic policies, 13 per cent see efforts but without clear results, while 61 per cent do not notice any activities of local governments aimed at the stimulation of local economic development (Swianiewicz 2002a).

15 Mayors, chief administrative officers, councillors, citizens, all interviewed in the Czech Republic, Hungary, Poland and Slovakia

16 An interesting example is provided by the recent conflict over construction of a residential area and retail-trade centre in the Warsaw district of Wilanow. Wilanow is a relatively loosely built and affluent part of Warsaw. The plan pursued by local authorities in coalition with international retail companies was to construct a huge shopping-mall and to intensify the land use in the housing zone. However, a strong opposition of Wilanow residents put a question mark on the plan. Initially it seemed that the growth coalition could win – in spite of protests the local council adopted a land-use plan allowing for such a construction. But further, continuous opposition resulted in a compromise proposal – the number of hypermarkets was reduced from three to one, and the size of the proposed housing construction was seriously reduced (Wojtczuk 2002).

17 Horvath and Peteri (2001) also provide examples of public-private partnership initiatives in CEE local governments.

18 Although it must not be forgotten that instruments used in the command economies before 1990 were drastically different from contemporary tools used to influence local economic development.

References

Albanian Ministry for Local Government and Decentralisation (2003) *Improvement of Administrative-Territorial Division*, Tirana.

Aziewicz, T. (1998) *Gospodarka rynkowa w usługach komunalnych*, Gdansk: The Gdansk Institute for Market Economics.

Baldersheim, H., Illner, M., Offerdal, A., Rose, L. and Swianiewicz, P. (eds) (1996) *Local Democracy and the Process of Transformation in East–Central Europe*, Boulder, CO: Westview Press.

Bończak-Kucharczyk, E., Cousins, L., Herbst, K. and Stewart, M. (1996) *Lokalne strategie rozwoju gospodarczego*, Warszawa: Brytyjski Fundusz Know-How – Fundusz Współpracy.

Brud, A. (2002) 'Wspolpraca samorzadu terytorialnego z organizacjami pozarzadowymi w wykonywaniu zadan publicznych', MA dissertation, Catholic University of Lublin/Institute of Economics.

Caulfield, J. (2002) 'Local Government Finance in OECD Countries', in: J. Caufield and H. Larsen (eds) *Local Government at the Millennium*, Opladen: Leske + Budrich: 153–169.

Clark, T. N. (1993) 'Local Democracy and Innovation in Eastern Europe', *Environment and Planning: Government and Policy*, Vol. 11: 171–198.

—— (2000) 'Old and New Paradigms for Urban Research', *Urban Affairs Review*, Vol. 36, No. 1: 3–45.

—— (ed.) (2003) *The City as an Entertainment Machine*, Research in Urban Policy Vol. 9, New York: JAI Press/Elsevier.

Coulson, A. (ed.) (1995) *Local Government in Eastern Europe*, Aldershot: Edward Elgar.

Council of Europe (1995) *The Size of Municipalities, Efficiency and Citizen Participation*, Local and Regional Authorities in Europe No. 56, Strasbourg: CoE.

DEXIA (2001) *Local Finance in the Fifteen Countries of the European Union*, Paris: Dexia, 2001.

Gaspar, M. and Wright, G. (1996) 'Organisational Culture Barriers of Local Government Management Development: The Hungarian Experience', in: J. Jabes (ed.) *Developing Organizations and Changing Attitudes: Public Administration in Central and Eastern Europe*, Bratislava: NISPAcee.

Hambleton, R. (1998) 'Competition and Contracting in UK Local Government', in: N. Oatley (ed.) *Cities, Economic Competition and Urban Policy*, London: Paul Chapman: 58–77.

—— (2001) 'The New City Management', in: R. Hambleton, H. Savitch and M. Stewart (eds) *Globalism and Local Democracy*, London: Palgrave: 147–169.

Hesse, J. J. and Sharpe, L. J. (1991) 'Local Government in International Perspective: Some Comparative Observations', in: J. J. Hesse (ed.) *Local Government and Urban Affairs in International Perspective*, Baden-Baden: Nomos: 603–621.

Horvath, T. (ed.) (2000) *Decentralisation: Experiments and Reforms*, Budapest: Open Society Institute/Local Government Initiative.

Horvath, T. and Peteri, G. (2001) *Navigation to the Market: Regulation and Competition in Local Utilities in Central and Eastern Europe*, Budapest: Open Society Institute.

Illner, M. (2003) 'Thirteen Years of Reforming Subnational Government in the Czech Republic', in: N. Kersting and A. Vetter (eds) *Reforming Local Government in Europe*, Opladen: Leske + Budrich: 261–281.

John, P. (2001) *Local Governance in Western Europe*, London: Sage.

Jurlina-Alibegovic, D. (2002) *The Model of Local Government Financing in Croatia*, Zagreb: Croatian Law Centre.

Kandeva, E. (ed.) (2001) *Stabilisation of Local Governments*, Budapest: Open Society Institute/Local Government Initiative.

Kulesza, M. (2002), 'Methods and Techniques of Managing Decentralisation Reforms in CEE Countries: The Polish Experience', in: Peteri G. (ed.) *Mastering Decentralisation and Public Administration Reforms in Central and Eastern Europe*, Budapest: Open Society Institute/Local Government Initiative: 189–217.

Larsen, H. (2002) 'Directly Elected Mayors: Democratic Renewal or Constitutional Confusion?', in: J. Caulfield and H. Larsen (eds) *Local Government at the Millennium*, Opladen: Leske + Budrich: 111–135.

Leach, S. and Wilson, D. (2000) *Local Political Leadership*, Bristol: The Policy Press.

Maenpaa, O. (2002) *Report on Administrative Decentralization in Macedonia*, unpublished report for the Council of Europe.

Mouritzen, P. E. and Svara, J. H. (2002) *Leadership at the Apex*, Pittsburgh, PA: University of Pittsburgh Press.

Newton, K. and Karran, T. J. (1985) *The Politics of Local Expenditure*, London: Macmillan.

Page, E. C. and Goldsmith, M. (eds) (1987) *Central-Local Government Relations: A Comparative Analysis of West European Unitary States*, London: Sage.

Pakoński, K. (2001) *Zintegrowane zarządzanie finansowe*, Warszawa: Municipium.

Peteri, G. and Zentai, V. (2002) 'Lessons on Successful Reform Management', in: G. Peteri (ed.) *Mastering Decentralization and Public Administration Reforms in Central and Eastern Europe*, Budapest: Open Society Institute: 13–31.

Pigey, J. (1999) *Fiscal Decentralisation and Local Government Finance in Hungary*, Washington, DC: Urban Institute.

Potkański, T. (2002) 'Systemy zarządzania jakością a rozwój instytucjonalny jednostek samorządu terytorialnego', unpublished material of the Ministry of the Interior and Public Administration, Warszawa.

Regulski, J. (2000) *Samorzad III Rzeczpospolitej: koncepcje i realizacja*, Warszawa: PWN.

Sagan, I. (2000) *Miasto: scena konfliktów i współpracy*, Gdańsk: Gdańsk University.

Sharpe, L. J. (ed.) (1993) *The Rise of Meso Government in Europe*, London: Sage.

Siedlecka, E. (2002) 'Spoleczeństwo mało obywatelskie', *Gazeta Wyborcza*, 23 September 2002.

Soos, G. (2003) 'Local Government Reforms and the Capacity for Local Governance in Hungary', in: N. Kersting and A. Vetter (eds) *Reforming Local Government in Europe*, Opladen: Leske + Budrich: 241–260.

Soos, G., Toka, G. and Wright, G. (eds) (2002) *The State of Local Democracy in Central Europe*, Budapest: Open Society Institute.

Stoker, G. (1991) 'Introduction: Trends in Western European Local Government', in: R. Batley and G. Stoker (eds) *Local Government in Europe: Trends and Developments*, New York: St. Martin Press: 1–21.

Swianiewicz, P. (ed.) (2001) *Public Perception of Local Governments in Central and Eastern Europe*, Budapest: Open Society Institute.

—— (2002a) 'The Investment Attractiveness of Polish Cities', paper prepared for the EURA Conference in Turin, 18–20 April 2002.

—— (ed.) (2002b) *Consolidation or Fragmentation? The Size of Local Governments in Central and Eastern Europe*, Budapest: Open Society Institute.

——— (2003a) 'The Values of Local Democracy as Seen by Mayors in East–Central Europe', in: H. Baldersheim, M. Illner and H. Wollman (eds) *Local Democracy in Post-Communist Europe*, Urban Research International Series, Opladen: Leske + Budrich: 263–273.

——— (2003b) 'Reforming Local Government in Poland: Top-Down and Bottom-Up Processes', in: N. Kersting and A. Vetter (eds) *Reforming Local Government in Europe*, Opladen: Leske + Budrich: 283–309.

——— (2003c) 'Partisan Cleavages in Local Governments in Poland After 1990', in: T. Zarycki and G. Kolankiewicz (eds) *Regional Issues in Polish Politics*, SSEES Occasional Papers No. 60, London: School of Slavonic and East European Studies, University College: 179–201.

Swianiewicz, P. and Klimska, U. (2003) 'Czy wielkie miasta są sterowalne? Wpływ sytuacji politycznej na warunki zarządzania największymi miastami Polski', *Samorząd Terytorialny*, No. 3: 12–28.

Verheijen T. (2000) 'Redefining Accountability Systems in Public Management; A Challenge for Central and East European Reformers', unpublished manuscript.

Winder, I. (2002) 'Zarządzanie jakością w administracji: normy ISO 9000', *Gazeta Samorządu i Administracji*, No. 13.

Wojtczuk, M. (2002) 'Przesądzone: Auchan powstanie', *Gazeta Stołeczna*, 8 October 2002.

Wysocki, S. and Buchacz, T. (2003) 'Zarządzanie jakością w administracji', *Służba Cywilna*, No. 5 (Autumn 2002–Winter 2003).

6 Cities in the multi-level governance of the European Union

Laurence Carmichael

Introduction

Local and national factors remain key variables in influencing the institutional design of local systems of governance and local political culture. However, the European Union (EU) context is increasingly encroaching on the way cities across Europe are run and the policies they can implement. The basic question of this chapter is to identify what roles cities currently play in the EU multi-level governance: are they emerging as key players or do they still remain minor entities, pushed aside by the other players? What are the implications of this role with respect to urban leadership and community involvement, especially concerning their complementarity and interplay?

First, this chapter identifies the EU competences in the area of urban sustainability. Despite its lack of explicit urban policy and its lack of competence in the area of urban public administration, the EU has recently developed a sustainable urban development agenda. This agenda – following key criteria identified by the Commission, including local empowerment, economic prosperity and employment, social inclusion and environmental protection – focusses attention on a number of EU policies that normally require the involvement of different levels of public authority in policy implementation. This establishes a hypothesis that the EU could, potentially, present both policy and governance challenges, which could in turn impact on the nature of the local interplay between leadership and community involvement.

Second, the chapter examines whether the EU criteria and rules identified above equate to a new model of urban governance enhancing democratic participation, effective problem solving and accountable agency in a broader multi-level governance context. The EU has encouraged new webs of relationship between the various levels of government through, for instance, the open method of coordination. It has also encouraged the rise of new business and voluntary actors in the policy process at local level. However, the EU influence at local level does not aim to fill an institutional and policy vacuum. Its impact rather depends on a number of factors, including the constitutional, legal and economic nature of domestic centre–local relationships and on the strength and power of local leaders and local networks. In effect this amounts to the complementarity of leadership and community involvement. EU legislators must therefore be aware of the immediate imbalance in the benefits of integration across the EU, despite their search for territorial cohesion.

Cities, EU and sustainability

Generally speaking, the search for sustainability, policy efficiency and effectiveness at EU level has increased in recent years, as has the emphasis of subsidiarity and proportionality. In 1998, the European Commission defined four preconditions to sustainable urban development: economic prosperity, social inclusion, protection of the environment and local empowerment (Commission 1998). The basic assumption was that those public authorities closest to citizens must be involved in policy making (in particular urban policy, employment, social inclusion and structural funds and the emerging European Spatial Development Perspective (ESDP)) in order to achieve several interlinked objectives. These included local democracy (developing local democratic structures able to enhance community participation in the policy process), efficient policies (generating value for money) and renewed social integrative structures (offering effective social inclusion). The Commission clearly linked governance and policy issues in its search for sustainability and, at the same time, tried to justify the process of EU integration and promote changes in domestic power sharing within the new EU governance. The Commission's communication offered, in itself, no legally binding definition of sustainability. Yet, it introduced a useful thread linking all the ingredients of sustainability generally accepted both at domestic and international levels, as well as some indication of the policies in which the EU would like to intervene in the future.

Good governance and local empowerment

In recent years, a combination of socio-economic change, globally as well as in Europe, have put pressure on the EU to start a process leading to a review of its governance system and the sustainability of its policies, leading in turn to a rethink of the involvement of sub-national tiers of government. Globalisation has led to the resurgence of cities as centres of growth, with implications for governance itself as policy makers see local institutions as the key to urban competitiveness (Jouve and Lefèvre 2002). In addition, the Commission has clearly stated in its White Paper on European Governance that there must be 'a stronger interaction with regional and local governments and civil society' (European Commission 2001a). National governments are left with the need to reconsider the role of their sub-national tiers within a system of EU governance, to facilitate the implementation of ever-increasing EU policies, address pressures for more local democracy and tackle global economic pressures.

Demands for regionalisation were expressed across Europe from the 1970s, but for the EU, the trigger for promoting a 'Europe of the Regions' was the advent in 1992 of the Single Market, when it was feared that economic disparities between regions would be exacerbated by increased liberalisation of trade across the EU. This led to increased funding for structural activities in the early 1990s (Hooghe 1996; Heinelt 1996).

An important event for EU Heads of States was the recognition in 1989 that social exclusion was a Europe-wide phenomenon (Council of the EU 1989). This marked the arrival of a European social agenda, including the development of employment and social inclusion strategies and other policies with definite local dimensions. However, the use of soft legislation rather than the setting up of a regulatory framework for social Europe means that member states are key players in a balancing act between a Europe of solidarities and cohesion and a more neo-liberal Europe. Economic pressures have emphasised the importance of global competitiveness, while privatisation and reductions in governmental capacity have weakened state welfare systems. But the possibility has emerged of a third way, a more liberal route along which the state would not be all powerful, but only one actor among others (Giddens 1998).

In parallel, the EU had to face a number of issues concerning its own status. First, the democratic deficit has been, for a long time, seen as a major drawback to EU legitimacy, and events of recent years have exacerbated the image of an EU remote from its citizens (Atkinson 2002). Second, against this background of stormy relationship with its citizens, how could the EU keep up the momentum of integration necessary to ensure successful enlargement to the east? The EU had to introduce new integrative strategies in social fields, involving both soft legislation to facilitate political consensus and encouragement of a greater involvement of sub-national authorities. Third, in the age of a search for grand political ideas, how could the citizens of Europe be offered a system of governance able to deliver sustainable policies?

Since the 1997 Treaty of Amsterdam, sustainable development has been one of the objectives of the EU. From then on, a number of political and legal processes at EU level supported the emergence of European strategies for sustainable development, in particular in the fields of employment through the Luxembourg process (European Council 1997a, 1997b), social inclusion policy through the Lisbon process (European Council 2000a) and environment through the Cardiff process (European Council 1998). These strategies required both a European wide framework, as well as the coordination of national approaches to sustainable development. The European Commission's proposed strategy for sustainable development, subsequently discussed by the Gothenburg European

Council (European Council 2001), introduced interesting, if thought by some to be weak (Colwell 2001) governance and policy propositions. First, it justified EU involvement in a number of policy areas, but also acknowledged the need to involve all the layers of the multi-level governance, including local government and citizen participation (Commission 2001a). In addition, it set out the policy obstacles to sustainable development, including over-emphasis on sectoral policies and economic incentives, short-termism, ignorance and outdated policies.

While participation in the democratic process is seen by the EU as essential to obtain sustainability, the EU has no competences in reforming domestic centre–local relations, but can only encourage partnership and consultation. Three other ingredients were thus deemed necessary by the Commission to ensure a sustainable future for cities – economic prosperity, social inclusion and protection of the environment. It is through these policy arenas, and the challenges they pose to urban governance, that cities can hope to develop their own policy making and implementation role.

Strengthening economic prosperity and employment in towns and cities

Towards the end of the 1980s, the decision to tackle territorial disparities came as a reaction to the creation of the single market where there would be losers at the periphery while inners at the core as the central regions of the EU became even more dynamic growth poles (Hooghe 1996). More recently, territorial dynamics have been seen in a more positive light as an instrument of competitiveness. In particular, polycentric development and labour force employability have been two instruments in the search for global competitiveness, emphasising the importance of the urban dynamics of the EU (Commission 1997, 1998). Consequently, economic prosperity and employment are seen as key instruments of urban sustainable development.

Spatial planning is one policy area where the EU is now trying to reconcile the role of the urban core with the regions in which they are situated. The European Spatial Development Perspective (ESDP) was adopted in 1999 as an intergovernmental strategy to address the peripherality of certain areas of the EU (Commission 1999). While the EU in any strict sense has no supranational competence in spatial planning, the Council of Ministers saw spatial planning as a means of promoting sustainable growth, economic and social cohesion and solidarity between member states – all goals of the EU under article 2 of the Maastricht Treaty. Growing recognition of the importance of the EU in relation to territorial planning (Faludi 2000; Williams 2000) is enhanced by the threat to economic and social cohesion across the EU posed by enlargement to Eastern Europe. The growing emphasis on territorial issues also supports the principles of subsidiarity and the role of local and regional communities.

For cities, the ESDP is an important document as one of its key object-ives is the development of polycentric and balanced urban systems (Com-mission 1999) whereby cities would cooperate both with rural areas and regions. Despite its obvious integrationist agenda and support for some kind of multi-level governance in territorial development with cities as key partners, the ESDP remains a voluntary framework between national authorities and it will be interesting to evaluate the top-down impact of this process at the local level in EU member-states, keeping in mind that national actors and factors can also interfere in the process (Eser and Konstadakopoulos 2000). For instance, in the UK, the EU interest in plan-ning policy during the period of a Euro-sceptic Conservative government had an impact on local authorities, yet with little changes in the UK plan-ning guidance at national and regional levels (Tewdwr-Jones *et al.* 2000). By contrast with a Labour government since 1997 the ESDP has been referred to in UK planning policy (Faludi 2001). In addition, while the EU has moved towards a more social agenda in the last decade, the ESDP suggests that the key approach to EU territorial cohesion is to prepare cities and urban systems to compete more efficiently in a globalised market place, hence creating *dynamic zones of global economic integration* (Commission 1999). Such an approach, until it delivers results, could be tagged as idealistic by those who see the EU's prime objective to be polit-ical and to create an area of even economic development to ensure internal EU cohesion (Krätke 2001). For those who see the EU as a neo-liberal project, putting the emphasis on global competitiveness as a key objective implies accepting the cost that territorial cohesion will be diffi-cult to achieve (Agnew 2001).

The ESDP, by offering an alternative to the core-periphery model of development, yet by focussing on world competitiveness of cities and regions, lies at the crossroads of two major political paths. Given its volun-tary nature, it will be up to member states to decide which direction they want to take.

The Commission, following the Potsdam Council of Ministers which agreed the ESDP, started to refine the concept of territorial cohesion, in terms of both governance and policy development in the first report on economic and social cohesion (Commission 2001b). The Commission reiterated the need for greater territorial cohesion in the application of sector-based policies in its second cohesion report, suggesting a shift from 'Regional Europe' to more generally 'Territorial Europe', where regional policy addresses urban problems as well, and good governance means decentralised implementation (Commission 2002). The Commission also highlighted the need to gather more data on local indicators as well as more intelligence on urban areas (Commission 2002).

Last but not least, the territorial component of sector-based policies, including employment, but also social inclusion and equal opportunities, must be emphasised in the search for cohesion and acknowledged in structural activities (Commission 2002). As far as employment policy is concerned, the 1997 Employment Summit in Luxembourg focussed on four key sectoral priorities or pillars. It was left to member states, as key players of national structural and macro-economic policies, to set up national administrative structures and measures to transpose these priorities into practical action (Carmichael 2001; Kongshøj Madsen and Munch-Madsen 2001).

Since then, the EU has moved towards a more actor-centred approach to employment policy. In Nice, the member states agreed to support both the local and the regional dimensions of EU employment policies. However, they only referred to target policies for different regions in order to meet the Lisbon objectives for territorial cohesion (European Council 2000b). As for the Commission, it was more forceful in acknowledging that the mobilisation of local actors (local authorities, enterprises, NGOs and voluntary sector, social partners, state agencies, training providers) is a key factor for successful employment policies (Commission 2001c). For instance, in England, local strategic partnerships (LSPs) between public, private, voluntary and community sectors are being introduced to coordinate different initiatives meeting neighbourhood needs. A Community Empowerment Fund and a Community Chest enable communities to build capacity to participate in multi-actor arenas and to run their own projects (UK Government 2001).

Promoting equality, social inclusion and regeneration in urban areas

Another key EU activity for urban sustainability is the promotion of social inclusion and regeneration in urban areas. In the past, the EU, under the impetus of the Delors Commission, has cautiously addressed the issue of the negative impacts of economic integration through the application of the 1987 and 1992 reforms of structural funds. But the redistributive capacity of the EU is limited, and in any case with future enlargements, it is improbable that structural activities have the capacity – financial or political – to deliver territorial cohesion.

Social exclusion, partly a consequence of economic integration, affects urban centres because the concentration of population exacerbates the causes of exclusion – segregation, discrimination, racism and sexism, lack of education and social facilities. Ironically, economically dynamic regions can breed poor areas (e.g. London), hence regional indicators can miss local social problems, and regional policy can ignore the most acute forms of deprivation. Until 1997 social exclusion and urban decline did not play a large part in the EU social agenda, but from the late 1990s the agenda moved on.

The social solidarity of the European social model was emphasised in the Treaty of Amsterdam, a concept borrowed from the French approach to social exclusion (Durhkeim 1986, first edition 1893; Glorieux 1999). At the Lisbon European Council in March 2000, Heads of States and Governments agreed that the search for economic competitiveness should be accompanied by a fight for greater social cohesion. In particular they agreed to take steps to eradicate poverty and social exclusion. The European Council, without being prescriptive in an area where the EU has no power encouraged the greater involvement of local authorities in combating exclusion and promoting the mobilisation of local actors, NGOs and social services.

The Nice European Council (European Council 2000b) put the fight against poverty and exclusion firmly on the European Social Agenda (ESA) by requiring member states to develop national plans to eradicate poverty and exclusion. Again, the Council was careful not to prescribe any changes to domestic governance, even reiterating that subsidiarity suggested flexibility in the national implementation of ESA to acknowledge national differences in systems of employment services and social welfare.

However, the open method of coordination (OMC) agreed to implement the ESA also requires member states to develop policies with definite territorial dimensions (including assessment of regional and local needs and development of local and regional policies). The OMC was first introduced for implementing the Luxembourg process in 1997, but spread to other social areas. While circumventing the high politics issue of sovereignty, fiscal or otherwise, as well as other more politically-sensitive issues, the soft legislation approach is a politically acceptable instrument to steer member states towards a common, yet flexible, approach to social problems in general, and to urban problems in particular. Many of the issues are common to cities across Europe, so justifying a European wide approach stimulated by the Commission (Commission 1997). Member states can share a European social model, reinforced by peer pressure, with the Commission developing monitoring instruments recording national programmes of anti-exclusion activity and reviewing national achievements, and finding new allies at sub-national levels by encouraging member states to develop territorial policies.

The Commission has also been active in developing an explicit urban rationale, focussing on social exclusion and the need to address urban regeneration (Commission 1997, 1998). The 1998 document gave a definition of the four key ingredients to urban sustainability. Atkinson, appraising the emerging urban agenda of the EU, suggested that the Commission saw it as a chance to expand its activities and create a consensus on urban policy among other key players. However the Commission was careful not to increase EU regulatory or redistributive powers at the expense of national and sub-national authorities, but simply to assess how current policies affect urban areas. Atkinson sums it up when he refers to the role of the Commission to be one of *leadership and vision* (Atkinson 2001).

Altogether the Commission seems more forceful than the European Council in encouraging the rise of an urban sustainability agenda, but its own role is complementary to that of the European Council. The latter is more about politics, the former about policy making. While the OMC may appear a key EU instrument in the fight against exclusion, the EU regulatory powers remain very limited, except perhaps in the area of anti-discriminatory legislation. The EU can also focus some of its redistributive capacity to deliver the European Social Agenda, and through this route address urban social exclusion.

Structural activities aim primarily to strengthen economic prosperity and employment. Following the 1999 reform of the structural funds, however, a number of initiatives reinforce the urban dimension of structural activities. The Community initiative URBAN (covering priority urban areas) was maintained, and altogether 165 out of 283 structural programmes (at December 2002) aim at urban regeneration and industrial conversion.

However, urban activities still represent a very small share of EU redistributive policies. URBAN II involves funding of €728.3 million between 2000–2006, barely equivalent to 0.1 per cent of the EU budget per annum, to share between 53 programmes. The capacity of structural funds to tackle urban economic and social disparities is thus limited given that bidding structure for funding favours 'successful cities' (Chorianopoulos 2002). Yet, the Commission has acknowledged that more than three-quarters of the EU population live in urban areas. Its means do not seem to match its ambition in tackling urban issues.

Protecting and improving the urban environment

Last but not least, urban sustainable development requires that the urban, environment be protected and enhanced. Through the 1990s environmental issues have been closely linked with sustainable development with sustainability, like exclusion, requiring a cross-cutting approach and coordination between economic, social and environmental aspects of policies.

Sustainable development has been, since the Treaty of Amsterdam in 1997, one of the aims of the EU (article 6 of the EC Treaty). Since the early 1990s, with the Fifth Environmental Action Programme 'Towards Sustainability', a process has existed to integrate the environment into EU policies, and since the European Council in Vienna in 1998, EU institutions have had to systematically take account of environmental considerations in all their policies. The current Sixth Environmental Action Programme (2001–2010) aims at implementing this approach (European Parliament and Council 2002), and through spatial planning and urban development policies, the Commission wishes to enhance the role of the EU as a key global player in relation to the environment (Commission 2001d).

Cities are central to EU environment and sustainable development policies. In 1990, this role was acknowledged by *the Green Paper on the Urban Environment* (Commission 1990). The European Sustainable Cities Project was introduced in 1993 to promote urban sustainability across the EU, in particular through exchange of good practice and involving cities in the EU policy process. In 1996, the Expert Group on the Urban Environment, established in 1991 to develop the EU urban environment strategy outlined in the 1990 Green Paper, published a report outlining the capacity building tools for urban sustainability, including institutional development. Indeed, one of the preconditions for sustainable urban development was the setting up of efficient urban management structures, that is structures that can implement sustainable policies, including socio-economic development and urban regeneration, based on five principles – collaboration and partnership, policy integration, market mechanisms, information management and measuring and monitoring (Commission 1996).

EU impact on urban governance

Impact on policies

In all these ways the EU can potentially have an impact on the way city authorities conduct their business. In Chapter 2 the theoretical model upon which this book is based identified a set of possible impacts both on policy and on governance (in terms of input, throughput and output). As far as policies are concerned, EU policies linked to urban sustainability suggest impacts on cities across Europe at three levels: the substantial level (referring to the content of policies), procedural (referring to the interactive processes) and institutional/organisational (referring to the formal and informal 'rules of the game') levels. Table 6.1 synthesises the policy impacts so far identified above (pages 131–137). Policies are divided into those having a direct impact (e.g. *structural funds*) in italic and those with an indirect or secondary impact at local level (e.g. ESDP) in regular type.

Impact on urban governance

The European context as developed through the Council and Commission has generated other impacts – on urban governance. New choices and opportunities for cities are offered, through a number of the policies already discussed. These encourage cooperation and partnership across the various public authority levels, engaging changing agendas through new administrative structures. The EU Commission has now indeed introduced formally a qualitative link between its policies and what we could refer to as a more broadly based participatory democracy through the notion of 'European Governance' (Commission 2001a). Although it does not refer explicitly to the involvement of local or city authorities, the

Table 6.1 EU policy impact at the local level

Substantial impact	*Structural activities* • *concentration: focussing on problem areas* • *programming: establishment of multi-annual strategic planning (e.g. SPDs)* • *defining integrated/intersectoral strategies (training, employment, infrastructure regeneration etc.)* Planning/ESDP • defining integrated strategies • defining added value city specialism to city network *Competition Policy* • *implementing public procurement legislation* Employment • employability, entrepreneurship, equal opportunity, adaptability • planning: defining local employment needs Social Inclusion • improve employability • *anti-discrimination legislation* *Environment* • *implement EU environment legislation (including environment impact assessment, clean beaches, sewage etc.)* • policy integration
Procedural impact	*Structural activities* • *partnership working of local actors* • *additionality: vertical integration* ESDP • development of city networks, trans-border networks • development of private/public partnership working Competition • *bidding* Employment/National Action Plan • *local partnership working (public/private/third sector)* Social Inclusion • local partnership working Environment • partnership working • information and involvement of the general public
Institutional/ organisational impact	*Structural activities* • *change in role of local agencies* • *local government leadership: chairing over partnership, steering and monitoring committees.* • *information management: creation of shared databanks, networked information systems* • *new staff: European officers, funding and bidding 'experts'* • *financial management: setting-up new financial management methods to cope with EU funding mechanisms*

Table 6.1 continued

• *monitoring: developing monitoring instruments* • *quality control: setting-up monitoring of training providers* • *find additional funding* ESDP • communications: facilitate transfer of expertise (trans-border, across city network) Employment • *managing and leading local partnerships* • *change in role of local agencies* Social inclusion environment • information management • measuring and monitoring

Commission includes, in the five principles of good governance, the principle of participation, which implicitly requires the intervention of the sub-national level in the policy process. In itself, the implementation of the participation principle could affect some aspects of local governance in areas where the EU has competence to act. So, while the EU has no constitutional power to affect the institutions of local government – a purely domestic matter for national governments – the move from government to 'good European' governance, by focussing on the synergy between policies and decision-making process could potentially empower the local level. In particular, it could influence local leaders to lobby for more local involvement in EU policies. In view of the key economic role of cities in a global market, city leaders would have powerful arguments for involvement in European policies addressing pressures of globalisation. The role of cities at the core of social inclusive and environmentally-friendly policies is legitimised by the fact that it is at the level of urban space that citizens live and work. By enhancing the new opportunities given by the EU, city governance has the potential to develop a full social and environmental agenda. These newly found powers of the city cannot exist in isolation to global forces, but in conjunction with them. Indeed, we must share the confidence that the new network governance and the rise of more informal arrangements brought about by globalisation offers an opportunity for cities to contribute *to the on-going social construction of sustainability* (Guy and Marvin 1999). Table 6.2 summarises EU impact on urban governance.[1]

Cities in the EU multi-level governance: poor relation or unavoidable partner?

The developments identified in this chapter so far make European policies a potential driver for urban change, offering significant impacts for

Table 6.2 EU impact on urban governance

	Direct impact	*Indirect impact*
Input (democratic participation)	*None* EU has no constitutional power to debate participation and enfranchise communities in member states	*Limited* EU instruments: OMC, Committee of the Regions (COR), EES, ESA, Urban Communications. Local and regional voice in EU policy process through COR. Consultative voice only Local v. regional representation. Association of cities.
Throughput (policy process)	*None* EU has no power over transparency and accountability of partnership arrangements	*Limited* EU instruments: OMC. EU encourages partnership, but their representativity is left to member states. EU arrangements and links with local level are opaque.
Output (effectiveness)	*Limited* Effectiveness is ensured to a limited extent through COR, MEPs	*Yes* EU instruments: OMC, EES, ESA, ESDP, Urban Communications Vertical and horizontal partnership are encouraged by EU. Vertical partnerships required (structural funds). Horizontal partnerships required: problem solving sought through local capacity building (structural funds, employment, social inclusion).

policy and governance. The EU appears to support cities as allies in the fight for integration. Indeed, cities seem to have gained from the recent steps taken by the EU in a number of directions, including promotion of subsidiarity, of looser forms of arrangements encouraging multi-level partnerships, of policies with local dimensions and of a new polycentric model of economic development. With growing EU competences, local authorities are also asked to implement an increasing number of EU policies, bearing the costs of competition rules and social legislation, and benefiting from structural activities. With more than three-quarters of EU residents living in urban areas, cities seem to have a de facto legitimate political role to play in the EU, to ensure that human capital remains at the core of the debate on European multi-level governance and policies, and to bring issues of sustainability, accountability and democracy to the fore.

Yet, the EU rationale for urban sustainable development poses a number of problems for city empowerment. In the end, city power depends on the weight of the urban agenda over other EU policy agenda, on their autonomy vis-à-vis the other multi-level actors (in the domestic arena in particular), and more importantly on the role that cities are expected to play within a cohesive Europe. Hence the real impact of the European Union on urban governance cannot be evaluated outside the broader context of multi-level governance structures and processes. In practice these structures and processes establish three obstacles to an enhanced role for cities in multi-level governance.

First, the apparent EU support to urban areas and cities present in EU documentation is not reflected in the EU budget where rural concerns get the majority of EU expenditure. In addition, assistance to urban area is only part of a broader regional agenda in the EU structural policy.

Second, EU rules and processes do not reach down to the city level in an even fashion across the EU because central government control remains the dominant influence affecting levels of local autonomy. Indeed, despite the Europeanisation of domestic policies, the EU interest in the role of cities has so far been fundamentally at the policy implementation stage, with national authorities retaining policy formulation and decision-making powers.

Third, increased power and influence at the city level (and indeed at the neighbourhood level below the city) is legitimised by the fact that nearly 80 per cent of the EU population lives in urban areas. Greater local autonomy could thus respond to the democratic deficit. Enhanced local democracy, exercised through representative democratic government, may run counter to the forces which support a new governance dominated by economic actors. If cities are key institutions which can assist economic actors to help Europe maintain or develop its economic competitiveness within global markets, European pressures may encourage the enlargement of their economic role and governmental alliances with non-governmental actors. Cities could become the territory where economic and political actors fight for power and influence, but with adverse consequences for their welfare role and for the pursuit of social cohesion.

Cities squeezed between rural Europe and Europe of the regions

While there are indications that the rationale for a European urban focus is taking shape, Commission expenditure remains so far dominated by regional and rural considerations, with the Common Agricultural Policy (CAP) and Structural Funds accounting for 8 per cent of the EU budget. In addition, the EU has in the past seemed to lean towards a Europe of the regions through, for instance, the establishment of the Committee of the Regions. Rural areas and regions have already a strong national, as well as a more particular, rural and regional leadership. This not only helps to retain their engagement with EU decision making but also allows for the possibility of shaping policies to their own advantage. Le Galès, for example, points to the German *Länder* opposing urban anti-poverty programmes (Le Galès 2002). In addition, in the light of considerations of scale and function in many European states, the regional level seemed more appropriate than the lower city level with respect to the implementation of European territorial policies in policy areas such as planning, transport, the economy and technolgy (John 2001). This regional focus has been reinforced also by integrationist authors who have focussed on bottom-up integration and the triangular region–nation–EU as the basis for a multi-level approach to EU integration (Marks 1992; Heinelt 1996; Smith 1997; Hooghe and Marks 2001; Jeffery 2000). Yet, this emphasis on regions is partly cosmetic and not representative of an EC interest in city–regions as functional areas. Local governments are significant beneficiaries of structural funding aimed at the regeneration of traditional industrial and often urbanised areas. In addition, the Committee of the Regions represents all sub-national authorities.

Research has demonstrated that structural funding acts as a strong incentive for local interest in EU affairs. In particular cities and metropolitan authorities seem the most pro-active sub-national local government actors on European issues, with consequently greater influence for urban political and administrative institutions than rural ones. In the Netherlands, for example, local involvement in EU affairs increases with the size of the municipality. Enschede is more pro-actively involved in lobbying for funds than medium-sized authorities who deal with the EU in a more passive way and even more so than villages with no obvious involvement in EU affairs at all (de Rooij 2002). In the mid 1990s in the UK local authorities involved in EU affairs were most likely to focus on structural funding than any other EU policy, in particular metropolitan areas being the most pro-active (Goldsmith and Sperling 1997).

With funding the key driver of local involvement, cities that are not likely to be recipients of EU funding will have less interest in EU activities. Equally, cities that focus on funding may be less interested in policy issues. The pro-active Enschede was uninterested in attempting to influence EU regulation, but only in the acquisition of funding (de Rooij 2002). Those competing for funding will devise different strategies to access funding. Some cities have joined forces to open a Brussels Office representing their converging regional interests. Uneven access to funds, arising because of the incidence of the criteria for funding, may lead to uneven impacts at local level with consequences for local strategies within the multi-level context. Cities not only have to compete with regions and rural areas but also against each other for a slice of the EU cake.

Uneven impact of 'Europe' and central–local relationships

Central–local relations vary from country to country reflecting differences in power-dependencies between centre and periphery (Rhodes 1999), and differences in the degree of central control on local government generally (Wollman and Goldsmith 1992; Goldsmith 2002). Given the different levels of constitutional, legal, financial and political resources available, the degree of Europeanisation of urban interests is uneven across the EU member states. Central government actors still hold the key for future European empowerment of the local level. By preventing or limiting the access of cities to EU decision-making processes and funding, the national context not only slows down Europeanisation and integration, hence creating uncertainty in the implementation of EU policies, but more importantly, also creates inequalities between EU cities. Some cities have more power, more autonomy or more resources than others to take up EU opportunities, and are more successful at implementing EU policies and perhaps even at influencing them. A survey of British local government authorities in the mid 1990s revealed that central government's pressures on their expenditure and consequent lack of financial resources was the most critical key barrier to local authorities' participation in the EU (Goldsmith and Sperling 1997).

In addition, multi-level governance can have a perverse impact on central–local relationships and territorial power sharing. The pursuit of a multi-level solution may put pressure on national governments to decentralise. It may also, however, justify the decision of central governments to recentralise power, if negotiations with Brussels – generally handled centrally – involve policy areas which are normally within the jurisdiction of sub-national authorities (Smith 1997). German *Länder*, for example, saw the danger when, following the Maastricht Treaty, they demanded an amendment of the German Basic Law to retain the German power sharing balance. Cities – with less power than regions – have less recourse against recentralisation.

The EU cannot interfere in domestic power sharing arrangements. Any resulting focus on national systems of intergovernmental relations may thus exaggerate the barriers to the role of cities in European affairs. This fails to recognise, however, the broader changes brought about by the growth of multi-level intergovernmental relations, where the synergy between institutional rules, processes and behaviour become more important in defining policies than the institutional context itself.

Conclusion

The European Parliament, Council and Commission must think carefully about the level of strategic integration between the various territories and actors involved in multi-level governance if it wants, on the one hand, to improve competitiveness while, on the other hand, to define a social cohesion rationale. It is difficult to decide whether cities have been empowered by the EU. The EU has developed an urban agenda, and seems to encourage the participation of the sub-national level in policy making. This is limited, however, by sector-based competences as well as by national constitutional and legal power sharing arrangements which inhibit anything beyond the encouragement of vertical partnerships. Yet, in order to meet EU economic and social ambitions, cities have a role to play in any European multi-level governance, taking into account the responsibilities of the city vis-à-vis other actors and constituents. These responsibilities include the following:

1   *The global city*: cities have a role to play in world trade to alleviate global competitive pressures. Most services are based in cities and towns. Local autonomy offers flexibility to address local economic situations, to market a territorial identity, and to develop powerful strategic economic alliances.

2   *The business city*: from its creation, the EU has, above all, pursued economic objectives. The Commission now sees cities as the key to future economic development and EU world competitiveness. The development of the ESDP acknowledges this fact, suggesting further that the EU cities are expected to compete, hence to enhance the presence of business within a new local governance. The importance of business interests in the political system and the opportunities for development of stronger links between city administrations and business are further reinforced by the move towards multi-level governance, including the overall decentralisation trends across the EU and the rise of new actors, including private interests, in the policy process (see, for instance, John 2000). Since the EU has no influence on local democracy, it can only put pressure on governments to open up the policy process to non-governmental actors, including business.

3   *The welfare city*: arguments against any move towards business dominated regimes in Europe highlight the social responsibilities of public bodies. Putting a heavy emphasis on business interests tends to ignore a European Social Model, which despite variations between national protection systems across Europe leading to differences in state-market relationships (Esping-Andersen 1990), still retains principles of solidarity and welfare through collective action. Cities and other local actors are seen as key actors of social policies, including employment and social inclusion policies.

4   *The autonomous city*: EU policy makers want to ensure the prosperity and well being of all EU citizens, requiring a certain level of policy integration at national or EU level. This may imply the dilution of local autonomy, but sustainable local democracy means that local

leaders and communities should have some control over the territorial resources necessary to respond to local problems (Lamy 2002). In relation to the overarching goals of sustainability, there may be inevitable tensions and conflicts between competitiveness, social cohesion and environmental policies. Such conflicts reinforce the dilemma of where power lies with the city regime or at least with semi-autonomous local actors, with national governments at whose level the key welfare functions largely remain, or with an EU which strives to establish the territorial cohesion in Europe through a multi-level governance system within which the various levels are complementary (Le Galès 2002).

5   *The networked city*: as the policy process has become a forum for interest intermediation, interest groups compete within policy networks. Such a 'competitive symposium' (Atkinson and Davoudi 2000) may do little to protect *weaker interests*, but rather *privileges the more efficient ones* (Middlemas 1995). By contrast, it will be more appropriate to privilege the collaborative behaviour of a constellation of city actors, who are ready, within the new EU governance, to seize power at local level (Ache 2000). Indeed, the role of the rich and business class must be examined just as much as the role of disadvantaged communities and their participation in the policy process. For Pahl, for instance, 'whose city?' relates more to the rich entrepreneurial class that, through its active participation in urban development, can threaten social cohesion within the city walls (Pahl 2001). In the end, the network governance encouraged by the European Commission means a real and efficient empowerment of communities.

In short, for the success of the global, business, welfare, autonomous, networked city, finding a balance between economic competitiveness and social inclusion must depend on the achievement of a complementary engagement of actors from neighbourhood, city, region, national and European levels – the epitome of multi-level governance.

Note

1 For the different dimensions of legitimation see the considerations presented in Chapter 2 of this book.

References

Ache, P. (2000) 'Cities in Old Industrial Regions between Local Innovative Milieu and Urban Governance – Reflections on City Region Governance', *European Planning Studies*, Vol. 8, No. 6: 693–709.

Agnew, J. (2001) 'How Many Europes? The European Union, Eastward Enlargement and Uneven Development', *European Urban and Regional Studies*, Vol. 8, No. 1: 29–38.

Atkinson, R. (2001) 'The Emerging "Urban Agenda" and the European Spatial Development Perspective: Towards an EU Urban Policy?', *European Planning Studies*, Vol. 9, No. 3: 385–406.

—— (2002) 'The White Paper on European Governance: Implications for Urban Policy', *European Planning Studies*, Vol. 10, No. 6: 781–792.

Atkinson, R. and Davoudi, S. (2000) 'The Concept of Social Exclusion in the European Union: Context, Development and Possibilities', *Journal of Common Market Studies*, Vol. 38, No. 3: 427–448.

Carmichael, L. (2001) 'The EU and the Fight against Exclusion: Maximising the Means to Match its Ambitions', in: D. Mayes, J. Berghman and R. Salais (eds) *Social Exclusion and European Policy*, Cheltenham: Edward Elgar: 233–254.

Chorianopoulos, I. (2002) 'Commenting on the Effectiveness and Future Challenges of the EU Local Authority Networks', *Regional Studies*, Vol. 36, No. 8: 933–939.

Colwell, A. (2001) 'The EU Strategy for Sustainable Development: A False Dawn?', *Town and Country Planning*, September 2001: 256–257.

Commission of the European Communities (1990) *Green Paper on the Urban Environment, COM 218 (1990)*, Brussels: Commission of the European Communities.

—— (1996) *European Sustainable Cities – Report of the Expert Group on the Urban Environment*, Brussels: Commission of the European Communities.

—— (1997) *Towards an Urban Agenda in the European Union, Communication from the Commission COM (1997) 197 final, 28 October 1998*, Brussels: Commission of the European Communities.

—— (1998) *Sustainable Urban Development in the European Union: A Framework for Action, Communication from the Commission COM (1998) 605 final, 28 October 1998*, Brussels: Commission of the European Communities.

—— (1999) *European Spatial Development Perspective: Towards Balanced and Sustainable Development of the Territory of the EU*, Luxembourg: Office for Official Publications of the European Communities.

—— (2001a) *White Paper on European Governance, COM (2001) 428 final*, Brussels: Commission of the European Communities.

—— (2001b) *First Progress Report on Economic and Social Cohesion, COM (2001) 46 final*, Brussels: Commission of the European Communities.

—— (2001c) *Strengthening the Local Dimension of the European Employment Strategy, COM (2001) 629 final*, Brussels: Commission of the European Communities.

—— (2001d) *A Sustainable Europe for a Better World: A European Union Strategy for Sustainable Development COM (2001) 264 final*, Brussels: Commission of the European Communities.

—— (2002) *Second Progress Report on Economic and Social Cohesion*, Brussels: Commission of the European Communities.

Council of the EU (1989) *Resolution of 29 September 1989 on Combating Social Exclusion, OJ C 277*, Luxembourg: Office for Official Publications of the EC.

Durhkeim, E. (1986, first edition published in 1893) *De la division du travail social*, Paris: Presses Universitaires de France.

Eser, T. and Konstadakopoulos, D. (2000) 'Power Shifts in the EU? The Case of Spatial Planning', *European Planning Studies*, Vol. 8, No. 6: 783–798.

Esping-Andersen, G. (1990) *The Three Worlds of Welfare Capitalism*, Princeton: Princeton University Press.

European Council (1997a) *Conclusions of the Presidency of the European Council of 16 and 17 June 1997*, Amsterdam: European Council.

—— (1997b) *Conclusions of the Presidency of the Extraordinary European Council – Employment – of 20 and 21 November 1997*, Luxembourg: European Council.

—— (1998) *Conclusions of the Presidency of the European Council of 15 and 16 June 1998*, Cardiff: European Council.

—— (2000a) *Conclusions of the Presidency of the European Council of 23 and 24 March 2000*, Lisbon: European Council.

—— (2000b) *Conclusions of the Presidency of the European Council of 7–9 December 2000*, Nice: European Council.

—— (2001) *Conclusions of the Presidency of the European Council of 15–16 June 2001*, Gothenburg: European Council.

European Parliament and Council of the EU (2002) *Sixth Community Environment Action Programme, OJ L 242, 10/09/2002*, Luxembourg: Office for Official Publications of the EC.

Faludi, A. (2000) 'The European Spatial Development Perspective – What Next?', *European Planning Studies*, Vol. 8, No. 2: 237–250.

—— (2001) 'The Application of the European Spatial Development Perspective: Evidence from the North-West Metropolitan Area', *European Planning Studies*, Vol. 9, No. 5: 663–675.

Giddens, A. (1998) *The Third Way and the Renewal of Social Democracy*, Cambridge: Polity Press.

Glorieux, I. (1999) 'Paid Work: A Crucial Link Between Individuals and Society?', in: P. Littlewoods (ed.) *Social Exclusion in Europe: Problems and Paradigms*, Aldershot: Ashgate: 67–87.

Goldsmith, M. (2002) 'Central Control over Local Government – A Western European Comparison', *Local Government Studies*, Vol. 28, No. 3: 91–112.

Goldsmith, M. and Sperling, E. (1997) 'Local Governments and the EU: the British Experience', in: M. Goldsmith and K. Klaudi Klausen (eds) *European Integration and Local Government*, Cheltenham: Edward Elgar: 95–120.

Guy, S. and Marvin, S. (1999) 'Understanding Sustainable Cities: Competing Urban Futures', *European Urban and Regional Studies*, Vol. 6, No. 3: 268–275.

Heinelt, H. (1996) 'Multi-level Governance in the European Union and the Structural Funds', in: H. Heinelt and R. Smith (eds) *Policy Networks and European Structural Funds*, Aldershot: Avebury: 9–25.

Hooghe, L. (1996) 'Introduction: Reconciling EU Wide Policy and National Diversity', in: L. Hooghe (ed.) *Cohesion Policy and European Integration: Building Multi-level Governance*, Oxford: Oxford University Press.

Hooghe, L. and Marks, G. (2001) *Multi-Level Governance and European Integration*, Boulder: Rowman and Littlefield.

Jeffery, Ch. (2000) 'Sub-National Mobilization and European Integration: Does It Make any Difference?', *Journal of Common Market Studies*, Vol. 38, No. 1: 1–23.

John, P. (2000) *A Europe of Regimes? Urban Collective Action in the Global Era*. ESRC Cities Workshop on Urban Governance, 25–26 September 2000, Bristol.

—— (2001) *Local Governance in Western Europe,* London: Sage.

Jouve, B. and Lefèvre, Ch. (2002) 'Metropolitan Governance and Institutional Dynamics', in: R. Hambleton, H. Savitch and M. Stewart (eds) *Globalism and Local Democracy – Challenges and Change in Europe and North America*, Basingstoke: Palgrave: 185–200.

Kongshøj Madsen, P. and Munch-Madsen, P. (2001) 'European Employment Policy and National Policy Regimes', in: D. Mayes, J. Berghman and R. Salais (eds) *Social Exclusion and European Policy*, Cheltenham: Edward Elgar: 255–276.

Krätke, S. (2001) 'Strengthening the Polycentric Urban System in Europe: Conclusions from the European Spatial Development Perspective', *European Planning Studies*, Vol. 9, No. 1: 105–116.

Lamy, P. (2002) 'Interview', *Pouvoirs Locaux*, Vol. IV, No. 55: 91–98.

Le Galès, P. (2002) *European Cities: Social Conflicts and Governance*, Oxford: Oxford University Press.

Marks, G. (1992) 'Structural Policy in the European Community', in: A. Sbragia (ed.) *Euro-Politics*, Washington: The Brookings Institute.

Middlemas, K. (1995) *Orchestrating Europe: The Informal Politics of the European Union 1973–1995*, London: Fontana.

Pahl, R. (2001) 'Market Success and Social Cohesion', *International Journal of Urban and Regional Research*, Vol. 25, No. 4.

Rhodes, R. (1999) (2nd edn) *Control and Power in Central–Local Government Relations*, Aldershot: Ashgate.

(de) Rooij, R. (2002) 'The Impact of the European Union on Local Government in the Netherlands', *Journal of European Public Policy*, Vol. 9, No. 3: 447–467.

Smith, A. (1997) 'Studying Multi-Level Governance. Examples from French Translations of the Structural Funds', *Public Administration*, Vol. 75: 711–729.

Tewdwr-Jones, M., Bishop, K. and Wilkinson, D. (2000) 'Euroscepticism, Political Agendas and Spatial Planning: British National and Regional Planning Policy in Uncertain Times', *European Planning Studies*, Vol. 8, No. 5: 651–668.

UK Government (2001) *National Action Plan on Employment 2001 – UK,* Brussels: European Communities.

Williams, R. (2000) 'Constructing the European Spatial Development Perspective – For Whom?', *European Planning Studies*, Vol. 8, No. 3: 357–365.

Wollman, H. and Goldsmith, M. (1992) *Urban Politics and Policy: A Comparative Introduction*, Oxford: Blackwell.

7 Collaboration in multi-actor governance

Murray Stewart

Disjointed government

It is widely recognised that good local governance implies cohesion between the various sectors – public, private, voluntary, community – and relies on the development of structures and processes which support collaboration. Effective leadership and inclusive participation are implicit in such structures and processes. The evidence is, however, that robust structures to integrate differing, and often conflicting, interests are difficult to establish and maintain. Indeed fragmentation is more evident than integration.

This is particularly obvious where the challenges facing localities involve complex, cross-cutting issues which impinge on the internal working of separate organisations. These cross-cutting issues – of which competitiveness and social inclusion are but two – are characterised by differing understandings and explanations of cause and effect, by multiple organisational engagement, by the failure to mobilise and integrate programmes, and by imperfect communication between policy and action. These cross-cutting – or 'wicked issues' (Rittel and Webber 1973) – have confounded the efforts of fragmented government to address their intractability. At the heart of this intractability lies the recognition that most organisations work to their own agendas, make the best use of their own resources and perform to standards and targets which inhibit joint working.

The fragmentation of systems of local governance has been accentuated by particular changes in the national contextual circumstances within which individual cities are located, and cross-national generalisations about the emergence of a new local governance are dangerous. Nevertheless it is possible to identify a number of features of European urban life which provide a common backdrop against which to look at the specificities of particular cities.

Within a general process of globalisation a number of features combine to homogenise the city – the revolution in communications technologies, the growth of the knowledge economy, the collapse of the command economies of eastern Europe, and the emergence of individual and group life styles which challenge traditional attitudes and behaviours (Hutton and Giddens 2000). This leads to a struggle between homogenisation in the face of common external forces and diversification in the search for local identity and urban meaning (Ascher 2002).

Common to much of this is the changing role of the welfare state and the consequent role for cities in support for the lower income, often disadvantaged, sometimes excluded populations. The very existence, far less the nature, of the welfare state varies widely across European states, and it is clear that welfare systems – whether these be the formalised systems of central and local state or the less formalised support of families and communities, are under stress. Two pressures combine, on the one hand the growing numbers and needs of the disadvantaged and marginalised, on the other the decreased resource base from which support may come. Clearly the history of welfare systems in the United Kingdom, in Denmark, in France and in Greece are very different, but their declining capacity represents a significant challenge to local governance.

At the same time global forces impose demands for cities to be more competitive in an environment where investment, like labour, is ever more mobile. Public and private sectors together need to pool their energies and resources to demonstrate that their city is worthy of the rewards of competition, whether this be the market competition for mobile investment or the institutionalised competition of governments – as for example for international festivals or events such as European City of Culture.

The twin demands of addressing the needs of the marginalised groups and marketing the city in a competitive international environment place heavy demands on local governance, demands which are reinforced by the unwillingness and/or inability of central states to fulfil many of what have traditionally been their obligations to localities.

The devolution of responsibility has not meant, however, the devolution of power. Indeed the retention of influence by central states confounds the hollowed state thesis, the argument (Rhodes 1994; Jessop 1995) that there is a shift of power upwards to Brussels, outwards to arm's length agencies, and downwards to region and locality. Hollowing out is more a redistribution of function with many of the same functions exercised at different territorial levels and in different organisational forms, with little devolution of state control but significant devolution of responsibility for delivery and little devolution of resources (Holliday 2000; Taylor, A. 2000). Holliday argues that 'the state may be to an extent fragmented but this does not mean it is disabled. The British core is more substantial than ever before'.

In many instances the devolution of responsibility has led to the establishment of new institutions and agencies together with a range of centrally initiated but locally delivered programmes. This institutional proliferation, reinforced in some cases by a pursuit of special initiatives, weakens both the local capacity to deliver integrated services and the ability of the centre to control. What emerges is a planning and implementation vacuum. The difficulty in filling this vacuum allows – often encourages – individual planning and providing agencies, central and local, to follow their own priorities, and a complex battle of organisational politics occurs with everyone pursuing single and selfish goals. Well-used methods for controlling implementation begin to break down, and compliance with policy intention is less rarely observed. In such a situation the centre attempts to retain or regain control, while localities attempt to gain autonomy.

In short local governance confronts a realignment of state role and function, the dismantling of long-standing institutions, moves towards a new economy of welfare, an increased vulnerability to global competition and increased visibility of some of the more problematic issues of contemporary urban life. In terms of urban administrative processes there has also been the co-existence of, but tension between, hierarchy, market and network as the ideologies and practices of national governments shift in terms of the most appropriate and effective methods of allocating and managing resources. The net consequence is that in many cities there now exists a multiplicity of governmental and non-governmental agencies accountable to different central departments for different targets, each with different professional cultures and with different systems of accountability, different financial regimes and many with considerable operational autonomy. It is difficult to overstate the organisational complexity that results. While there are not only a large number of important organisational actors involved in the policy process, there arc also different combinations of these actors involved in the delivery process at local and neighbourhood levels, giving rise to problems of both vertical and horizontal integration. The outcome is governance failure at local levels.

This inevitably poses questions about the effectiveness of the cultural, organisational and administrative mechanisms which are in place to bring about the necessary new capacity building for integrated local governance. The 'new governance' emphasises the importance of collaboration and coordination as the means of building a local institutional capacity to counter the challenges outlined above.

The collaborative agenda

Collaboration and coordination, however, are hard to achieve. Webb (1991) identified three broad drivers for coordinated action – rational/altruistic drivers, mandated or imperative drivers and bureaucratic political drivers. Rationality and altruism produce voluntary collaboration, and the conditions under which such collaboration can emerge, and collaborative advantage extracted, have increasingly been researched in the context of partnerships, coalition and strategic alliances (for example, Huxham 1996; Schruijer 1999; Taillieu 2001; Purdue and Stewart 2002; Scott and Thurston 2003; Sullivan and Skelcher 2002). Voluntary collaboration relies in large respect upon trust, however, and where trust does not exist more formal methods to ensure coordination need to be employed. These methods vary but much emphasis has been laid on the market paradigm and on a culture of contractualisation and contract compliance as the method of enforcing conformance in the past twenty years (Oatley 1998), an approach to coordination which in some ways reflects the mandated mode identified by Webb. But this mode has in turn been overtaken by the emergence of 'network governance', more reliant on social relationships, more reliant on informal exchange, less hierarchically organised and more effective in recognising the variety of local stakeholders. Although the principles of network governance may be clear, reflecting the embeddedness of economic (and bureaucratic) action in social structures (Granovetter 1985), there is less evidence as to how networks actually achieve collaborative or coordinated action. Networks are not structures and seldom have formal decision-making powers. Moreover networks can be highly exclusionary simply because there are few rights of membership, protocols of behaviour or established accountabilities. Networks lack the means of enforcing the behaviour of their members and thus while offering many of the necessary attributes of collaborative working are in themselves not sufficient to ensure that collaboration occurs.

Many of the questions raised so far relate to the nature of vertical, multi-level governance (explored more fully in the preceding chapter by Carmichael), but the remainder of this chapter addresses the question of the forms in which horizontal integration occurs. It explores briefly three paradigms from which the nature of local integration may be explored. First there is a political science paradigm within which issues of power are central and which looks to the interests of the dominant stakeholders for explanations of the emergence of coalitions and regimes as mechanisms of integration. Second comes an ecological paradigm, mixed with a dash of operational research, which sees the interaction of actors within a systems approach. Third there is a hybrid approach which espouses joint working through partnership as the mechanism for collaboration and coordination. This mixes aspects of the political and institutional with a relational approach which echoes the literature of coalitions and regimes but relies less on power and more on the exploitation of local social capital.

Structures of integration

Coalitions and regimes

A wide US-based regime literature has now crossed the Atlantic and is increasingly, if hesitantly, being applied to European politics (Harding 1994; Stoker and Mossberger 1994; Owen 1994; Levine 1994; Peck and Tickell 1995; Stewart 1996; Srom 1996; Lauria 1997). Regime theory originally argued that private sector interests, in conjunction with public authorities, created some form of growth coalition (Logan and Molotch 1987; Stone 1989) which pushed forward the interests of the development sector. It is clear, certainly in the UK situation, that growth, or perhaps the threat of decline, has proved a major driver of the move towards collaborative action over the last decade. What is less clear (but has been discussed further in the conceptual chapter introducing this book) is the extent to which the strategic partnership building represents the formation of a regime, not least in the extent of the local autonomy open to such coalitions to act independently of a centralised state.

Bristol – for example – has attracted particular attention. The fluctuating and vacillating nature of an incipient Bristol regime over a period of six years was noted by DiGaetano and Klermanski (1994 and 1999) while Bassett (1996) found it hard to place the city within existing frameworks. For him, Bristol's 'network of partnership initiatives sprawls across the symbolic and instrumental categories' of Stoker and Mossberger (1994). Stewart (1996) also argued that the Bristol regime differed from its US counterparts in being more strongly dependent on the rules and regulation of central government – an institutionalised and imposed partnership structure. In the mid 1990s Bristol appeared to exemplify the extent to which a set of local leadership interests could coalesce to form, not simply a loose collection of ad hoc local do-gooders but a relatively coherent and integrated network of linked interests. Later work, however, stresses the fragility of the networks which linked Bristol public, private and voluntary sectors together (Malpass 1994; Miller 1999; Stewart 2003) as well as the weakness of leadership in articulating the joint interests of local stakeholders.

Regimes do not pretend to be inclusive, although they may well seek to incorporate the interests of those whom they perceive to be threatening or who might offer an alternative collaborative agenda. Regimes pursue and articulate dominant interests. Economic values predominate; power is central; democracy is not an issue; survival depends on authority not legitimacy. Leadership is thus crucial since leaders establish and maintain the cohesion of the regime; participation (in the sense of community participation) is less important.

Even those who doubt that the concept of the regime is appropriate to the European urban context (for example, Davies 2002), acknowledge evidence about the existence of select (if not elite) groupings with significant power and influence over local affairs. The utility of the regime model therefore is less its precise applicability in Europe and more its explicit articulation of ideas of stakeholder power, dominant interests, capacities to incorporate, abilities to exclude and opaque accountability.

Systems

An alternative perspective on integration is reflected in a more technical paradigm. There is increasing attention to 'whole system' approaches to governance (Stewart *et al.* 1999; Wilkinson and Appelbee 1999; Pratt *et al.* 1999; Six *et al.* 1999). These approaches, drawing on ecological models of interaction and interdependence, offer an alternative way to understand and plan intervention within a complex set of interactions. They are based on the premise that complex systems need to be understood in terms of the interactions between parts of the system and its environment. These interactions involve feedback loops, whereby elements in the systems feed influence and information to each other over time. Outcomes are the result of the interaction of a large number of organisations and agents each of which is attempting to respond to a changing environment, by adapting behaviour and by shaping the environment itself. The system is 'open' in the sense that there is constant interaction between each organisation or agent and all the other agencies that make up the environment they find themselves in.

In the context of joined-up governance, the 'system' must be thought of as inclusive – the totality of actors, including public, private, voluntary sectors and citizens. Effective policy implementation requires effectiveness within each component of the system and effective links between them. If one element in the system is not working well, this can have adverse consequences for other elements in the system, negative reinforcement or a vicious circle. Conversely virtuous circles can be set up in which effective working in one domain reinforces effective working in others. What matters is the extent to which different elements reinforce, complement and strengthen each other, or conversely the extent to which they dilute and undermine each other. Weakness in one area may not matter if it is counter-balanced by strength in another.

Whole systems models are useful in recognising the interdependence of parts of the system of governance, but are less helpful in deciding precisely where to intervene. Systems models are inherently liable to failure as disequilibrium sets in. Holism is desirable in principle, difficult to achieve in practice. In effect, as argued above, all systems have particular drivers which maintain the system in motion and mediate the relationship between the parts and the whole. Discussion of 'drivers' shifts systems approaches marginally towards recognition of power and the capacity of different interests to 'drive' the system. Leadership is crucial here of course. Who pulls the levers that makes the system work? What are the circuits of power within organisational and inter-organisational systems? In general, however, the systems model is apolitical, deriving from the view that there is a natural, perhaps Darwinian, process that governs system change. The cogs, wheels and levers are interlocking and interdependent; no actor within the system can achieve what he or she wants without carrying, pushing or driving others in concerted action.

Network governance and urban partnership

As discussed on pages 151–152 network governance emerged as an alternative to markets and hierarchy (Rhodes 1996, 1997) in recognition of the failures of bureaucratic models of government and the imperfections of the market. Networks are loose, informal, unaccountable and often exclusive. Above all they seldom have direct decision-making or resource allocation functions. The institutional manifestation of network governance has been either an array of talking shops which attempt to influence the silo-based behaviour of constituent agencies, or the establishment of more formal partnership arrangements to manage cross-cutting issues. Indeed partnerships have emerged as the panacea for the failures of urban government and for a number of years have been a requirement of local, national and European working, especially in relation to disadvantage and exclusion (Geddes 1998; Madanipour *et al.* 1998; Parkinson 1998; Geddes and Benington 2001). EU programmes themselves have been a strong stimulus to partnership working in the pursuit of inclusion. Yet despite the growth of partnership working, or perhaps as a result of it, the definition and meaning of partnerships has been debased. Sullivan and Skelcher (2002) identify the defining characteristics of partnership as negotiation between people from diverse agencies, delivery of benefits of added value, formal articulation of a binding purpose or plan. But they also remind us that partnerships are formed from constituencies with widely varying values and interests and with contrasting cultures of discourse and working methods. There are several ways of looking at partnerships. The early work of Mackintosh (1993) remains helpful. She distinguished between transformation (working in partnership to convince the other partner(s) of your own values and objectives), synergy (working to produce added value beyond what would have been achieved separately) and budget enlargement (achieved when partnerships generate extra resources). A different perspective looks at the evolution of partnerships over time as joint working moves from early collaboration through consolidation, delivery and ultimate termination or succession (Lowndes and Skelcher 1998). A different distinction is between the functions of facilitation, coordination and implementation (Stewart 1997).

Over the years there have been numerous UK studies looking at partnership working (Mackintosh 1993; Hastings 1996; Harding 1998; Lowndes and Skelcher 1998). The nature of partnership working is a function of a number of features of joint working, and it is possible to categorise partnerships along a number of descriptive variables – membership, status, structures, leadership, agendas, organisational cultures. Central to these is membership, with success a function of which stakeholders are allowed to participate. Partnerships can be distinguished by whether their membership is open or closed, and also by whether their members are chosen, appointed, selected, elected or invited. 'Participatory' groups (Joldersma 1997), and heterogeneous participatory groups in particular, are more likely to be open, thus increasing the scope for diversity and for generating wider understanding, but reducing the likelihood of agreement about aims and objectives. It is in more traditional areas of public policy responsibility, where strong and established professional groups exist, that cooperation, acceptable policy options and convergence are more likely to be evident. In newer areas of public policy – environmental protection, economic development, cultural development, the new public health for example – where professionalism is less entrenched, and where the norms and values of policy remain ambiguous, there is much more scope for open groups and participatory policy making. Thus in many Local Agenda 21 forums or alliances there are to be found a wide range of public, private and community groups debating the nature of the appropriate environmental policy response.

Few partnerships start from scratch. They build instead on past relationships and these foundations matter. In any locality – region, city, town or neighbourhood – there is a very particular past, and a unique geography. Every successful local intervention has to be based within the context of unique local circumstances. Research on area-based initiatives argued that there are five important dynamics that affect successful collaboration – political geography and impact of boundaries in joint working, shared identity and the presence or otherwise of common interest, the history of previous initiatives and the dynamics of changing inter-organisational relations, and the role of personalities in determining inter-agency relationships (DTLR 2002).

Equally significant in understanding partnership working is the nature of power relationships. Power is a central – if often unacknowledged – feature of partnership working. Partners bring different degrees of power to partnerships – skills, expertise, local knowledge, human resources but above all money. Those with resources carry most power and the evidence is that the big battalions prove to be the big players. Conversely those for whom many contemporary community or neighbourhood partnerships are intended to benefit, have less power and once more there is much evidence of the marginalisation of community sector interests in partnership working (Hastings *et al.* 1996; Skelcher *et al.* 1996; Hoggett 1997; Purdue *et al.* 2000; Taylor 2000).

Within this complex picture of partnership working lies the role of leaders. Leadership in collaborative arrangements differs from leadership within single organisations given the need to develop an integrative capacity. Joint arrangements such as partnerships are seldom hierarchical but instead involve a wide range of partners as discussed above. A range of leadership styles may therefore be appropriate for joint working dependent on the personal characteristics evident in the leader(s) reflecting the degree of charisma, commitment, persuasion, ambition etc. which rest within any individual. Many studies highlight the importance of individual psychological characteristics. The literature also emphasises the variety of styles that exist. Stone (1995) adapted what Burns (1978) had termed 'collectively purposeful causation' towards a more explicit discussion of power relations and the ability to initiate change. His classic distinction between power 'over' and power 'to' reflected a new awareness of the importance of influence in the exercise of leadership. Gray (1996) also focussed on those who 'entice others to participate' in joint action, and developed the role of the 'convenor' of collaborative action.

This recognition of the capacity of the leader to mobilise collaborative advantage echoes both Svara (1990) who pointed to the tendency for many US mayors to move towards a more facilitative style of leadership, and those who emphasise facilitative leadership as the basis for transformational collaboration (Himmelman 1996; Chrislip and Larson 1994). Skelcher *et al.* (1996) suggest that network participants may be enthusiasts, activists, pragmatists or opponents and these general attitudes towards network participation must of course affect the potential emergence of individuals as leaders. Skelcher *et al.* also identify three approaches to leadership – the charismatic, the fluid, and the coordinating role. Building on this typology, and prefiguring Chapter 8 which follows, it is possible to see a number of (non-exclusive) roles, or perhaps leadership styles, which might be adopted (Stewart 2001):

- champion – taking forward the goals of the partnership;
- salesperson – keen to sell the partnership and its achievements to others in order to generate more resources, support, partners;
- interpreter – moving between networks to carry the message of one set of interests to another;
- broker – again moving between networks but in the capacity of negotiator, bringing together resources, putting together packages or multi-organisational projects;
- coordinator – mediating, bringing together, ensuring information is shared;
- visionary – forcing the partnership to think long term;
- representative – reflecting the feelings and wishes of particular interests and ensuring that their voice is heard in the debates of partnership;

- agent provocateur – seeking to provoke action where it is felt unlikely to happen, stirring up controversy and/or conflict.

Individual leadership style, however, is mediated by the collaborative context within which leaders operate. Leaders manage the stages of partnership development – from partnership promotion, through the establishment of partnerships to operational maintenance and support, to attrition (as motivation falls and leaders become more wary of joining partnerships) into a final stage where the multiplicity of local partnership demands strategic rationalisation (Sweeting *et al.* 2004). Depending on context different models emerge. *Designed and focussed leadership* – typified by much of the experience of US and European mayoral cities – is only constrained at the margins by formal partnership or other collaborative arrangements. Much stronger is the influence of personal style which the individual leader may bring, and the relationship with followers upon whom the single leader depends. Alternatively, where partnership working is highly dependent on the external policy environment and where the arrangements are complicated and bureaucratic, personal style can count for less, and leaders struggle to achieve consensus in a situation of multi-organisational bargaining. Followers are largely missing since few are clear what the partnership is doing or where the leadership is going. Strong leadership may bring order to a complex web of joint arrangements through a *pivotal, integrative* style, but elsewhere the complexity of multiple partnership operation may result in a vacuum with leadership *invisible, implicit, fragmented.* Conversely leadership behaviour may be strongly influenced by the structures and processes of partnership working and by developmental influences, resulting in what might be called *formative and emergent* leadership (Sweeting *et al.* 2004). Personal style – building networks and trust – is important, as is the relationship with followers, in this case those who are willing to forge alliances for the delivery of action. However, action is driven by the exigencies of implementation rather than policy statements; strategic direction is weak. Leadership is less dependent on the policy environment; indeed local leaders set their own agenda, ignore the external policy environment and simply get on with the job (Huxham and Vangen 2000).

Multi-actor institutional arrangements

It is tempting, therefore, to take partnership arrangements as the focus for urban research which looks to horizontal multi-actor, multi-agency institutional arrangements for linking leadership to participation. Unlike regime theory or systems analysis, partnerships offer scope for examining the ways in which leadership and participation complement one another, and offer a formal setting – the local partnership arrangements – in which some interaction takes place. At the same time partnership is a peculiarly, though certainly not exclusive, UK phenomenon and many of the PLUS cities do not have formal partnership arrangements. The research question with respect to multi-actor settings, therefore, is that set out by Denters and Klok in Chapter 3 – what kinds of institutional arrangements exist in the cities to draw together the diverse interests of public, private, voluntary and community interests? What are the various structures – partnerships or their equivalent – that go beyond a simple combination of actors to exploit the complementarity of strategic leadership and community participation? How far do structures in practice provide the forum in which this potential for complementarity can be developed and strengthened, or do institutional arrangements do more to stifle relationships than foster them? Do joint arrangements such as partnerships operate in the same way in addressing competitiveness as they do in addressing exclusion?

In examining empirically the arrangements for collaborative working in the range of urban settings offered by the PLUS cities, there emerge four strands of ideas around which the relationships between leadership and participation can be organised.

Trust and social capital

All modes of governance involve transaction costs. Under market rules there are the costs of negotiation and exchange; in hierarchies there are the costs of establishing rules and of ensuring compliance; in network modes of governance (of which partnerships are the formal mechanisms) the costs are of time expended in meeting, communicating and sharing. The burden of transaction costs under any mode of governance can be lightened, however, if the parties know, like and trust each other. Granovetter (1985) argues that economic and/or administrative actions are embedded in social relations. Social norms substitute for the rules which hierarchy demands, the contracts which markets demand, and the interaction which networks demand, and produce a context within which collaboration and compliance occur without high transaction costs. Social capital is created. This is not the social capital of borrowing sugar from neighbours or going bowling with others. It is rather Granovetter's weak ties (1973) which link communities to the formal arrangements of governance and fill the space between state and civil society (Woolcock 1998; Taylor, M. 2000).

Central to the building of social capital is trust (Kramer and Tyler 1996; Coulson 1998; Hardy *et al.* 1998; Huxham and Vangen 2000). Indeed trust is often the common element identified as the essential attributes of a good partnership. It is less clear, however, whether trust is a necessary input to partnership or is an output from it. Huxham and Vangen (2000) observe that trust needs to be both formed and fulfilled to generate bilateral trust. They also remind us that trust can both be rooted in expectations (that something predictable will occur) and in experience (that something has occurred). It can be generated by both experience and reputation. It is also the basis upon which risk is shared. Where no one partner has the will, resources or capacity to carry through some task on his or her own, then trust in others minimises risk, since the possibilities of failure or resource wastage are spread. Trust ensures that risks are genuinely shared as opposed to being off-loaded in the case of failure. Furthermore trust reduces the risks of partisan interest group activity, partner disempowerment or leadership domination.

Participation and inclusion

The limited nature of much community participation in partnerships has already been noted. Agenda setting, timing and location of meetings, conduct of business, language and discourse, gender relations, and cultural insensitivity all combine to marginalise community interests. Power is not shared but is retained by the traditional actors – politicians, professionals, academics – whose language and behaviour does little to encourage participation or support inclusiveness. More research is needed as to whether this is because partnership remains novel to many of the participants and that new styles of working are only slowly learned by the traditional players. There has been much emphasis on capacity building for communities, and rightly so. Communities need skills, time, resources, experience and confidence to enable them to participate equally in partnership working with others. The real need for capacity building, however, lies in the larger organisations of traditional government whose behaviour towards residents, users, communities has been to view them simply as clients of a service provider.

The new public management has shifted the balance towards 'customers' and stops short of directly addressing rights other than those relating to rights to consumption or redress against unfair market impacts. It gives little emphasis to exclusion, therefore, other than exclusion from markets – predominantly the labour market. Indeed the European debate on exclusion has focussed predominantly on labour market exclusion. It had long been recognised that structural change would have adverse consequences for particular groups, most obviously those rendered jobless initially by the decline of the coal and steel industries but later by the wholesale restructuring of much manufacturing. Recognition of the disadvantaged position of coal and steel workers, and of migrant workers and their families, evolved into recognition of the impact of long-term unemployment on whole communities and in the 1970s, the First Poverty programme. It is widely accepted (Room 1997; Lee and Murie 1997) that the roots of the social exclusion debate are to be found in the literature of poverty studies. Room, however, points to two differing traditions, the existence of which goes some way to explaining the routes through which social exclusion has come to be articulated.

On the one hand there is a continental European tradition. This derives from a view of society and the distribution of power and resources which emphasises the semi-contractual nature of relationships between classes and groups, and the interdependence between such classes. There is thus a basic adherence to the notion of a cohesive society within which there are mutual rights and obligations. The absence of such rights and/or the non-fulfilment of obligations represents the breakdown of social cohesion and the failure of societal institutions (whether of church, family or education) to maintain an acceptable level of integration. Within a more liberal Anglo-Saxon approach to disadvantage more emphasis has been placed on the relative position of individuals in relation to acceptable levels of resources, financial or real, which provide the power to acquire goods or services from either state or market. The social exclusion literature however, has increasingly differentiated exclusion from poverty by emphasising the 'relational' factors inherent in the continental model, and by identifying a number of systemic factors which separately or in combination drive marginal individuals or groups into 'exclusion'. Among these factors, suggests Berghman (1997), may be the democratic/legal system, the labour market, the welfare system and the family/community system. Inclusion within these systems is evidence of a meaningful citizenship on Marshallian criteria (Marshall 1950), and the lack of access to the civic rights which enable participation in these systems may be the touchstone of exclusion.

Engagement and empowerment

If collaborative working is characterised by the creation of social capital, by the involvement of community actors and by active membership of partnership structures, what guarantees are there that promises made by 'leaders' will be kept and that a genuine complementarity between leadership and participation is achieved? The contract culture has been widely criticised for its negative impact on joined up working. The dominance of performance management, indicators and targets has diluted the willingness and ability of many agencies to engage in joint working. Agency outputs need to be attributable to their inputs, and resources swallowed up by joint working do not produce identifiable performance measures. The relational contracts entered into through network governance are often not worth the paper they are (not) written on, and there is widespread evidence that budgets are not realigned to meet mutual shared objectives, but remain dedicated to the perceived priorities of the constituent partner agencies.

There remains distrust, therefore, among disadvantaged communities, whether these are the communities of place and neighbourhood or the communities of interest such as minority ethnic groups or people with disabilities, whose concerns lie wider than the neighbourhood. This is a distrust which stems from the experience of successive governmental initiatives which offer much but fail to deliver long-term or sustainable change. How far then can a new complementarity of leadership and community assure a material and lasting change in the circumstances of urban residents? The PLUS research should seek to examine the mechanisms through which such assurances can be given and guaranteed. Within the UK as elsewhere there are shifts towards resident empowerment. In England the New Deal for Communities appears to offer significant resources to community based partnerships; tenant management organisations are gaining responsibility for estate based management and maintenance; service level agreements with the main provider agencies can provide a contractual basis for the delivery of improved local services; area budgeting can give local discretion over the allocation of (modest) resources. Urban leadership can offer such mechanisms to community interests; active participation can exploit them to generate local benefit.

Accountability and legitimacy

In the new governance of multi-sectoral working, accountabilities become blurred. Joint action and co-funding cloud the responsibilities and obligations of participant organisations in partnership and traditional expressions of accountability become unclear. Many consider partnerships to be opaque, and there are widespread pleas for more transparency. But collaborative working can be translucent – what you see depends on the light in which it is seen. Thus what someone sees as acceptable, another sees as unacceptable. Holding the partnership up to the light reveals a shifting kaleidoscope of pictures, each true, but each different. Accountabilities are ambiguous therefore. There can be confusion between accountability to the partnership machinery on the one hand and accountability to the 'original' local government, private sector or community interest represented in the partnership structures on the other. 'Directors' or partnership 'board members', from whatever sector they come, carry individual as well as collective responsibility and there is an acknowledged tension between accountability within the partnership (e.g. as director, trustee or board member) and accountability to the partner organisation(s). Representative responsibilities become intertwined with executive roles in new, often informal organisational forms. This clearly presents a challenge to traditional political accountability exercised through the democratic electoral processes which underpin representative democracy. It presents a challenge also to the political structures which seek to ensure adherence to political position and loyalty to party, and to the enforcement and disciplinary procedures of whipping and party groups, There are thus complex issues involved in the accountability of the new partnerships, coalitions and alliances which characterise urban governance, and into which the community is increasingly drawn

The accountability of local decision makers to democratic control through election, however, represents only one route through which accountability can be demanded or proffered. There are many situations in which local accountability may be expected – *professional* accountability (inculcated through professional education and experience, reinforced by restricted entry to employment), *financial* accountability (determined by accounting and audit practice), *legal* accountability (reflecting the obligation to behave within the law and to be brought to account in the courts if the law is broken), and *procedural* and/or administrative accountability (evident in the extent to which organisational processes conform to statute or to the rules and precedent of natural justice). In addition, and most importantly for sustainability there is a *temporal* accountability of generation to generation. In often non-specific and non-enforceable ways the present generation is accountable both retrospectively to past generations and prospectively to the future. Political accountability remains, however, the main focus for debate with the key issue being the relative merits of representative versus participative democracy. And it is in relation to democratic accountability that the tension and/or complementarity of leadership and participation re-emerge.

Competitiveness and inclusion

In summary, it is likely that the complementarity of leadership and participation may be enhanced if there is a social capital which binds communities to the leadership of joint structures, if there is meaningful community inclusion in the processes of collaboration, if there are mechanisms for implementing and enforcing the promises made by leaders to communities, and if there is transparency and accountability in the decision-making procedures of joint working.

This is an analysis which has drawn much of its logic from the experience and that of area-based partnerships directed towards goals of social inclusion. Many of the principles of partnership apply equally to those coalitions and partnerships which address competitiveness, but there are significant differences (OECD 2001). Most obviously the spatial scale at which competitiveness and exclusion have been typically addressed varies. Partnerships for inclusion are often neighbourhood based and aim to draw in all those from communities who have hitherto been excluded. Partnerships which address competitiveness by contrast are most often built at the city-wide or sub-regional level and draw in the stakeholders concerned with infrastructure, with inward investment, with place marketing and with labour market skills. Some of these initiatives have social inclusion objectives, most notably the integration of the disadvantaged or long-term unemployed into the active labour market. There are initiatives which bridge the competitiveness/inclusion boundary, initiatives concerned, for example, with intermediate labour markets or the social economy. But there is a challenge to city-wide partnerships and to city leadership to look both outwards to the larger picture of economic competitiveness and at the same time to look inwards to the needs of communities. Like the Roman god Janus, the city leader must look both ways at the same time.

References

Ascher, F. (2002) 'The Globalisation Process', in: R. Hambleton, H. Savitch and M. Stewart (eds) *Globalism and Local Democracy: Challenge and Change in Europe and North America*, London: Palgrave.

Bassett, K. (1996) 'Partnerships, Business Elites and Urban Politics: New Forms of Governance in an English City', *Urban Studies*, Vol. 33: 539–555.

Berghman, J. (1997) 'The Resurgence of Poverty and the Struggle Against Social Exclusion: A New Challenge for Social Security in Europe', *International Social Security Review*, Vol. 50, No. 1.

Burns, J. (1978) *Leadership*, New York: Harper Row.

Chrislip, D. D. and Larson, C. E. (1994) *Collaborative Leadership: How Citizens and Civic Leaders can Make a Difference*, San Francisco: Jossey Bass.

Coulson, A. (ed.) (1998) *Trust and Contracts*, Bristol: Policy Press.

Davies, J. S. (2002) 'The Governance of Urban Regeneration: A Critique of the Governing Without Government Thesis', *Public Administration*, Vol. 80, No. 2: 301–323.

Department of Transport, Local Government and the Regions (2002) *Collaboration and Co-ordination in Area Based Initiatives*, London: DTLR.

DiGaetano, A. and Klemanski, J. S. (1993) 'Urban Regimes in Comparative Perspective', *Urban Affairs Quarterly*, Vol. 29: 54–83.

—— (1999) *Power and City Governance*, Minneapolis: University of Minnesota Press.

Geddes, M. (1998) *Local Partnership: A Successful Strategy for Social Cohesion?*, European Foundation for the Improvement of Living and Working Conditions, Luxembourg: Office for Official Publications of the European Communities.

Geddes, M. and Benington, J. (2001) *Local Partnerships and Social Exclusion in the European Union: New Forms of Local Social Governance?*, London: Routledge.

Granovetter, M. S. (1973) 'The Strength of Weak Ties', *American Journal of Sociology*, 78: 1360–1380.

—— (1985) 'Economic Action and Social Structure: The Problem of Embeddedness', *American Journal of Sociology*, Vol. 91: 3.

Gray, B. (1996) 'Cross Sectoral Partners: Collaborative Alliances among Business, Government and Community', in: C. Huxham (ed.) *Creating Collaborative Advantage*, Thousand Oaks: Sage.

Harding, A. (1994) 'Urban Regimes and Growth Machines: Towards a Cross-National Agenda', *Urban Affairs Quarterly*, Vol. 29, No. 3.

—— (1998) 'Public-Private Partnerships in the UK', in: J. Pierre (ed.) *Partnerships in Urban Governance*, Basingstoke: Macmillan: 71–92.

Hardy, C., Phillips, N., and Lawrence, T. (1998) 'Distinguishing Trust and Power in Interorganisational Relations', in: C. Lane and R. Bachman, *Trust Within and Between Organisations*, Oxford: Oxford University Press.

Hastings, A. (1996) 'Unravelling the Process of Partnership in Urban Regeneration Policy', *Urban Studies*, Vol. 33, No. 2.

Hastings, A., MacArthur, A. and MacGregor, A. (1996) *Less Than Equal? Community Organisations and Estate Regeneration Partnerships.* Bristol: Policy Press.

Himmelman, A. (1996) 'On the Theory and Practice of Transformational Collaboration: From Social Service to Social Justice', in: C. Huxham (ed.) *Creating Collaborative Advantage*, Thousand Oaks: Sage.

Hoggett, P. (1997) *Contested Communities*, Bristol: Policy Press.

Holliday, I. (2000) 'Is the British State Hollowing Out?' *Political Quarterly*, Vol. 71, No. 2: 167–176.

Hutton, W. and Giddens, A. (2000) *On the Edge: Living with Global Capitalism*, London: Jonathan Cape.

Huxham, C. (ed.) (1996) *Creating Collaborative Advantage*, Thousand Oaks: Sage.

Huxham, C. and Vangen, S. (2000) 'Leadership in the Shaping and Implementation of Collaboration Agendas: How Things Happen in a (Not Quite) Joined Up World', *Academy of Management Journal*, Vol. 43, No. 6: 159–175.

Jessop, B. (1995) 'The Regulation Approach: Governance and Post-Fordism: Alternative Perspectives', *Economy and Society*, Vol. 24, No. 3.

Joldersma, F. (1997) 'Participatory Policy-Making: Balancing Between Divergence and Convergence', *European Journal of Work and Organisational Psychology*, Vol. 6, No. 2.

Kramer, R. N. and Tyler, T. T. (eds) (1996) *Trust in Organisations. Frontiers of Theory and Research*, London: Sage.

Lauria, M. (ed.) (1997) *Reconstructing Urban Regime Theory: Regulating Urban Politics in a Global Economy*, Thousand Oaks: Sage.

Lee, P. and Murie, A. (1998) *Poverty, Housing Tenure and Social Exclusion*, Joseph Rowntree Foundation Bristol: Policy Press.

Levine, M. A. (1994) 'The Transformation of Urban Politics in France: The Roots of Growth Politics and Urban Regimes', *Urban Affairs Quarterly*, Vol. 29, No. 1: 383–410.

Logan, J. R. and Molotch, H. L. (1987) *Urban Fortunes: The Political Economy of Space*, Berkeley: University of California Press.

Lowndes, V. and Skelcher, C. (1998) 'The dynamics of Multi-Organisational Partnerships: An Analysis of Changing Modes of Governance', *Public Administration*, Vol. 76: 313–333.

Mackintosh, M. (1993) 'Partnership: Issues of Policy and Negotiation', *Local Economy*, Vol. 7, No. 3.

Madanipour, A., Cars, G. and Allen, J. (1998) *Social Exclusion in European Cities: Processes, Experiences, and Responses*, London: Jessica Kingsley.

Malpass, P. (1994) 'Policy Making and Local Governance: How Bristol Failed to Secure City Challenge Funding (Twice)', *Policy and Politics*, Vol. 22: 301–312.

Marshall, T. H. (1950) *Citizenship and Social Class*, Cambridge: Cambridge University Press.

Miller, C. (1999) 'Partners in Regeneration: Constructing a Local Regime for Urban Management', *Policy and Politics*, Vol. 27, No. 3.

Oatley, N. (ed.) (1998) *Cities, Economic Competition and Urban Policy*, London: Paul Chapman Publishing.

OECD (2001) *Local Partnerships for Better Governance*, Paris: OECD Publications.

Owen, C. J. (1994) 'City Government in Plock: An Emerging Urban Regime in Poland?', *Journal of Urban Affairs*, Vol. 16, No. 1.

Parkinson, M. (1998) *Combating Social Exclusion. Lessons from Area-based Programmes in Europe*, Bristol: Policy Press.

Peck, J. and Tickell, A. (1995) 'Business Goes Local: Dissecting the Business Agenda in Manchester', *International Journal of Urban and Regional Research*, Vol. 19, No. 1.

Pratt, J., Pampling, D. and Gordon, P. (1999) *Working Whole Systems: Practice and Theory in Network Organisations*, London: The King's Fund 1999.

Purdue, D. and Stewart, M. (eds) (2002) *Understanding Collaboration: International Perspectives on Theory, Method and Practice*, Bristol: University of the West of England.

Purdue, D., Razzaque, K., Hambleton, R. and Stewart, M. (2000) *Community Leadership in Area Regeneration*, Bristol: Policy Press.

Rhodes, R. (1994) 'The Hollowing Out of the State: The Changing Nature of Public Service in Britain' *Political Quarterly*, Vol. 65, No. 2: 138–151.

—— (1996) 'The New Governance: Governing Without Government', *Political Studies*, Vol. 44, No. 4: 652–667.

—— (1997) *Understanding Governance, Policy Networks, Governance, Reflexivity and Accountability*, Buckingham: Open University Press.

Room, G. (ed.) (1997) *Beyond the Threshold: The Measurement and Analysis of Social Exclusion*, Bristol: Policy Press.

Schruijer, S. (ed.) (1999) *Multi-Organisational Partnerships, and Co-Operative Strategy*, Tilburg: Dutch University Press.

Scott, C.M. and Thurston, W. (2003) *Collaboration in Context*, Calgary: University of Calgary.

Six, P. *et al.* (1999) *Governing in the Round*, London: DEMOS.

Skelcher, C., McCabe, A. and Lowndes, V. (1996) *Community Networks in Urban Regeneration: 'It All Depends Who You Know'*, York: Joseph Rowntree Foundation.

Srom, E. (1996) 'In Search of the Growth Coalition: American Urban Theories and the Redevelopment of Berlin', *Urban Affairs Review*, Vol. 3.

Stewart, M. (1996) 'The Politics of Local Complacency', *Journal of Urban Affairs*, Vol. 18, No. 2.

—— (1997) 'Participatory Policy Making: Between Divergence and Convergence', *European Journal of Work and Organisational Psychology*, Vol. 6, No. 2.

—— (2001) 'La fonction de commandement dans le gouvernement urbain', in: T. Spector, J. Theys and F. Menard (eds) *Villes du XXI Siecle: Actes du Colloque de la Rochelle*, Lyon: CERTU.

—— (2003) 'Towards Collaborative Capacity', in: M. Boddy (ed.) *Bristol: The Integrated City*, (forthcoming).

Stewart, M., Goss, S., Clarke, R., Gillanders, G., Rowe, J. and Shaftoe, H. (1999) *Cross-Cutting Issues Affecting Local Government*, London: DETR.

Stoker, G. and Mossberger, K. (1994) 'Urban Regime Theory in Comparative Perspective', *Environment and Planning C. Government and Policy*, Vol. 12: 195–212.

Stone, C. (1989) *Regime Politics, Governing Atlanta*, Lawrence: University Press of Kansas.

—— (1995) 'Political Leadership in Urban Politics', in: D. Judge, G. Stoker and H. Wollman (eds) *Theories of Urban Politics*, Thousand Oaks: Sage: 96–116.

Sullivan, H. and Skelcher, C. (2002) *Working Across Boundaries: Collaboration in Public Services*, Aldershot: Palgrave.

Svara, J. H. (1990) *Official Leadership in the City. Patterns of Conflict and Cooperation*, Oxford: Oxford University Press.

Sweeting, D., Hambleton, R., Huxham, C., Stewart, M. and Vangen, S. (2004) 'Leadership and Partnership in Urban Governance: Evidence from London, Bristol and Glasgow', in: M. Boddy and M. Parkinson (eds) *City Matters. Competitiveness, Cohesion and Urban Governance*, Bristol: Policy Press: 349–366.

Taillieu, T. (ed.) (2001) *Collaborative Strategies and Multi-Organisational Partnerships*, Leuven-Apeldorn: Garant.

Taylor, A. (2000) 'Hollowing Out or Filling In? Taskforces and the Management of Cross-Cutting Issues in British Government', *British Journal of Politics and International Relations*, Vol. 2, No. 1.

Taylor, M. (2000) Communities in the Lead: Organisational Capacity and Social Capital, *Urban Studies*, Vol. 37, Nos. 5–6: 1019–1035.

Webb, A. (1991) 'Co-ordination: A Problem in Public Sector Management', *Policy and Politics*, Vol. 19, No. 4.

Wilkinson, D. and Appelbee, E. (1999) *Implementing Holistic Government*, Bristol: Policy Press.

Woolcock, M. (1998) 'Social Capital and Economic Development: Towards a Theoretical Synthesis and Policy Framework', *Theory and Society*, Vol. 21: 151–208.

8   Changes in urban political leadership

Leadership types and styles in the era of urban governance

Panagiotis Getimis and Despoina Grigoriadou

Introduction

The study of leadership has always been crucial to urban politics and government. However, in recent years, the discussion on leadership has become more prominent since the nature of urban political leadership has changed rapidly following local government reform. This chapter focusses on three issues. First, the new institutional types and practical styles of urban political leadership that have emerged following the shift from local government to local governance are captured. Second, an analytical framework focussing on the interrelation of the institutional settings with the actors' behaviour is presented. Using empirical evidence currently available, the authors classify different leadership types and styles, in order to explore the factors that influence political leadership and to formulate criteria for their measurement. Third, an assessment of the institutional settings and the enactment of leadership positions by leaders in relation to the policy-making process shall be attempted. This assessment will be based on the principles of effectiveness, efficiency and legitimacy (see Chapter 2 of this book).

By *leadership types*, we refer to the way the position of political leaders is institutionalised in the context of a city and the broader political system; by *leadership styles* we refer to the enactment of leadership roles by those actors who are holders of a leadership position. Focussing on leadership types and behavioural styles in the policy-making process enables one to avoid separated and isolated approaches that would not take into account the structural and/or intentional complementarity of political leadership and community involvement. As a result, the classification and the assessment of leadership types and styles are directly related to different forms of legitimation that refer to community involvement (especially input-, output- and throughput-legitimation; see Chapter 2 of this book).

In the first section, the conceptual framework is introduced. This is followed by a presentation of the new urban leadership's positional powers and behaviours, as these followed after changes in urban government.

The next section deals with a number of measurement criteria with respect to the positional power and the styles of leaders. These criteria are sufficiently broad in order to capture the different aspects of urban leadership in different settings of societal coordination. In the final section an assessment of leadership types and leadership styles is proposed in order to offer suggestions on those types and styles (or their mixed forms) that are suitable for an effective and democratic complementarity of urban leadership and community involvement.

Approaches to local political leadership

In addressing questions concerning the ways in which urban leadership is affected by changes in urban governance, the conceptual framework the authors opt for is based upon the theoretical assumptions of the interactionist approach (see Figure 8.1). According to this approach, political leadership is a process in which political leaders matter, shaping the course of the decision-making process but are, simultaneously, themselves shaped and constrained by a set of factors (Elgie 1995). The interdependence between the structures and rules that influence leadership and the personality of leaders is highlighted. As Judd (2000: 959) argues 'urban leaders have the ability to make choices, but within the parameters imposed both by local political arrangements and by external forces'. Therefore, leadership behaviour is strengthened and constrained by a number of external dynamics, as well as the personal characteristics of a leader that may impact upon her/his environment. The identification of the ways in which effective leadership ensues as a result of attuning the personality of the leader and the environment in which she/he acts is a matter of empirical analysis.

The styles of political leadership correspond to the manner in which leaders exercise leadership. 'Although every individual is unique, it is still possible to identify similarities between the kinds of ways that different political leaders behave in office' (Elgie 1995: 10). However, a single style of leadership is not always successful in any place at any time. Leaders may demonstrate different leadership styles across different arenas (party and

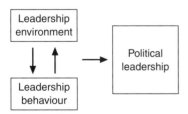

Figure 8.1 The interactionist approach to political leadership (source: adapted from Elgie (1995: 8)).

local government systems, policy areas) or at different moments in time. Many attempts have been made to develop classifications of leadership style (e.g. Barber 1977; Kavanagh 1990; Kotter and Lawrence 1974) since there exists an extensive relevant literature on political leadership. The most elementary way to distinguish leadership styles is the establishment of a dichotomy of leadership behaviour (Elgie 1995). The literature refers to distinctions such as between responsive and authoritarian leaders or between compromising and mobilising leaders.

The leadership environment essentially refers to those linkages to institutions and structures that reinforce or hinder the ambitions and behaviour of leaders. Similar to the case of leadership styles, there are various approaches to political leadership that classify and attach importance to different influential factors which set the framework in which leaders develop their styles. Elgie (1995) argues that two sets of factors influence leaders: the institutional structures and the needs of society. John and Cole (1999) identify four factors: the contextual factors, the institutional factors, the party organisation and system factors and finally other external factors. Judd (2000) focusses on the responses of the local leadership to national and local pressures; others (Hambleton 1998; Svara 1994) give priority to the relationship between mayor and municipal council or stress the particular importance of the relationship between political and organisational culture and the leader's own aspirations (Leach and Wilson 2000).

As far as the definition of political leadership is concerned, it is argued that although the concept of political leadership has been the subject of many books and articles, there is no consensus on a definition for this concept (Elgie 1995). On the contrary, there exist several definitions and numerous typologies of political leadership. According to Edinger (1993: 6) 'leaders are persons who exercise control over the behaviour of others so as to move them in a desired direction'. Leach and Wilson (2000: 11) argue that the main essence of leadership 'is the ability to inspire or persuade others to follow a course of action where there is at least some initial resistance to following'. In the light of how the term is used so far, leadership consists of the way that leaders, using their available resources and convincing others, shape the course of the decision-making process in order to provoke or prevent change.

Political leadership may be distinguished across two categories of leaders: positional and behavioural leaders (Edinger 1993). The positional leaders derive their powers from the formal position they occupy (e.g. mayors, council leaders) while the behavioural leaders derive their power from their own capacity to shape others' actions (e.g. experienced officers). Usually, leadership is a synthesis of position and behaviour. The institutional roles and rules as well as the actor's actual behaviour within these institutions form political leadership (Leach and Wilson 2000). For this reason, the synthesis of the leadership position and leadership behaviour has to be reconstructed empirically, case by case.

Concerning the question of who could be called a political leader,[1] Leach and Wilson (2000) remark that potential leaders may be not only leading politicians but also senior officers in local authorities. Chief executives or senior officers may take initiatives and may influence elected members to adopt a particular course of action. All mayors, to a greater or lesser extent, have a formal or informal cabinet, committees or appointed vice-mayors that 'control and determine the outcome of public policy decisions' (Kellerman 1984: 71). The focus of this book claims a more restricted use of the concept of urban political leaders. Here, the concept of political leader is reserved for publicly accountable actors. Usually, these actors are elected directly or via representation, some may also be appointed but are strongly connected to elected bodies.

This does not mean, however, that the administrative actors mentioned by Leach and Wilson can be dismissed. Within the context of the shift from government to governance, non-elected administrative actors (e.g. head officers in municipal services or in local development agencies, urban planners) play a crucial role in local decision making. For this reason, one has to include in leadership practice, the *delegated leaders* who represent political leaders in certain settings. Such delegated leaders have extensive contact with citizens, heads of organisations and interest groups from the locality as well as with organisations and actors from the higher government levels. They also enjoy considerable influence in shaping the behaviour of mayors and may take decisions regarding their delegated sector of responsibilities. These leaders are not publicly accountable themselves, but personally accountable to political leaders as their position depends directly upon the will of the latter (e.g. the mayor).

The new urban political leadership

Based on the theoretical discussion surrounding the shift from government to governance, there is growing evidence that the progression of local authorities from a hierarchical and bureaucratic exercise of power to a more enabling and modernised mode leads to new institutional forms and behavioural styles of political leadership (John 2001; Leach and Wilson 2000; Leach and Percy-Smith 2001; see also the contribution of Hambleton in this book). These changes refer to institutional reforms such as the consolidation of executive leadership and the emergence of strong political leaders and the strengthening of those leadership styles to cope with the urban environment and develop a strategic direction. Although these developments are not apparent at the same level in all countries because of their historic and socio-political particularities, there are still similarities that demonstrate an overall shift of local authorities from government to governance leading to new urban leadership types and styles that correspond to these changes.

Implications of the new urban political leadership

Over the last two decades the growing economic interdependence characterised by globalisation (Dunford and Kafkalas 1992; Jessop 1993), the increase of public deficits and the rise of new demands from local communities for more power in urban politics have strengthened local authorities and endowed them with new fields of intervention. The emergence of the entrepreneurial city and the development of partnerships and networks along with the questions of who governs and how, have all been well documented in the literature over recent years (see, for instance, Stewart and Stoker 1995; Hall and Hubbard 1998). According to this literature, the emergence of a variety of public private and voluntary organisations in the late 1990s has played an important role in local policy making and in the provision of services. In this new complex environment, local government – in other words democratically elected authorities – can not govern the local community on its own but has to work in partnership with the non-governmental sector of the community towards the solution of problems and conflicts. Besides the emergence of new actors, the pragmatic recognition by local authorities that no single actor has the capacity or resources to realise multi-sectoral policies, such as sustainable urban regeneration policies, has led to a more flexible and open role for local authorities in the political management of urban affairs.

However, the cooperation of local government with non-elected bodies of the community is not the only concern of local authorities (Leach and Percy-Smith 2001). They must also make internal and external political and administrative arrangements in order to ensure more efficiency and accountability. Local government reforms refer to the introduction of New Public Management (NPM) into local authorities' services and policy making, which according to Leach and Percy-Smith (2001), is related to the introduction of private management practices in local authorities such as the development of a more business-like approach of public services provision, the introduction of strategic management, a concern over consumer satisfaction and the introduction of performance criteria.

In addition, the rise of the New Political Culture – which is accompanied by a shift from the hierarchical political organisations and the class/race politics to a broadened citizen participation and the emergence of 'issue politics' (Clark 2002: 83) – as well as the government and governance failures concerning a democratic deficit and a lack of legitimacy (Burns 2000) correspondingly lead to a stream of new initiatives which intend to render local institutions more responsive to local needs and to offer more opportunities for participation to citizens. As a result, neighbourhood councils and community-based non-governmental organisations became essential actors in the local political process.

These developments have important implications for the institutional position and the practice of political leadership in local authorities. First,

the organisational fragmentation within local authorities and the development of a complex network of diverse objectives create an increasing need
for strong central direction by individual municipal leaders who, alone or
with a small executive (Leach and Percy-Smith 2001), will (i) oversee the
extended fragmentation of non-elected organisations, (ii) improve the
quality and speed of decision making and (iii) be directly accountable to
their constituencies. In fact, the political leader needs to create a strong
pro-active strategic agenda that develops as a response to the policy
environment. The development and endorsement of a strategic direction
requires genuine skills of management beyond 'governing' (in a traditional way), including setting standards, strategic aims and performance
evaluation.

Second, the introduction of NPM has led to the reinforcement of chief
executives that break the traditional distinction between policy formulation and policy implementation leading to a more shared leadership
where the mayor, the council and the chief executives take collaboratively
the political decisions. The chief executive as 'a dynamic executive leader
who is capable of working closely with elected members and brokering
community interests' (Hambleton 2002: 163) is appointed to manage the
local authority on behalf of the elected members. There is a convergence
between elected political leaders' role and chief executives' role by which
their relationship becomes crucial with respect to the effectiveness of
policy making and implementation (see also the contribution of Hambleton in this volume). While the political leaders move towards a more innovative entrepreneurial and managerial role, the chief executives extend
their role beyond their traditional task of serving the administration
towards the more overtly political task of working closely with elected
bodies and the community.

A further impact refers to the increased dependence of urban political
leadership on the external environment. In view of the fact that the local
authorities should operate more entrepreneurially in partnership with a
wider range of external organisations (public, private or voluntary) in
order to respond to local issues, there is also a need for a more outgoing
and inclusive style of leadership (Hambleton 2002; John 2001). Effective
urban leadership is not possible without leaders who work alongside a
plethora of non-elected bodies. Consequently, new leadership tasks
emerge. The leaders should possess collaborative skills but also a steering
capacity to strongly influence the structures and processes of partnership
formations, in order to shape the participants' behaviour in favour of
community well-being.

Pressures favouring the reform of political leadership have appeared
across many western European local governments and have promoted (i)
the emergence of dynamic leaders and (ii) institutional changes in
decision-making systems. Concerning the first type of reform, the practice
of more visible and strong local leadership is evident in European

countries such as France, Italy, the UK and Holland. New generations of local politicians use the changes in institutional contexts and political scenes in order to construct for themselves a strong political constituency, while gaining a large degree of independence from political parties (Jouve and Lefevre 2002: 191–194). These changes are also obvious in Greece. The recent weakening of the significance of the national political parties has led to the emergence of new mayors being independent of local parties and traditional elites' milieus (Lyritsis 2000). Even if the emergence of these economy-driven leaders has been accompanied in many cases by corruption scandals and disgraced resignations, they have nevertheless created development coalitions and have sought to become local boosters of regeneration and growth. Most surprisingly, strong leaders are not only emerging in South European countries (like France, Greece and Italy), which have traditionally supported powerful leaders, but also in northern countries such as the Netherlands, Germany and the UK (John 2001: 134–153). This development is complemented by the reforms of the decision-making system in Scandinavian countries strengthening the position of the executive,[2] and in Germany and the UK where directly elected mayors have been introduced.

If the criteria for an effective and democratic leader are (i) the promotion of a strong direction of public policies in a fragmented organisational urban environment to ensure problem-solving (effectiveness), (ii) the enhancement of public support through the strengthening of citizens' deliberation and joint policy implementation (legitimacy) and (iii) the mobilisation of local resources through interactive arrangements between various local actors and participatory management (efficiency), changes in urban political leadership have not always proved responsive to effective and democratic policies deriving from the complementarity of urban leadership and community involvement (John 2001: 134–153; Burns 2000). As Haus and Heinelt (in Chapter 2) underline with reference to Jessop's conceptualisation of 'governance failure', governance may bear considerable advantages in relation to other modes of societal coordination, yet it may also fail in terms of effectiveness and accountability (Jessop 2002; Getimis and Kafkalas 2002). Consequently, new types of urban political leadership demonstrate not only good practices related to being able to steer and generate capacity but also weaknesses embedded in governance. In many cases, the strengthening of the executive may contribute to the decisiveness and the effective implementation of political decisions, but could also demonstrate little awareness for the demands of the community. In other cases, a consensual leader whose decisions depend on dispersed and fragmented interests and citizen's demands could lose a clear sense of direction of the community's future. Finally, in cases where the system of local accountability is very weak, vesting considerable power in leading figures could result in the abuse of such power and in corruption scandals.

The new urban leadership in comparative perspective

Generalisations of impact of these changes on urban leadership in all countries must be carefully carried out. A cross-national comparison must take into account that responses can differ due to different government traditions, institutional contexts and histories.

European local government systems are classified into different types or families. According to Page and Goldsmith (1987) one may distinguish between the South European government systems (applied in France, Italy, Belgium, Spain, Portugal and Greece) and the North European government systems (covering the United Kingdom, the Scandinavian countries and Denmark). Comparative studies have demonstrated that these two families comprise different types of political leaders followed by different types of legitimation (John 2001). In the southern systems, the political leaders play an important role in the balance of powers and in the local decision-making process. For example, in France, the mayors are very important in acting as administrative brokers towards the mobilisation of resources from the national government and in building inter-municipal cooperation (Crozier and Friedberg 1977). In Greece, mayors are equally very powerful figures, elected directly by the people and controlling the majority seats in the council. They mediate between the centre and the locality and make use of clientelistic relations and of the party support to promote their policies (Hlepas 1994). By comparison, in the northern system, power is shared between the leader and the executive committees and promotes a more collective process of decision making. For example, in Scandinavian countries, the municipalities are run by a political leader in close cooperation with executive committees composed of politicians.

Concerning new public management John (2001) notes that the idea is not equally spread in all European countries, with the local government systems in Southern Europe being less affected. The rationalisation of the local administrative system in these countries is more difficult because of its close relations with the local political and economic system and its organisational deficiencies.

In addition, the construction of local partnership arrangements between local authorities and the socio-economic sector is not something all countries are familiar with and, where these emerge, they could assume different institutional forms (networks, subcontracting/out-sourcing, privatisation, etc.) involving different actors. In some cases, the partnerships are dominated by technocratic arrangements that restrain the role of political leaders while in others political leaders acquire a crucial role due to the partnerships' institutional form.

Finally, particular kinds of leadership are also promoted by particular characteristics in the political culture. For example, in Germany, the introduction of directly elected mayors has so far not led to corruption as in other countries since institutional and cultural factors have apparently served as 'checks and balances' to ward off possible power distortions (Wollman 2004). These factors are reflected in some *Länder* both in the electoral law and in the traditionally independent non-partisan local groups that do not privilege a partisan leadership profile, as well as in the mayor's term in office that is significantly longer than that of the council's.

Factors influencing political leadership and criteria to measure them

The absence of a sufficiently robust analytical framework to make sense of the new challenges that an urban political leader has to cope with makes effective comparison among them difficult (Leach and Percy-Smith 2001; Elcock 2001). However, as highlighted above, the analysis of urban leadership requires the understanding of the following key influences: the leader's personal characteristics and ideology/values, the leadership's role in urban governance, the leader's position in horizontal (local) political structures, and finally the vertical political structures (see Figure 8.2).

The vertical political structures refer to formal and informal national rules that shape the power, identity and context in which leadership is

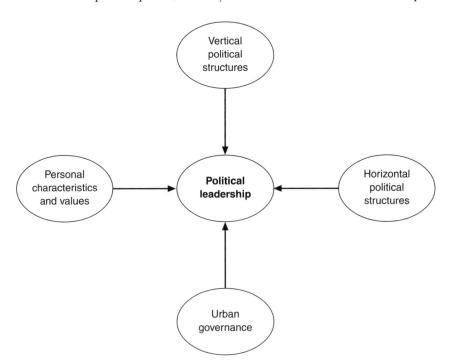

Figure 8.2 Factors influencing local leadership.

exercised. It includes local–central government relations and the relation-ship of leaders to political parties, addressing the extent to which leader-ship depends on the local–national dimension within parties.

The horizontal political structures refer to the local institutional environment, i.e. the relation of the urban political leader to the council and the municipal administration, but also to more informally structured aspects like the local party system.

The personal characteristics of the leaders refer to those personal traits and capacities, which convince others to follow their lead. Charisma (according to Max Weber) is a familiar example of such a personal trait. The ideology and values of leaders represent mainly their personal atti-tude towards the exercise of power and their policy orientation.

Finally, the leadership's role in urban governance reflects the relation-ship maintained by the leaders to a wider range of external bodies, whether from the public, private or voluntary sector in order to exercise responsiveness towards local issues.

The first two factors, i.e. the vertical and horizontal political environ-ment, structure the leadership types. Together with this structural side of leadership the last two factors, i.e. the personal characteristics of leaders and their networking with the local community, shape leadership styles. Urban political leadership is the result of the interaction between leader-ship types and styles. Although institutions matter because they constitute the political structure of local authorities, persons occupying political offices interpret these structures differently and shape the specific fea-tures of urban leadership in each context. In other words: their behaviour makes a difference in the exercise of political authority.

Leadership types

To get a clearer idea of different leadership types, it is necessary to examine the vertical and horizontal political environment by addressing the following dimensions:

1   the relationship between central and local government (the level of financial assistance, the level of decentralisation of powers),
2   the endogenous economic potential of the city,
3   the formal powers of urban political leadership defined by the legal framework regarding the balance of power between mayor, council and chief executives,
4   the impacts of voting systems regarding the influence of parties.

Regarding the degree of the local government's autonomy from the central state, it is important to define the extent to which urban leaders are embedded in an urban setting with autonomy from the state and have the possibility to influence this setting in order to achieve their policy objectives. In other words, it is necessary to measure the degree to which the leaders possess strategic competencies (the ability to define and pursue their objectives) and are offered the preconditions to pursue their objectives in their actions. Starting from this point, one could classify leadership in two categories: *empowered and disempowered leadership* (see also the contribution of Bäck in this book).

The factors defining the level of dependence of *local* government on the *central* state include the political, such as the level of the nationalisation of local elections, the access of local government to informal channels influencing on central government and the local authority's impact on the national system. They could include economic factors, such as the share of central government grants in the city budget, the percentage of central government grants in relation to the local tax income and the level of local autonomy in managing central government grants. Finally, legal factors could include the scope of allocation of competences by the state and the level of state supervision in the development of such competences.

Taking into account these variables, it may be assumed that a powerful leadership can derive ideally from a high level of local autonomy, i.e. financially independent local authorities with far-reaching competences across a wide range of policies, a low degree of involvement of the upper level of government in local politics and control over local interest groups and party demands. Regarding the last factor, empowered leaders do not have to respond to internal party group demands and adjust their vision and behaviour according to political parties' changes and interests groups' pressures.

By contrast, in the case of a disempowered leadership the mayor and/or the council have restricted powers and autonomy and develop a culture of dependency vis-à-vis the central state. The decision-making process in the face of weak leadership is dispersed and dependent on the 'retention of loyalty' from various actors and political parties while the mismatch between citizens' perceptions of leadership and the interpretation of this role by the leaders themselves causes conflict.

In addition to the aforementioned limits and constraints of power posed by vertical factors, one should also identify the variables decisive for the internal distribution of powers in the self-government of local authorities (horizontal political structures). By internal distribution of power we refer to the ways in which political power is shared among the mayor (or other political leaders), the council and the head(s) of the municipality. When developing a typology of government forms that illustrates the diversity of political power relations between these actors, it is important to identify where political power is centred in the municipality and what institutional types of leadership the particular form provides for.

Mouritzen and Svara (2002) distinguish four ideal types of municipal executive form which specify important aspects of the horizontal political structure in which different types of leadership can evolve:

1   The *strong-mayor form* is based on an elected mayor who controls the majority of the council and constitutes the central figure of the executive. The systems of local government in South Europe like France, Greece, Italy and Spain are close to this form of municipal organisation.

2   The *committee-leader* form is based upon the sharing of the executive powers between a central actor, who is clearly the political leader of the municipality, and several standing committees. The case of Denmark, Sweden and (traditionally) Great Britain can be more or less labelled as committee-leader form.

3   The *collective form* is based on the collective leadership by the executive committee of the council consisting of elected councillors and the mayor. Belgium and the Netherlands can be said to fall into this category.

4   The *council-manager form* features a city council and a city manager. The council is a relatively small body which has a 'general authority over policy but is restricted from involvement in administrative matters' (Mouritzen and Svara 2002: 56). The city manager, appointed by the city council, is a professional administrator who is responsible for all executive functions. The local government systems of Finland, Norway, Ireland, the United States and Australia share to differing degrees the characteristics of the council-manager form.[3]

Mouritzen and Svara (2002) set out to examine the balance of powers among the council, the mayor and the political/administrative executive. Their focus on the relations between the elected officials and the chief administrators and the linkages of the political and administrative dimensions of government has led them to put less emphasis on the issue of *election*. This factor is of special interest when political leadership is seen as a salient position subject to public accountability.[4] In order to go deeper into the aspect of urban political leadership, which constitutes a core issue in this book, the authors add the following questions: How are the members of the council and the mayor elected? Is the mayor elected directly by the citizens or is she/he elected by and among the council members by a proportional or majoritarian composed council? Answers to these questions could lead to conclusions about the characteristics of majoritarian (i.e. competitive) or consociational types of democracy in local government (see also Bäck in this book).

More specifically, the electoral system defines the extent to which the city council is controlled by one or more political actors (Mouritzen and Svara 2002: 53) as some electoral systems produce a situation where one party or a coalition of parties may create an effective majority. Particularly in the case of the indirect election of the mayor, i.e. where the mayor is elected by and among the members of the majority of the city council, or where a chief administrative officer is appointed by the majority of the council, the linkage between the leading political actor and the council can become very strong. This can result in a very dominant majority and a rather closed policy-making process. By contrast, the proportional selection of the council's members requires the agreement of parties over the distribution of the political positions. In that case, the indirectly elected mayor or the appointed chief executive officer has to act collaboratively with the council members.

The importance of electoral systems in the balance of power at the horizontal local government level can be demonstrated by the following example: Sweden, and Great Britain's former local government systems belong to the committee-leader type. On the one hand Sweden opted for the proportional election of the city councillors and the election of the executive committee on a proportional basis, therein promoting a more consensual style of decision making. On the other hand, the majoritarian election of the council members in Britain often awarded one party the control over the council and the executive.

However, the issue of election does not always determine the power relations between the mayor, the council and the executive. This is illustrated by countries that belong to the strong mayor form. The local governments of Italy, Greece, France and Spain fall into the category where the mayor is the central political leader, and is responsible for municipal administration and has a strong position vis-à-vis the council. Although these cases have different electoral systems concerning the election of mayor, they do not show differences in relation to the mayoral position in the municipality that results from the electoral system. In Italy and in Greece the mayor is directly elected by the citizens. Due to a majoritarian system of voting that favours the personification of elections, the mayor has full control over the council, whose role is restricted to operation control and approval of the main projects. The main governing body of the municipality is the executive body, labelled the City Board in Italy and the Mayoral Committee in Greece. The members of these bodies are selected and appointed exclusively by the mayor and are in charge of executive functions. In France and Spain, the mayor is indirectly elected by and among the council. However, the electoral system based on the majoritarian principle grants the mayor extensive powers in the council, and in the executive. Political power is heavily concentrated in the executive, formed by the mayor and deputy mayors who are, in the case of France, elected by the council following the recommendation of the mayor, or, in the case of Spain, appointed directly by the mayor.

To conclude, the different local government systems influence political leadership which lead to four ideal types. However, embedded in certain political and societal environments are factors that empower or disempower leaders.

Leadership styles

The four executive forms and the degree of local government autonomy described above imply different expectations over the role of leaders. In the empowered, strong mayor type of local political organisation, one could expect strong leaders that offer policy directions to the council and control the executive. In dispowered collective types of local political organisation by contrast, it is assumed that weak leaders with mainly ceremonial competencies would prevail. However, the reality leads us to less stereotyped considerations. In Greece and France, where the strong mayor type is dominant, one can detect weak mayors who reproduce the status quo without seeking to promote their strategies. Mouritzen and Svara (2002: 69) note that 'the share of weak mayors is by far the largest in a country that comes very close to the strong mayor ideal type'. Instead of the promotion of a strong strategy, they remain tied to party demands and give in to pressure groups. Another example is that of Denmark which is characterised in Mouritzen and Svara's typology (2002) as a committee-leader form of government. According to these authors, in this country there are examples of powerful mayors who have been in office since the mid 1960s and have effectively shaped the socio-economic development of their community. These examples demonstrate that the behaviour of leaders (and its success or failure) differs within positional types of leadership.

Consequently, in addition to the typology of positional powers of political leadership, this section will also identify the potential leadership styles that depend on the leaders' political values. By political values one refers to the political orientation in relation to the perceptions of social problems and ways of problem solving, as well as the attitude to the delegation of powers.[5] The personal enactment of the institutional leadership position will be analysed in relation to two dimensions: the leadership orientation/predisposition and the attitude towards the exercise of power (Leach and Wilson 2000: 26–32).

The first dimension reflects the way in which leaders envisage their role. There are some leaders that develop distinctive strategic policy agendas which they try to incorporate in the authority's policy-making processes. Others do not have any kind of agenda, preferring a more generalised policy framework which leaves more scope for the reproduction of the status quo. These leaders may have a leadership position, but have little desire to provide the lead in terms of new ideas and strategic direction; they do not have a clear vision for the future of their local society. The orientation of leaders towards leadership could be distinguished by the following set of variables (Leach and Wilson 2000; Kotter and Lawrence 1974):

- *Coping of leaders with policy change.* Two styles of leader may be distinguished in relation to policy change: the *proactive* and the *reactive*. In the first case, the leader has a positive attitude towards the emergence of controversial issues in the policy arena by proposing innovative plans and projects and by establishing new institutions that enable innovative policy making. Furthermore, the proactive leader evaluates and institutionally redesigns the rules of the policy arenas. In the second case, the reactive leader responds with continuity and stability in each policy arena and she/he does not consider the formulation of new policies.

- *Generating capacity and problem solving.* There again arise two styles of leader: the *competent* and the *consensual* leader styles. In the first case, the competent leader mobilises and attracts resources from various actors (local authority, political actors from other territorial level, resourceful actors – not at least the business community), solves the main problems of the authority and helps citizens to resolve complaints they bear towards the municipal government. The consensual leader has a low interest in mobilising the available resources and expresses inertia towards the basic problems of the municipality.

- *Developing a clear personal agenda.* One can distinguish between the *programme politicians* and *caretaker* styles of leader. The programme politicians establish clear objectives and introduce them in the municipal policy-making process. The programme politicians support a coherent programme and a long-term strategy. Finally, they design the authority's dominant ideology (they have a clear answer to the question: what kind of authority are we and where are we going?) and they lessen party influence. The caretaker, by contrast, has no clear agenda, which results in inertia and a drift in council affairs between parties, councillors and executives. She/he has no clear vision over the conduct of the municipal affairs and the way in which the municipality will develop in the future.

- *Cohesiveness.* One may distinguish between the *negotiator* and the *confrontational* styles of leadership. The negotiator realises effective coordination by mediating conflicts inside the local authority and pursuing conflict resolution (between administration and politicians). She/he has the capacity to cope with administrative fragmentation and to create an identity (vision) for the community. The confrontational leader does not easily cope with opinions and viewpoints of others and she/he is motivated by a strong political drive.

- *Accomplishment of tasks concerning executive action.* One could distinguish between the leader as *city manager* and the leader as *politician*. The first one is more keen to define orientations towards transforming the administrative structure (e.g. introduction of NPM principles), to guide the staff in their daily activity, to control policy output (monitoring, reporting, evaluating), to appoint individual staff and to ensure the correct operation of the politico-administrative process. The politician leader does not get involved in the accomplishment of policies and she/he does not control the programme implementation. She/he restricts her/his involvement in the policy design leaving the city management to the executive officers.

With respect to the second dimension, namely the exercise of power, the key distinction here lies between the desire to act authoritatively ('power over') and the desire to act through empowerment ('power to'), reflecting Stone's (1995) theory of the narrow exercise of power and the empowering exercise of power. The leader's behaviour that promotes the empowerment of the community could be distinguished by the following set of variables (Leach and Wilson 2000; John and Cole 1999):

- *Generating support from the community.* The leaders who generate support from the community play a crucial role in the mobilisation of the local civil society through the reinforcement of existing procedural rules or the establishment of new ones enabling actors to participate and interact. They embark in collaborations with the community, exchanging resources and creating links between citizens and local government, therein improving accountability, responsiveness and the public's trust towards its governors. In this case, the leaders advocate the citizens' views to municipal political bodies, share information with citizens and integrate the views of citizens in their policy design.
- *Leading and coordinating partnership.* There are different responses by leaders in the establishment of partnerships according to the extent to which leaders are mobilised in favour of their partners' empowerment. One can identify the coordinator and the champion style of leader. The coordinator tries to build networks of trust by negotiation and sharing information, developing integrative capacity by moving between networks, carrying the message of one set of interests to another and, finally, mediating and bringing together competitive interests. The champion has a more active role. She/he mobilizes collaborative advantage by bringing together resources, invites actors to participate, takes forward the goals of the partnership, provokes action where it is felt unlikely to happen and finally she/he forces the partnership to think long term.

By contrast, the leaders acting authoritatively are characterised by top-down approaches of command and control. They prefer more hierarchical practices of power exercise assigning less significance to the institutions of citizens' participation and to the establishment of partnerships and networks between local authority and community.

The above two dimensions regarding the leadership orientation and the exercise of power lead to the identification of the following typology of leadership styles (John and Cole 1999: 102) (see Figure 8.3):

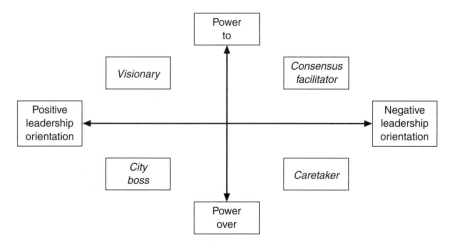

Figure 8.3 Ideal leadership styles (source: adapted from John and Cole (1999) and elaborated by the authors).

a   The *visionary* mixes strong leadership and capacity generation to form a powerful and effective coalition, bringing together different sides and establishing innovative policies and effective coordination.

b   The *consensual facilitator* is adaptable and generates capacity through influence and bringing out the contribution of others. However, this type of leader finds it hard to develop a consistent approach, and decision making is hampered by the presence of other influential local actors and parties.

c   The *city boss* is uncomfortable in complexity of networks and copes poorly with rapid policy change. She/he is a strong leader who does not anticipate capacity building in local actors but is characterised by strong determination. In addition, she/he promotes her/his policies by-passing conflicts and disagreements in the party network.

d   The *caretaker* is a comparatively ineffective leader who also encounters difficulties in coping with policy change. Networks in local governance remain beyond the scope of this type of leader and this leader prefers to maintain the status quo.

It should be noted that the empirical evidence will most likely identify a more refined view of leadership, perhaps entailing a mixture of styles. In addition, leadership styles are unlikely to be fixed during the entire policy process. Following Ostrom's approach of institutional analysis in successive policy arenas (Ostrom *et al.* 1994, see also the chapter by Denters and Klok in this book), the authors suggest that in each arena leadership behaviour is likely to change. As far as leadership types are concerned, although leadership types are more difficult to change during the process of policy making, it is nevertheless possible to identify slight changes that could result for instance from decentralised state policies.

Preliminary hypothesis on combinations, benefits and risks of leadership types and styles

Although it is possible to find different combinations of leadership types and styles across different countries, the authors suggest that specific leadership types encourage specific leadership styles. However, such hypotheses must be tested empirically.

The first hypothesis of possible elective affinities refers to the significance of the voting system and thus the election of political leaders for their behaviour towards the council and the political parties. Regarding the strong mayor executive form, it is argued that the direct election of the mayor and the majoritarian election of the council lead to top-down, authoritarian leadership behaviour owing to the lack of counterbalancing institutions of accountability that restrain the (ab)use of mayoral power. Alternatively, in the collective leadership type, the division of power between the local assembly and the local executive requires a more collaborative leadership style in order to establish a more consensual environment for promoting decisiveness and maintaining cohesiveness and coordination. In addition, the dependency of leaders on the parties is lower because of the proportional electoral system that presupposes co-operation of parties in the council.[6]

A second hypothesis refers to the relation of the majoritarian or consensual type of decision making with the leaders' behaviour towards community involvement. Taking into account that the stronger the consensual character of local politics, the stronger the norms of citizen integration in local politics might be, we assume that these constitutional settings presuppose leadership styles with a more empowering attitude towards power ('power to'). On the other hand, in the majoritarian types of decision making, where the executive and the assembly are in the hands of a simple majority, more authoritarian styles of leaders could characterise local politics.

A third hypothesis refers to the relation of the institutional separation of powers with the leadership behaviour regarding its role in promoting cohesiveness. One could argue that in cases of separation of executive powers, leaders are challenged to develop a more collegial attitude towards power in order to counteract the complexity and the fragmentation deriving from the dispersion of power between the assembly and the executive. On the other hand, in cases where the powers are concentrated in one political body, the leaders may develop more autonomous policies and adopt their own solutions since the cohesiveness of the authority is not threatened by the fragmentation of powers.

To consider ideal leadership types and styles and their possible combinations an assessment has to be made regarding benefits and risks. The assessment is realised according to *effectiveness, legitimacy* and *efficiency*. It includes also the three different forms of legitimation, i.e. input-, throughput- and output-legitimation (see Chapter 2). Tables 8.1 and 8.2 provide an overview of such an assessment.

Even if the idea of a strong, directly elected mayor were to be derived from the necessity for more responsiveness and participation in local authorities, it would run the risk of reinforcing the dominance of the executive and of diminishing the influence of the council and the citizens' demands. However, it offers the opportunity for more decisiveness and efficiency since the mayor is a visible political person that concentrates powers enhancing the governing capacity in local politics. Alternatively, in the case of a collaborative leadership style in a collective leadership type,

Table 8.1 Assessment of leadership types

Leadership type	Benefits	Risks
Strong mayor type	Input legitimation by election Effectiveness through decisiveness and strong direction Efficiency through personal accountability for governance Visible political leadership	Risk of 'solitary hero', personalised leadership, executive 'closure', 'one man show' Dominance of the executive to the detriment of council and citizens Lack of throughput-legitimation and citizens' involvement due to potential personalised access to decision making (clientelism etc.)
Committee-leader type	Accountability through internal checks and balances Efficiency through close cooperation with the executive Input-legitimation by better representation of the community Visible political leader	Difficulties in decision making (delays caused by collaboration) Danger of increased role of non-elected actors Lack of throughput-legitimation due to dispersed responsibilities
Collective type	Input-legitimation by vote and consensual negotiations Internal checks and balances	Problems of delays in the decision-making and the implementation process Dispersed responsibilities
Council-manager type	Efficiency due to the importance of the executive Internal checks and balances	Conflicts between political and managerial strategies Lack of input-legitimation due to the role of the city manager

Table 8.2 Assessment of leadership styles

Leadership styles	Benefits	Risks
Visionary	Innovative, capacity generation, increased legitimacy, efficiency Political accountability Visible political leadership	Risk of overload Disappointment of failure
Consensual facilitator	Facilitator of capacity generation Increase of efficiency and legitimacy	Dependence of the interest intermediation balance Lack of strategic direction Risk of ineffectiveness
City boss	Effectiveness, capacity to solve problems Visible political leadership	Authoritarian, non-accountable, executive closure, lack of legitimacy and efficiency
Caretaker	Maintaining cohesion because of upholding the status quo	No capacity generation No change and innovation due to the lack of flexibility and adaptation

the leader has the advantage to support and promote different interest groups and citizens' demands. She/he may not be dominated by her/his political party but is obliged to respect all parties in order to preserve coherence and avoid conflicts in the council. However, this combination of leadership type and style could lead to lack of decisiveness and efficiency in the leader's efforts to compromise different interests inside and outside the local authority.

From the analysis of the tables it may be argued that the best combination of leadership type and style could be a collective form of local government with a visionary leader. It seems that this combination enhances the legitimation and the effectiveness of decision making. Such an institutional context offers input- and throughput-legitimation, while the visionary style of the mayor increases effectiveness, counterbalancing the inherent risks of the collective type of local government executive such as delays in decision making and conflicts inside the municipal council.

Notes

1 See also the discussion of Hambleton in this volume in the section called 'Who are the local leaders?'.
2 An example of strong executive leadership is the case of Bergen (Norway) where the City Parliament has recently introduced a politically elected body, the City Government that is the city's executive organ.
3 For more details see the contribution of Bäck and Hambleton in this book who refer also to Mouritzen and Svara (2002).
4 Furthermore, the term of the mayor can offer important insights. For example,

188 *Panagiotis Getimis and Despoina Grigoriadou*

in Germany, the mayor has a longer term than the city council; this institutional arrangement supports the independence of the mayor from party constraints.
5 In contrast, the personal attributes and resources of the leaders like charisma, charm or social intelligence will not be included to this classification of styles due to the difficulties encountered in observing and even measuring them.
6 The strong correlation of the local government organisation with leaders' behaviour in parties is stressed by Mouritzen and Svara (2002: 71). According to them, most mayors from strong mayor and committee-leader cities bring a strong commitment to promote their political party position, while in collective cities the leaders are less associated with party politics.

References

Barber, J. (1977) *The Presidential Character: Predicting Performance in the White House*, Englewood Cliffs, NJ: Prentice-Hall.

Burns, D. (2000) 'Can Local Democracy Survive Governance?', *Urban Studies*, Vol. 37, Nos. 5–6: 963–973.

Clark, T. N. (2002) 'Globalization and Transformation in Political Cultures', in: R. Hambleton, H. V. Savitch and M. Stewart (eds) *Globalism and Local Democracy: Challenge and Change in Europe and North America*, Hampshire: Palgrave: 67–89.

Crozier, M. and Friedberg, E. (1977) *L'acteur et le systeme. Les contraintes de l'action collective*, Paris: Seuil.

Dunford, M. and Kafkalas, G. (eds) (1992) *Cities, Regions and the New Europe*, London: Belhaven.

Edinger, L. (1993) 'A Preface to Studies in Political Leadership', in: G. Sheffer (ed.) *Innovative Leadership in International Politics*, Albany, NY: State University of New York Press: 3–20.

Elcock, H. (2001), *Political Leadership*, Cheltenham and Northampton, MA: Edward Elgar Publishing.

Elgie, R. (1995) *Political Leadership in Liberal Democracies*, London: Macmillan Press.

Getimis, P. and Kafkalas, G. (2002) 'Comparative Analysis of Policy-Making and Empirical Evidence on the Pursuit of Innovation and Sustainability', in: P. Getimis, H. Heinelt, G. Kafkalas and R. Smith (eds) *Participatory Governance in a Multi-Level Context: Concepts and Experience*, Opladen: Leske + Budrich: 155–171.

Hall, T. and Hubbard, P. (1998) *The Entrepreneurial City*, West Sussex: John Wiley & Sons.

Hambleton, R. (1998) 'Strengthening Political Leadership in UK Local Government', *Public Money and Management*, January–March: 1–11.

—— (2002) 'The New City Management', in: R. Hambleton, H. V. Savitch and M. Stewart (eds) *Globalism and Local Democracy: Challenge and Change in Europe and North America*, Hampshire: Palgrave: 147–168.

Hlepas, N. (1994) *Local Government: Theoretical Research and Instructional Reforms*, Athens-Komotini: Sakoulas.

Jessop, B. (1993) 'Towards a Schumpeterian Workfare State? Preliminary Remarks on Post-Fordist Political Economy', *Studies in Political Economy*, Vol. 40: 7–39.

—— (2002) 'Governance and Metagovernance: On Reflexivity, Requisite Variety and Requisite Irony', in: P. Getimis, H. Heinelt, G. Kafkalas and R. Smith (eds) *Participatory Governance in a Multi-Level Context: Concepts and Experience*, Opladen: Leske + Budrich: 33–58.

John, P. (2001) *Local Governance in Western Europe*, London: Sage.

John, P. and Cole, A. (1999), 'Political Leadership in the New Urban Governance: Britain and France Compared', *Local Government Studies*, Vol. 25, No. 4: 98–115.

Jouve, B. and Lefevre, Ch. (2002) 'Globalism and Local Democracy', in: R. Hambleton *et al.* (eds) *Globalism and Local Democracy*, Hampshire: Palgrave: 185–200.

Judd, D. (2000) 'Strong Leadership', *Urban Studies*, Vol. 37, Nos. 5–6: 951–961.

Kavanagh, D. (1990) 'From Gentlemen to Players: Changes in Political Leadership', in: D. Kavanagh (ed.) *Politics and Personalities*, London: Macmillan.

Kellerman, B. (1984) 'Leadership as a Political Act', in: B. Kellerman (ed.) *Leadership: Multidisciplinary Perspectives*, Englewood Cliffs, NJ: Prentice-Hall: 63–89.

Kotter, J. P. and Lawrence, P. R. (1974) *Mayors in Action: Five Approaches to Urban Governance*, New York: John Wiley.

Leach, R. and Percy-Smith, J. (2001) *Local Governance in Britain*, Hampshire: Palgrave.

Leach, S. and Wilson, D. (2000) *Local Political Leadership*, Bristol: Policy Press.

Lyritsis, N. (2000) 'Parties and Local Elections', *Greek Journal of Political Sciences*, No. 15: 7–24.

Mouritzen, E. and Svara, J. (2002) *Leadership at the Apex. Politicians and Administrators in Western Local Governments*, Pittsburgh, PA: University of Pittsburgh Press.

Ostrom, E., Gardner, R. and Walker, J. (1994) *Rules, Games and Common-Pool Resources*, Ann Arbor, MI: The University of Michigan Press.

Page, E. and Goldsmith, M. (1987) *Central and Local Government Relations*, Beverly Hills: Sage.

Stewart, J. and Stoker, G. (1995) *Local Government in the 1990s*, London: Macmillan.

Stone, C. N. (1995) 'Political Leadership in Urban Politics', in: D. Judge (ed.) *Theories of Urban Politics*, London: Sage: 96–116.

Svara, J. (1994) *Facilitative Leadership in Local Government*, San Francisco, CA: Joey Bass.

Wollman, H. (2004) 'Urban Leadership in German Local Politics: The Rise, Role and Impact of the Directly Elected (Executive) Mayor', *International Journal of Urban and Regional Research*, Vol. 28, Issue 7: 150–165.

9   Leading localities
Rethinking the agenda

Robin Hambleton

Introduction

'If only we had real leadership – then things would improve.' How often have we heard this cry not just in the context of government and public service, but also in the corridors of private companies and not-for-profit agencies? 'Leadership' is widely touted as a panacea for organisational and societal failings – particularly if it is 'real leadership'. Sometimes the rhetoric about leadership has a negative 'blame the boss' spin. It suits those who are not performing their jobs very well to develop an explanation that attempts to locate the blame for their ineffectiveness elsewhere. More positively the plea for leadership can represent a genuine desire to see a clear vision articulated for the organisation – one that can shape clear standards for performance as well as inspire collective commitment to shared values and aspirations. Rhetoric aside – and despite the widespread agreement that leadership is very important – there is a startling degree of confusion over what leadership actually means.

This chapter attempts to map the broad contours of the leadership agenda now facing those involved in leading cities and localities in western democracies.[1] The first section discusses theories and concepts relating to leadership by drawing on various disciplines. This discussion suggests that there are very different ways of conceptualising leadership and that much of the thinking relating to leadership is impaired by attachment to out of date models. One point, given emphasis here, is that effective leadership is situational – that successful leadership is shaped by and responds to the context within which leadership is exercised. The next two sections outline two shifts that are reshaping the context for the exercise of local leadership – the move from local government to local governance and the shift from public administration to 'new public management'. These two shifts are not uniform across all countries but they do appear to have some kind of momentum in most OECD countries. It follows that forward-looking leadership needs to respond to these changes.

'Who are local leaders?' and 'How is local leadership exercised in practice?' are questions addressed in the next two sections. Here the argument draws on recent research in the fields of urban politics and public management. Local leadership takes place in particular places and in the context of local power structures that have been built up over a long period. It will be suggested that leadership ideas derived from advances in management theory need to be adapted and tuned to these local power systems.

Understanding leadership

Leadership is widely studied in psychology, sociology and political science as well as organisation theory. While there is disagreement about what constitutes good leadership there is widespread agreement on two points. First, the personal characteristics of individual leaders matter. Qualities like vision, strength, stamina, energy and commitment are associated with successful leadership. As Jones (1989) observes the biographical, or case study, approach to the study of leadership can, by examining the conduct and behaviour of known leaders, provide valuable insights on the exercise of leadership. Burns rightly argues in his classic book that: 'The study of leadership in general will be advanced by looking at leaders in particular' (Burns 1978: 27). In the field of urban politics there is, in fact, a considerable body of literature built around this approach. For example, the 'fly on the wall' study of Ed Rendell when he was Mayor of Philadelphia in the period 1992 to 1997 provides an excellent, albeit journalistic, picture of personal emotion and energy in city leadership (Bissinger 1997). Other more academic studies of US city leaders include books on Robert Moses of New York City (Caro 1975), Mayor Richard J. Daley of Chicago (Cohen and Taylor 2000) and Mayor Harold Washington also of Chicago (Rivlin 1992). A similar tradition exists in Europe with, for example, studies of Joseph Chamberlain, the Mayor of Birmingham (Garvin 1932).[2]

The second point of agreement in the leadership literature is that context matters. An effective approach to leadership in one setting might not be appropriate in another. On this analysis the accomplishments of individual leaders may be less important than forces – economic, political, institutional and cultural – shaping the context within which they exercise leadership. Sometimes called situational leadership, at other times contingent leadership, this approach has become popular within the field of management studies as well as political science.

If we take the management literature first, it is clear, for example, that leadership is different for first-level supervisors in an organisation than for chief executives. To illustrate the situational leadership approach in a management context we can refer to the model developed by Hersey (1984). This uses two dimensions of leadership, essentially the two familiar dimensions of management – the task dimension and the people (or relationship) dimension. The task dimension refers to the extent to which the leader engages in spelling out the duties and responsibilities of an individual or group. The people dimension concerns the extent to which the leader engages in two-way or multi-way communication. Hersey combines task and people into a two-by-two chart to generate four possible 'leadership styles': telling, selling, participating and delegating (see Table 9.1).

When is each style appropriate? The model says it depends on the subordinates' 'readiness level'. This readiness level stems from subordinate attitudes (how *willing* are they to do a good job) and level of skill (how *able* are they to do the job well). The model envisages four levels of subordinate readiness and argues that different styles are appropriate for different situations. For subordinates at the lowest level (unable and unwilling) the model suggests managers need to give strong direction 'telling' them what to do. At the next level up (unable but willing) the model suggests leaders explain what is needed and provide subordinates with an opportunity for clarification. At the next level, where subordinates are able but unwilling, the leader is advised to share ideas and have a participative discussion. At the highest level, where subordinates are both able and willing the leader should simply delegate – the subordinates will self manage rather well. This is not to suggest that this is a flawless model. Indeed, as noted by Bolman and Deal (1997), research has suggested that leadership by 'telling' is likely to demotivate staff. The more general lesson to draw from Table 9.1, however, is that the approach to leadership needs to be tuned to the particular situation.

A similar conclusion emerges from research on local leadership in urban politics. A recent UK study of leadership in urban governance, built around an examination of approaches to leadership in three localities, highlights the impact of contextual factors (Sweeting *et al.* 2004). By comparing experience in different parts of the country this study shows that the institutional design of the governance system of a city can be critical in shaping the leadership approach. The research shows, for example, that the constitution of the Greater London Authority provides a platform for

Table 9.1 A situational leadership model

Relationship (Degree of two way communication)	Task (Degree to which task is spelt out)	
	low	*high*
high	*Leadership through participation* Use when followers are able but unwilling	*Leadership through selling* Use when followers are unable but willing
low	*Leadership through delegation* Use when followers are able and willing	*Leadership through telling* Use when followers are unable and unwilling

Source: Adapted from Hersey (1984).

high profile, outgoing leadership by the directly elected mayor of London (Sweeting 2002). This institutional design provides both a strong legitimacy for leadership and a clear focus for leadership – the mayor enjoys a mandate from the citizens of the entire metropolis and is recognised by all concerned as the leader of the capital. This design contrasts with the governance arrangements in Bristol where confusion reigns – hardly anybody knows who the political leader of any of the local authorities is. The poor institutional design of the governance of Bristol – a fragmented city region with confusing municipal boundaries and a proliferation of complex partnerships with overlapping responsibilities – constrains leaders. They are forced into an endless process of negotiation with diverse stakeholders. Nobody has the legitimacy to exercise strong leadership for the locality as a whole with the result that even modest changes require leaders to participate in a delicate dance.

So far so good – leaders matter and context matters. But what is the nature of the leadership task? Burns (1978) draws a very helpful distinction between transactional and transformational approaches to leadership. Stated simply the old paradigm has defined leadership as a 'transaction' between a leader – often described as the 'boss' – and a follower, or 'subordinate'. A typical exchange is pay for doing a job but other exchanges can take place – such as the favours and feelings psychologists suggest are traded in social exchange theory. Transformational leadership is different in nature from transactional leadership. It has been described as a process of 'bonding' rather than 'bartering' (Sergiovanni 2000). Burns argues that leadership is about transforming social organisations, not about motivating employees to exchange work efforts for pay. Sashkin and Sashkin (2003) build on the argument advanced by Burns and suggest that a shared approach to vision building is crucial. In addition transformational leaders couple self-confidence with an orientation towards the empowerment of others and recognise the importance of building a caring organisational culture.

Sashkin and Sashkin (2003) also take the analysis of leadership a step further by unpacking the personal characteristics dimension outlined earlier into two parts – personality and behaviour. Thus, they outline research that suggests that leaders tend to have certain traits or personality characteristics – for example, they are often described as confident, persistent, patient, creative, intelligent, friendly and so on. Max Weber was the first social scientist to explore a trait that has been widely associated with leadership – charisma. This is an illusive concept but research by McClelland and others has shown that charisma often derives from a desire to have an impact on others. On this analysis the desire to gain and use power underpins the motivation of many leaders (McClelland 1987).

Turning to leadership behaviour Sashkin and Sashkin (2003) have, over a period of twenty years and through a variety of studies, articulated four transformational behaviours: communication leadership (focussing attention and making complex ideas clear by using metaphors), credible leadership (keeping promises and fulfilling commitments), caring leadership (valuing individual's special skills and abilities) and creating opportunities (producing empowered followers who become self-assured and confident of their own abilities).

Lastly, and it is a point we return to later as it is central to local government leadership, it is useful to consider the distinction that is now often made between 'leadership' and 'management'. As Bennis and Nanus (1985: 21) put it 'managers do things right, and leaders do the right thing'. Kotter (1988) sees managers planning, organising and controlling while leaders focus on the change-oriented process of visioning, networking and building relationships. But Gardner counsels against contrasting management and leadership too much:

> Every time I encounter utterly first-class managers they turn out to have quite a lot of the leader in them. Even the most visionary leader is faced on occasion with decisions that every manager faces: when to take a short-term loss to achieve a long-term gain, how to allocate scarce resources, whom to trust with a delicate assignment.
>
> (Gardner 1990: 4)

This interplay between leadership and management is vital in local government. It is, as we shall see later, misguided to claim that politicians 'lead' and officers 'manage'. Both have roles in leadership and management but the received models of political/administrative relations fail to recognise this. It has reached the point where these out of date models are impairing the development of effective local leadership in many countries. We return to this theme shortly but first we review two shifts that are reshaping the context within which local leadership takes place.

From local government to local governance

The term 'governance' is used in a variety of ways (Rhodes 1997; Andrew and Goldsmith 1998; Pierre and Peters 2000). For the purpose of this discussion it is sufficient to use these words in the way they are commonly used in practitioner as well as academic debates. *Government* refers to the formal institutions of the state. Government makes decisions within specific administrative and legal frameworks and uses public resources in a financially accountable way. Most important, government decisions are backed up by the legitimate hierarchical power of the state. *Governance*, on the other hand, involves government *plus* the looser processes of influencing and negotiating with a range of public and private sector agencies to achieve desired outcomes. A governance perspective encourages collaboration between the public, private and non-profit sectors to achieve mutual goals. While the hierarchical power of the state does not vanish, the emphasis in governance is on steering, influencing and coordinating the actions of others. There is recognition here that government can not go it alone. In governance relationships no one organisation can exercise hierarchical power over the others. The process is interactive because no single agency, public or private, has the knowledge and resource capacity to tackle the key problems unilaterally (Kooiman 1993, 2002).

Moving to the local level *local government* refers to democratically elected councils. *Local governance* is broader – it refers to the processes and structures of a variety of public, private and voluntary sector bodies at the local level. It acknowledges the diffusion of responsibility for collective provision and recognises the contribution of different levels and sectors (Andrew and Goldsmith 1998; Wilson 1998; John 2001). In most situations the elected local council is the only directly elected body in the local governance system and this is of critical importance. The rhetoric about governance can be viewed as a way of shifting responsibility from the state onto the private and voluntary sectors and civil society in general. This displacement of responsibility can also obscure lines of accountability to the citizen and the shift to governance certainly poses a major challenge to local democracy (Kearns and Paddison 2000). The movement to local governance can, however, be welcomed as an overdue shift from a perspective which sees local government simply as a vehicle for providing a range of important public services to a new emphasis on community leadership. This interpretation envisages the role of the local authority being extended beyond the tasks of service provision to embrace a concern for the overall well-being of an area (Clarke and Stewart 1998). This shift from government to governance is striking in the UK but it is also visible in other countries, for example, Germany (Banner 1999; Hambleton *et al.* 2002; Heinelt 2004).

The move from government to governance has profound implications for the exercise of local leadership. Out goes the old hierarchical model of the city 'boss' determining policy for city council services and imposing it on the bureaucracy, and in comes the facilitative leader reaching out to other stakeholders in efforts to influence decisions in other agencies that affect the local quality of life. Recognition of the shift from government to governance requires leading politicians and senior managers to adopt an outward looking approach and, crucially, to engage with the economic and other interests which influence the current and future well-being of the locality. Clarence Stone argued in 1980 that local politicians operate 'under *dual pressures* – one set based in electoral accountability and the other based in the hierarchical distribution of economic, organisational and cultural resources' (Stone 1980: 984, emphasis in original). Stephen Elkin refined this approach arguing that the division of roles between the state and the economy means that government must continually deal with the mandates of popular control and economic well-being. The way the division of roles develops and is handled gives rise to specific 'regimes'

(Elkin 1987). These depend, basically, on the strength of political elites relative to economic elites. Modern approaches to local leadership need to understand these local power structures and use the unique positional power of local government to intervene in these processes.

The academic study of urban politics and local power structures has benefited in recent years from valuable research on 'urban regimes' carried out, initially, by scholars in the USA (Stone 1989a; Lauria 1997). The regime approach, and Stone's work in particular, suggests that the power to command or dominate over others under modern conditions of social complexity in cities and communities is illusive: 'The power struggle concerns, not control and resistance, but gaining and fusing a capacity to act – *power to*, not *power over*' (Stone 1989a: 229; emphasis in original). In other words, power is structured and exercised in an effort to obtain results through cooperation, not to gain control over other agencies. This implies a very different approach to local leadership than top-down command and control.

From public administration to new public management

In parallel, and overlapping with, the movement from government to governance there has been a significant shift in the way public services are organised and run. In the UK context it is possible to discern two overlapping phases of change in local government: from public administration to corporate management (Hambleton 1978); and from corporate management to 'new public management' (Hoggett 1991; Dunleavy and Hood 1994; Pollitt and Bouckaert 2000). There is a good deal of rhetoric about these changes. Bold claims have been made about the virtues of private management practice and about the desirability of developing a more businesslike approach to the running of public services. But there is considerable confusion in the debate. In particular, the phrase 'new public management' has several meanings (Heinelt 1998; Wollman 2003). Because of the confusion, there is a risk that management-led reforms may come to lose sight of the underlying social purpose of public services. Researchers have also shown that 'new public management' is taking different forms in different countries.[3]

Figure 9.1 provides a way of unpacking the rhetoric surrounding 'new public management'. It identifies the three currents of change that have characterised public service reform strategies in the last twenty years or so.[4] The first broad alternative, associated in the 1980s with the radical right, seeks to challenge the very notion of collective and non-market provision for public need (Walsh 1995). Centring on the notion of privatisation it seeks to replace public provision with private. The second alternative, shown on the right of Figure 9.1, aims to preserve the notion of public provision, but seeks a radical reform of the manner in which this provision is undertaken. Thus, it seeks to replace the old, bureaucratic

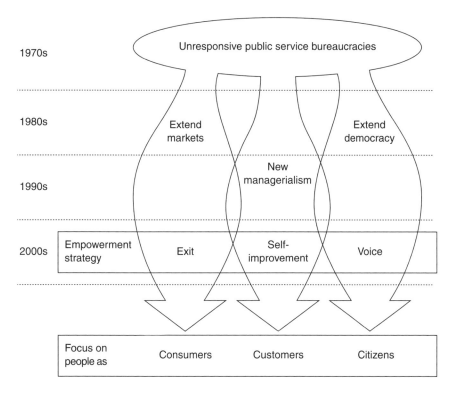

Figure 9.1 Public service reform strategies.

paternalistic model with a much more democratic model, often involving radical decentralisation to the neighbourhood level (Burns *et al.* 1994). The market approach treats people as consumers and the democratic approach treats people as citizens.

In Hirschman's terms the political right sought to give individuals the power of *exit* and the political left sought to give citizens the power of *voice* (Hirschman 1970). In the market model the consumer, dissatisfied with the product of one supplier of a service, can shift to another. The democratic model recognises that many public services cannot be individualised – they relate to groups of service users or citizens at large. Such collective interests can only be protected through enhanced participation and strengthened political accountability (Barber 1984). Hirschman is at pains to point out that, while exit and voice may be strongly contrasting empowerment mechanisms, they are not mutually exclusive.

The third broad strategy for public service reform shown in Figure 9.1 – and this is particularly important for the emerging leadership agenda for local government – attempts to distinguish a managerial as opposed to a political response to the problems confronting public service bureaucracies.

This response borrows from the competing political models in a way that simulates radical methods but in a form that preserves existing power relations between the producers and users of services. Citizens are redefined as customers. In place of the sometimes violent and unpredictable signals of exit and voice the model introduces a variety of managerial techniques (market research, user satisfaction surveys, complaints procedures, customer care programmes, focus groups, call centres, interactive websites etc.) to provide more gentle and manageable 'feedback'.

On this analysis the 'new public management' can be seen to be associated with two of the strands in Figure 9.1 – the market and managerialist reform strategies. This interpretation is consistent with the analysis put forward by Hood (1991) who suggests that 'new public management' involves a marriage of two streams of ideas: the new institutional economics and business-type managerialism. But this is a narrow agenda for public management reform as it fails to recognise the vital importance of the third strand in Figure 9.1. Enhancing democratic vitality is also part of the *management* task in modern local government. Democratic renewal requires managers as well as politicians to focus on people as citizens, not just customers or consumers. Recognition of the importance of active citizen participation in local governance has profound implications for the managerial leadership as well as political leadership of local government. Elsewhere I have named this broader approach the 'new city management' and explained how it can bring about a new and more sophisticated level of interaction between politicians, managers and citizens (Hambleton 2002).

Who are the local leaders?

It is a simple question to ask 'Who are the local leaders?' but answers will vary depending on country and context. At a conceptual level it is possible to distinguish between three sets of institutions which, together, provide the capacity to govern any given city or locality: 1) government itself, 2) corporate business and 3) the network of civic organisations which can be very influential in shaping public debate on policy issues and spurring voluntary activity in the community (Stone 1989b: 147). All three sectors can provide platforms for the emergence of local leaders. The relative power and influence of leaders based in these various sectors varies from country to country and city to city. For example, the power of elected politicians to effect change might be expected to be greater in countries with a strong welfare state and a long established commitment to public service – say Norway – as compared with countries where the role of government is seen as less important and is less well funded – say the USA. Conversely, and not surprisingly, we can expect that the power of business elites in the city leadership of, say, Dallas to be greater than in Oslo. Context, traditions, public expectations, culture – these all have a bearing on who is in a position to exercise local leadership. The variation in the balance of power between the three sets of institutions is shaped not just by the national context, but also by regional economic factors. Thus, city leadership in a declining region can be expected to have a different configuration from leadership in an area experiencing an economic boom, not least because the private sector enthusiasm to invest in the area will vary.

As noted earlier research comparing different 'urban regimes' throws light on these issues – this research maps the way power is configured in different localities. Building on earlier approaches to the study of 'community power' (Dahl 1961; Hunter 1953; Bachrach and Baratz 1970; Stone 1989a) DiGaetano and Klemanski (1999) compared the governance of Birmingham and Bristol in England with Detroit and Boston in the USA. From this and other urban research they identify four 'modes of governance': 1) pro-growth, 2) growth management, 3) social reform and 4) caretaker. These are not watertight categories but it is clear that different kinds of leaders tend to move to the fore depending on which mode of governance has dominance. Thus, for example, in a caretaker regime, where the governing strategy is limited to routine service provision, the leaders are likely to be fiscally conservative politicians and officials partnering with small property owners. In a social reform regime, where the focus is on community development rather than business development, elected politicians, progressive development and planning professionals and lower class community activists are likely to be the significant players.

This literature raises interesting questions for city leaders and for social movements aspiring to generate political platforms for the emergence of new leaders. The research suggests that urban regimes do, indeed, shape patterns of governance and, as a consequence, the political space available for local leaders. But perhaps the reverse is also true. Innovation in local politics can certainly generate change in urban regimes, and even the overthrow of a once dominant regime. It follows that effective leaders may be able to build new regimes or, at least, re-orient established regimes.

Within government there are two main sets of players – elected politicians and appointed officers. It is normally the elected politicians who are seen as the main leadership figures in a locality. They enjoy a political mandate from local citizens and, even if voter turnout in local elections is not very high, their legitimacy to speak out on behalf of local people is difficult to challenge. In practice, elected politicians take on a variety of roles ranging from voicing local concerns and responding to the grievances of constituents through to major leadership responsibilities as, say, a committee chair, cabinet member or directly elected mayor. All elected politicians exercise leadership roles in their locality but the nature of this leadership varies considerably – from representation of a neighbourhood through leadership on a key topic to leadership of the whole local authority (Audit Commission 1997). The nature of party politics can have a profound impact on local political leadership. In some situations most of the important public policy decisions are taken in secretive party group meetings, in others the conflict between parties can lead to a kind of 'points scoring' approach to local debate and discussion. Discussions with leading councillors in UK local government in the mid 1990s revealed growing recognition of the governance dimension of local leadership referred to earlier (Hambleton and Holder 1995). Thus, many local authority leaders felt that strengthening civic leadership and promoting the image of the area to outsiders deserved more attention.

A long-standing myth in local government is that there is a sharp separation of roles between politicians and officers. The old adage that politicians decide on policy and officers implement it was challenged over twenty years ago by research on policy implementation. This showed that implementation is an interactive and negotiative process between those seeking to put policy into effect and those upon whom action depends (Barrett and Fudge 1981). More recently Svara (2001) has demonstrated how early contributors to the field of public administration acknowledged a policy role for administrators that has often been ignored partly because, over the years, the dichotomy became a 'useful myth' (Miller 2000: 314–315). The dichotomy idea shields administrators from scrutiny and serves the interest of politicians who can pass responsibility for unpopular decisions to administrators (Peters 1995: 177–178). A more sophisticated conceptualisation of the politician/officer interface recognises that *both* groups contribute to both policy development and local leadership.

Mouritzen and Svara (2002) provide a valuable cross-national analysis of 'leadership at the apex' of local government in fourteen countries. The authors do not examine the role of leaders outside the institution of local government, rather they provide a detailed and fascinating picture of the roles of mayors (and other leading politicians) and the way they interface with their Chief Executive Officers (CEOs). This research shows that overlapping leadership roles between senior politicians and CEOs is the norm. The leadership partnership can take different forms and the research categorises different ways of pairing the leadership roles. Sometimes the CEO is dependent, sometimes interdependent and sometimes independent. In most situations, however, there is a complementarity of politics and administration. Complementarity implies separate roles, but roles that come together in a mutually supportive way (Mouritzen and Svara 2002: 248–256).

A study of managerial leadership for the UK Society of Local Authority Chief Executives (SOLACE) suggested that chief executives have a key role in leading change and developing the organisation of the authority (Hambleton 1999). Four leadership roles were identified: providing strategic advice to politicians; managing processes relating to decisions; taking decisions on behalf of the council; and influencing other agencies. Chief executives interviewed for the research suggested that the fourth role was expanding quite quickly and this chimes with the shift from government to governance discussed earlier (Travers *et al.* 1997). In the UK context the development of continuous learning opportunities for chief executives has identified five key capacities: working with the political dimension; leading the organisation; developing self knowledge; developing effective external relationships; and maintaining a focus on strategic and long-term issues (Broussine 1998).

Moving outside local government attention needs to be given not just to the business interests highlighted by urban regime theory but also to a variety of other players who may, depending on the local context, be in a position to exercise decisive leadership. Sometimes these figures are to be found outside local government but inside other organs of the state. It may be, for example, that regional state bodies contain key actors who play a significant local leadership role. Certainly, as it becomes clearer that regions form the effective spatial unit in an era of global economic competition, leadership for relatively large metropolitan regions is now receiving increased attention in many countries (Jouve and Lefevre 2002).

In some countries the non-profit (or third sector) plays a vital role in local leadership. Religious groups, trade unions and, at times, universities as well as charitable foundations can make a significant contribution in helping to set the local agenda as well as in relation to specific community projects. At the local level community based leaders can come to play a particularly important role, not least in situations where higher levels of government – perhaps national government, perhaps the European Community – have chosen to target regeneration or neighbourhood renewal funds on particular localities. Research on community leaders in area regeneration partnerships in the UK suggests, however, that state agencies are still not that skilled at working with local people in ways which support their neighbourhood leadership role (Purdue *et al.* 2000). Taylor (2003: 132–134) also shows how community based leaders can be caught in a kind of no man's land between their communities and the decision makers, accused on the one hand of failing to deliver and on the other of being unrepresentative.

In summary, local leaders comprise a mixed bag. In some situations a powerful, directly elected mayor or council leader can give the impression of exercising decisive leadership of the locality with other actors having relatively minor roles. This discussion of 'Who are the leaders?' has suggested, however, that it is more than likely that, in any given locality, there is a pattern of *dispersed leadership*. In modern conditions of social complexity power is fragmented and this means that leadership involves a process of connecting the fragments. Elected politicians, appointed officers, business leaders, non-profit organisations, religious groups, community representatives and figures from higher education can all be found carrying out leadership roles in modern systems of urban governance. However, as discussed more fully in Chapter 2, while all these players can make a significant contribution to local leadership, their legitimacy to exercise formal leadership varies. In democratic societies there can be no argument with the view that accountability to the citizens has to underpin the formal exercise of power by local leaders. It follows that elected politicians should be expected to play the decisive role. Local elections matter not least because they provide the legitimacy for the exercise of local leadership.

Locality leadership in action

Borrowing from Fainstein (1990) it can be suggested that there are two ways of entering a discussion of locality (or city) leadership in action. The global approach scrutinises the wider context within which cities operate and draws attention to the constraints on local leadership. Some, but not all, commentaries adopting this approach conclude that the scope for local leadership is trivial. Thus, according to one influential study (Peterson 1981), cities are constrained by local and regional economic competition and must give priority to policies that promote economic growth. Cities that do not comply with these forces will be punished by loss of private investment, jobs and tax revenue. The second approach, which works from the inside out, examines the forces creating the particularities of a specific place – its economic base, its social make up, its constellation of political interests and so on. In this formulation local political leaders and civic elites may turn out to have a considerable impact on the fortunes of the city and this is certainly the position adopted by Judd (2000). In practice both perspectives are helpful. The same city can be regarded as part of a totality and as a unique outcome of its particular history. Comparative academic studies that combine both a global and a local perspective are now on the increase and this combination of perspectives is leading to a better understanding of the scope for and limits on local leadership (Savitch and Kantor 2002).

Recognising this wider context for the exercise of leadership, what options for local leadership are available? The literature on mayoral leadership provides a starting point for this discussion, although a warning note is needed as much of this literature is based on analysis of US cities and, as mentioned earlier, the national context can have a profound effect on local leadership (see the contribution of Bäck in this book). Yates (1977) provides one formulation based on the argument that mayors differ along two central dimensions: 1) the amount of political and financial resources that they possess and 2) the degree of activism and innovation that they display in their daily work. This approach generates a two-by-two matrix envisaging four 'leadership styles': 1) crusader, 2) entrepreneur, 3) boss, and 4) broker (see Table 9.2).

Crusaders lack resources and political clout but they want to make a difference. They rely heavily on dramatising issues and seeking to develop

Table 9.2 Some possible mayoral leadership styles

Political power base	Activism/innovation	
	high	*low*
strong	Entrepreneur	Boss
weak	Crusader	Broker

Source: Adapted from Yates (1977).

support through the force of principles and personality. Entrepreneurs are, for Yates, the strongest mayors – they have sufficient political and financial resources to allow them to act decisively on substantive policy issues and usually give a high level of attention to economic development policy. They can push and deliver on big projects. Boss mayors also have substantial financial and political resources but they focus their efforts on maintaining control rather than on setting new policy agendas. Finally, broker mayors lack financial and political resources and limit their vision to mediating conflicts between various interest groups.

This framework provides a helpful starting point but it should be noted that there is a substantial US literature on mayoral leadership (Kotter and Laurence 1974; Ferman 1985; Svara 1990). In particular, it should be noted that more recent research on US mayors has suggested a shift towards facilitative leadership (Svara 1994). This does not mean that earlier conceptualisations of mayoral leadership should be discarded out of hand. Rather we need to recognise the importance of the move from government to governance referred to earlier. Leadership models developed in the 1970s were formulated at a time when the monolithic power of city halls was greater.

Now, in most OECD countries, effective city governance requires a high level of partnership working among agencies. In this changed context leadership has less to do with followership than with collaborative endeavour (Chesterton 2002). Effective leaders now work to find ways of discovering diverse views and strive to build consensus among multiple actors. This means that facilitative leadership styles are being adopted by a growing number of local political leaders, mayors, CEOs and agency heads.

In the UK context the issue of local leadership started to attract serious interest in public policy circles in the mid 1990s. Tony Blair, as Leader of the Opposition made several speeches arguing that local authorities needed stronger and more outgoing leadership (Hambleton 1998). In 1996 I was commissioned to examine possible leadership models and I was fortunate to be able to carry out this study in partnership with one of the leading local authority politicians in the UK – Steve Bullock (Hambleton and Bullock 1996).[5] In carrying out this research we asked leading figures in UK local government what they thought constituted successful local authority leadership. The indicators of good leadership that emerged are summarised in Table 9.3.

More recently a similar framework has been developed by Leach and Wilson (2002). Informal soundings with local leaders in other countries suggest that the indicators listed in Table 9.3 are relevant to an international conversation about local leadership. They provide the outlines of a set of aspirations for local leadership. Whether local leaders are able to deliver good performance as measured by these criteria is a question that can only be answered through empirical research.

What about the role of the chief executive or city manager? Earlier it was suggested that it is misleading to believe that there is a sharp demarcation in roles between politicians and officers. Senior officers and particularly the CEO or city manager are not mere servants of the elected politicians. They have great professional skill and experience and exercise important leadership roles alongside the politicians. Cross-national research on local government CEOs has drawn a distinction between two approaches to leadership. These are the 'classical' and the 'political' bureaucrat (see Klausen and Magnier 1998).

The classical bureaucrat is more of a background figure and, in terms of the distinction between management and leadership drawn earlier, he/she lies at the 'management' end of the spectrum – the classical CEO focusses on 'doing things right'. The political bureaucrat has a more proactive style

Table 9.3 Indicators of good local political leadership

- *Articulating a clear vision for the area*
  Setting out an agenda of what the future of the area should be and developing strategic policy direction. Listening to local people and leading initiatives
- *Promoting the qualities of the area*
  Building civic pride, promoting the benefits of the locality and attracting inward investment
- *Winning resources*
  Winning power and funding from higher levels of government and maximizing income from a variety of sources
- *Developing partnerships*
  Successful leadership is characterised by the existence of a range of partnerships, both internal and external, working to a shared view of the needs of the local community
- *Addressing complex social issues*
  The increasingly fragmented nature of local government and the growing number of service providers active in a given locality means that complex issues which cross boundaries, or are seen to fall between areas of interest, need to be taken up by leaderships which have an over view and can bring together the right mix of agencies to tackle a particular problem
- *Maintaining support and cohesion*
  Managing disparate interests and keeping people on board are essential if the leadership is to maintain authority

---

Source: Adapted from Hambleton and Bullock (1996: 8–9).

on 'doing things right'. The political bureaucrat has a more proactive style and is more towards the 'leadership' end of the spectrum – the political CEO is still concerned with 'doing things right' but she or he is even more concerned with 'doing the right thing'. It would be unwise to suggest that features of the classical bureaucrat are simply old hat and can be discarded in favour of the more political approach. Rather the fascinating challenge now confronting all local government leaders – whether they are politicians or officers – is how to strike the right balance in relation to their local situation. Having said that the idea of the town clerk 'administering' local authority services is now surely an out of date concept. The local government town clerk is, in most western democracies, being replaced by a CEO (or city manager). This person is appointed to 'manage', not administer, the local authority on behalf of the elected members. In the best local authorities the CEO is a dynamic executive leader who is capable of working closely with elected members and brokering community interests. The political CEO wants to work closely with the political leaders to help the politicians achieve high performance on the indicators of good political leadership set out in Table 9.3.

How do local leaders relate to local citizens? Earlier it was suggested that the old, hierarchical models of leadership are out of date. A top-down approach in which the 'boss' hands down instructions to a grateful – or not so grateful – band of subordinates or followers is anachronistic. We have seen how the politician/officer relationship in modern local governance is better seen as a kind of partnership with benefits flowing from mutual respect and role sharing. The same is also true in relation to citizen involvement in decision making. In all Western democracies well-informed and confident citizens are putting new demands on local government, as well as other public agencies, to be more open, more responsive and more accountable. As Table 9.1 makes clear the bureaucratic paternalism of the past – in which politicians and officers made decisions over the heads of local people – has been challenged by new approaches to user and citizen empowerment. These changes have profound implications for the exercise of local leadership.

Three points stand out. The first need is for leaders to develop their listening and learning skills. In a complex and rapidly changing society it is essential for leaders to be really well tuned in to the concerns of all groups in society. The discussion above has suggested that good political leadership is associated with listening as well as leading (see Table 9.3). And Table 9.4 shows how the political bureaucrat is well informed about citizens' viewpoints. Second, it is important to recognise the legitimacy of different viewpoints. Politicians, officers and citizens draw on different sources of legitimacy – elected members enjoy a political mandate from citizens, officers bring managerial and professional skills as well as impartiality and citizens have a democratic right to be heard and to hold

Table 9.4 The classical and the political bureaucrat

The classical bureaucrat	The political bureaucrat
• Guide subordinate staff in day-to-day handling of activities • Manage economic affairs, accounts and budgetary control • Ensure that rules and regulations are followed • Provide the mayor with legal, economic and other kinds of technical advice	• Formulate ideas and visions • Promote and encourage new projects in the community • Provide the mayor with political advice • Be informed about citizens' viewpoints • Develop and implement norms concerning the proper roles of politicians vis-à-vis bureaucrats • Influence decision-making processes in order to secure sensible and efficient solutions

Source: Adapted from Klausen and Magnier (1998: 13).

government to account. Much of the management literature on leadership is built around practice in the private sector and this limits its usefulness in the context of democratic institutions where citizen rights are altogether different from the rights of the consumer or customer (Marshall 1950). Acceptance of this argument means that leaders need to do much more than listen – they need to empower neglected voices in the democratic process if decisions are not to be dominated by the powerful and the connected. Third, it seems clear that local leaders should adopt a transformational rather than a transactional approach. As explained earlier this means, inter alia, developing credible leadership (keeping promises and fulfilling commitments) and creating opportunities for *others* to exercise power. Striving to gather all decision-making power to the centre merely creates an overloaded and ineffective centre. The effective modern leader recognises the value of decentralising authority not just to officers but to citizens as well (Burns *et al.* 1994).

Conclusion

This chapter has examined the nature of local leadership in conditions of modern social complexity. It has been suggested that a number of academic disciplines can throw light on the nature of the local leadership task. More than that it can be claimed that a multi-disciplinary approach is essential if we are to understand local leadership and, in the light of that understanding, develop advice for those involved in or aspiring to local leadership roles. The literature on leadership – in management studies, political science and psychology – suggests that both leaders and context matter. This is encouraging. Leaders *can* make a difference. But their success will, to a great extent, be determined by how well they adapt their approach to the local context. It follows that off-the-shelf advice on leadership from private sector management consultants is likely to miss the mark.

Two major trends have been outlined which are reshaping the context for local leadership – the shift from local government to local governance and the move from public administration to new city management. The former brings home the importance of recognising that government cannot go it alone. Leaders need to see themselves not as having *power over* events but as having *power to* influence events (Stone 1989a). This reframing puts a premium on partnership working and alliance building. Top-down leadership does not work in a partnership setting – hence the need to rethink traditional models. The second shift – this one in the world of administration and management – takes thinking beyond the limiting concepts of the 'new public management' to open up a new set of possibilities for politicians and officers in the local governance system. Instead of trying to redefine local people as either consumers or customers the new city management puts democratic renewal high on the managerial, not just the political, agenda. In this model new and constructive relationships between politicians, officers and citizens are being created.

In any given city or locality there will be a range of local leaders – some will be elected politicians, others will be significant players in the business sector, yet others will be civic leaders based in non-profit organisations, trade unions, religious institutions and so on. The chapter has suggested that appointed officers in local government constitute an important group of leaders who have been neglected in the literature. In particular, CEOs or city managers have a vital role to play not just in developing the organisation of the authority but also in contributing to the overall leadership of the locality. It is a complete myth to suggest that politicians lead and officers follow. Officers, and particularly senior officers, are better seen as full partners with local politicians in the local leadership task. There are different ways of handling the relationship between the top elected official and the top officer. But in all cases it is imperative that appointed officials are fully accountable to the elected politicians – without clarity on this point accountability of the city government to the citizenry will crumble.

The chapter has set out some indicators of good political leadership – as derived from the views of existing local leaders in the UK – see Table 9.3. There is no suggestion that these represent a definitive checklist, rather they are advanced to provoke fresh thinking about the local leadership agenda. In relation to officers it has been suggested that values associated with the 'classical bureaucrat' need updating to accommodate ideas associated with what has been described as the 'political bureaucrat' (Klausen and Magnier 1998). The chapter has examined various models of mayoral leadership and, while more collective approaches to leadership are common in some European countries, this largely US literature can pose helpful challenges and questions for local leaders in any context.

Arguably the most important message of this chapter is that citizens – their needs, their aspirations and their rights – should lie at the heart of the new local leadership agenda. At times it may be appropriate to treat public service users as consumers of products or customers of services but these conceptualisations of members of the public are profoundly limiting in the context of a democratic institution. This is because they are built around the notion that government should become more like a business when, in practice, this is a misguided view. Most of the important decisions in government involve complex trade-offs between competing interests – they have different impacts on different groups of citizens. Government is also required to regulate behaviour in society. A range of government activities – land use planning, social work, environmental health, safety standards, policing, the courts, the prison service – limit the freedom of the individual in order to achieve benefits for the community as a whole. These major choices relating to the distribution of benefits and control of behaviour in society can only be addressed through a political process. In his analysis of the role of business and management concepts in public service Mintzberg suggests that the current malaise about government stems from it being *too much* like business rather than not enough: 'I am not a mere customer of my government, thank you' (Mintzberg 1996: 77).

A prize to strive for – and this is where bold innovation in practice in particular cities is so important – is to blend managerial innovation with democratic revitalisation. Two flawed approaches to local government reform need to be challenged: first, the idea of enlightened politicians fighting to impose change on recalcitrant and incompetent city hall bureaucracies and, second, the reverse scenario of bright and able local government professionals striving to transform public services against the wishes of slow moving and out of touch elected officials. There may be localities where these stereotypes apply but they do not reflect the mainstream of local government in Europe and North America. The task of leading localities in the coming period should draw strength from being citizen focussed – from working with local communities in new and inventive ways. Old-style politics involving a politician-dominated approach to decision making and new-style managerialism, which undervalues the political contribution to public service, are both past their 'sell by' date. Creating new ways of combining political and managerial innovation to enhance responsiveness to citizen concerns is now the central challenge for all those concerned to improve city leadership.

Notes

1 I use the terms 'city' and 'locality' interchangeably in this chapter as the leadership agenda for those leading cities, counties, towns and rural areas have much in common.
2 For a German–USA comparison of mayors and other urban political leaders see Gissendanner 2001 and for the German debate Gissendanner 2002.
3 See Naschold (1997) and his work for the Bertelsmann Foundation (see also Wegener 1998) and as a recent analysis of public service reform comparing Norway, Sweden, New Zealand and Australia, Christensen and Laegreid (2001).
4 I would like to acknowledge the contributions of Danny Burns and Paul Hoggett in developing this framework in the early 1990s (Burns *et al.* 1994: 22).
5 Steve Bullock was the leader of the London Borough of Lewisham in the early 1990s. He later became one of the very first directly elected mayors in UK history when he was elected as Mayor of Lewisham in 2002.

References

Andrew, C. and Goldsmith, M. (1998) 'From Local Government to Local Governance – and Beyond?' *International Political Science Review*, Vol. 19, No. 2: 101–117.
Audit Commission (1997) *Representing the People. The Role of Councillors*, Management paper. London: The Audit Commission.
Bachrach, S. B. and Baratz, M. (1970) *Power and Poverty*, London: Oxford University Press.
Banner, G. (1999) 'From Government to Governance: German Local Authorities Between Regulation, Service Provision and Community Development', *The Annals of Public Administration Research*, No. 17, (1999–2000), The Research Institute for Public Administration, Hanyang University, Seoul, Korea.
Barber, B. R. (1984) *Strong Democracy. Participatory Politics for a New Age*, Berkeley, CA: University of California Press.
Barrett, S. and Fudge, C. (eds) (1981) *Policy and Action*, London: Methuen.
Bennis, W. G. and Nanus, B. (1985) *Leaders: Strategies for Taking Charge*, New York: Harper Collins.
Bissinger, B. (1997) *Prayer for the City*, New York: Vintage Books.
Bolman, L. G. and Deal, T. E. (1997) *Reframing Organisations. Artistry, Choice and Leadership*, San Francisco, CA: Jossey-Bass.
Broussine, M. (1998) *A Scheme for Continuous Learning for SOLACE Members*, Bristol: Bristol Business School, University of the West of England.
Burns, D., Hambleton, R. and Hoggett, P. (1994) *The Politics of Decentralisation*, London: Macmillan.
Burns, J. M. (1978) *Leadership*, New York: Harper and Row.
Caro, R. A. (1975) *The Power Broker*, New York: Vintage.
Chesterton, D. (2002) *Local Authority? How to Develop Leadership for Better Public Service*, London: Demos.
Christensen, T. and Laegreid, P. (eds) (2001) *New Public Management*, Aldershot: Ashgate.
Clarke, M. and Stewart, J. (1998) *Community Governance, Community Leadership and the New Local Government*, York: Joseph Rowntree Foundation.

Cohen, A. and Taylor, E. (2000) *American Pharao*, Boston: Little Brown.

Dahl, R. (1961) *Who Governs?*, New Haven: Yale University Press.

Di Gaetano, A. and Klemanski, J. S. (1999) *Power and City Governance. Comparative Perspectives on Urban Development*, Minneapolis, MN: University of Minnesota Press.

Dunleavy, P. and Hood, C. (1994) 'From Old Public Administration to New Public Management', *Public Money and Management*, Vol. 14: 9–16.

Elkin, S. (1987) *The City in the American Republic*, Chicago, IL: University of Chicago Press.

Fainstein, S. (1990) 'The Changing World Economy and Urban Restructuring', in: D. Judd and M. Parkinson (eds) *Leadership and Urban Regeneration*, London: Sage.

Ferman, B. (1985) *Governing the Ungovernable City*, Philadelphia, PA: Temple University Press.

Gardner, J. W. (1990) *On Leadership*, New York: The Free Press.

Garvin, J. L. (1932) *The Life of Joseph Chamberlain*, London: Macmillan.

Gissendanner, S. (2001) *Strategic Action in Hard Times. Local Responses to Deindustrialization in the United States and Germany*, unpublished PhD Thesis, University of Georgia.

—— (2002) 'Die bedeutung des Bürgermeisters für die strategische Entscheidungsfähigkeit deutscher Großstädte', in: J. Bogumil (ed.) *Kommunale Entscheidungsprozesse im Wandel. Theoretische und empirische Analysen*, Opladen: Leske + Budrich: 91–109.

Hambleton, R. (1978) *Policy Planning and Local Government*, London: Hutchinson.

—— (1998) 'Strengthening Political Leadership in UK Local Government', *Public Money and Management*, January–March: 41–48.

—— (1999) *Modernisation: Developing Managerial Leadership*, Merseyside: SOLACE.

—— (2002) 'The New City Management', in: R. Hambleton, H. V. Savitch and M. Stewart (eds) *Globalism and Local Democracy. Challenge and Change in Europe and North America*, Basingstoke: Palgrave.

Hambleton, R. and Bullock, S. (1996) *Revitalising Local Democracy – the Leadership Options*, London: Association of District Councils/Local Government Management Board (now Local Government Association/Improvement and Development Agency).

Hambleton, R. and Holder, A. (1995) *Shaping Future Authorities. Achieving Successful Organisational Change*, Luton: Local Government Management Board.

Hambleton, R., Savitch, H. V. and Stewart, M. (eds) (2002) *Globalism and Local Democracy. Challenge and Change in Europe and North America*, Basingstoke: Palgrave.

Heinelt, H. (1998) *Recent Debates on the Modernisation of Local Politics and Administration. An Attempt at a Systematic Overview*, Paper to the Third European Conference on Public Administration Modernisation, May, University of Lille (also published as 'Neuere Debatten zur Modernisierung der Kommunalpolitik. Ein Überblick', in: H. Heinelt and M. Mayer (eds) *Modernisierung der Kommunalpolitik*, Opladen: Leske + Budrich: 12–28).

—— (2004) 'Governance auf lokaler Ebene', in: A. Benz (ed.) *Governance. Eine Einführung*, Opladen: Leske + Budrich (forthcoming).

Hersey, P. (1984) *The Situational Leader*, New York: Warner Books.

Hirschman, A. O. (1970) *Exit, Voice and Loyalty*, Cambridge, MA: Harvard University Press.

Hoggett, P. (1991) 'A New Management in the Public Sector?', *Policy and Politics*, Vol. 19, No. 4: 243–256.

Hood, C. (1991) 'A Public Management for all Seasons', *Public Administration*, Vol. 69: 3–19.

Hunter, F. (1953) *Community Power Structure*, New York: Doubleday.

John, P. (2001) *Local Governance in Europe*, London: Sage.

Jones, B. D. (ed.) (1989) *Leadership and Politics*, Lawrence, KN: University Press of Kansas.

Jouve, B. and Lefevre, C. (2002) 'Metropolitan Governance and Institutional Dynamics', in: R. Hambleton, H. V. Savitch and M. Stewart (eds) *Globalism and Local Democracy – Challenge and Change in Europe and North America*, Basingstoke: Palgrave.

Judd, D. (2000) 'Strong Leadership', *Urban Studies*, Vol. 37, Nos. 5–6: 951–961.

Kearns, A. and Paddison, R. (2000) 'New Challenges for Urban Governance', *Urban Studies*, Vol. 37, Nos. 5–6: 845–850.

Klausen, K. K. and Magnier, A. (1998) *The Anonymous Leader. Appointed Chief Executive Officers in Western Local Government*, Odense: Odense University Press.

Kooiman, J. (1993) 'Social-Political Governance: Introduction', in: J. Kooiman (ed.) *Modern Governance*, London: Sage.

—— (2002) 'Governance. A Social-Political Perspective', in: J. R. Grote and B. Gbikpi (eds) *Participatory Governance. Political and Societal Implications*, Opladen: Leske + Budrich: 71–96.

Kotter, J. P. (1988) *The Leadership Factor*, New York: The Free Press.

Kotter, J. and Laurence, R. (1974) *Mayors in Action. Five Approaches to Urban Governance*, London: John Wiley and Sons.

Lauria, M. (ed.) (1997) *Reconstructing Urban Regime Theory*, Thousand Oaks, CA: Sage.

Leach, S. and Wilson, D. (2000) *Local Political Leadership*, Bristol: Policy Press.

—— (2002) 'Rethinking Local Political Leadership', *Public Administration*. Vol. 80, No. 4: 665–689.

Marshall, T. H. (1950) *Citizenship and Social Class*, Cambridge: Cambridge University Press.

McClelland, D. C. (1987) *Human Motivation*, New York: Cambridge University Press.

Miller, G. (2000) 'Above Politics: Credible Commitment and Efficiency in the Design of Public Agencies', *Journal of Public Administration Research and Theory*, Vol. 10, No. 2, 289–327.

Mintzberg, H. (1996) 'Managing Government, Governing Management', *Harvard Business Review*, May–June: 75–83.

Mouritzen, P. E. and Svara, J. H. (2002) *Leadership at the Apex. Politicans and Administrators in Western Local Governments*, Pittsburgh, PA: University of Pittsburgh Press.

Naschold, F. (1997) 'Binnenmodernisierung, Wettbewerb, Haushaltskonsolidierung. Internationale Erfahrungen zur Verwaltungsreform', in: H. Heinelt and M. Mayer (eds) *Modernisierung der Kommunalpolitik*, Opladen: Leske + Budrich: 89–117.

Peters, B. G. (1995) *The Politics of Bureaucracy*, White Plains, NY: Longman Publishers.

Peterson, P. (1981) *City Limits*, Chicago, IL: University of Chicago Press.

Pierre, J. and Peters, B. G. (2000) *Governance, Politics and the State*, London: Macmillan.

Pollitt, C. and Bouckaert, G. (2000) *Public Management Reform. A Comparative Analysis*, Oxford: Oxford University Press.

Purdue, D., Razzaque, K., Hambleton, R. and Stewart, M. (2000) *Community Leadership in Area Regeneration*, Bristol: Policy Press.

Rhodes, R. A. W. (1997) *Understanding Governance*, Buckingham: Open University Press.

Rivlin, G. (1992) *Fire on the Prairie*, New York: Henry Holt.

Sashkin, M. and Sashkin, M. G. (2003) *Leadership that Matters*, San Francisco, CA: Berrett-Koehler Publishers Inc.

Savitch, H. V. and Kantor, P. (2002) *Cities in the International Marketplace*, Princeton, NJ: Princeton University Press.

Sergiovanni, T. J. (2000) *The Lifeworld of Leadership*, San Francisco, CA: Jossey-Bass.

Stone, C. (1980) 'Systematic Power in Community Decision Making', *American Political Science Review*, Vol. 74: 978–990.

—— (1989a) *Regime Politics: Governing Atlanta 1946–1988*, Lawrence, KN: University Press of Kansas.

—— (1989b) 'Paradigms, Power, and Urban Leadership', in: B. D. Jones (ed.) *Leadership and Politics*, Lawrence, KN: University Press of Kansas.

Svara, J. H. (1990) *Official Leadership in the City. Patterns of Conflict and Cooperation*, Oxford: Oxford University Press.

—— (ed.) (1994) *Facilitative Leadership in Local Government. Lessons from Successful Mayors and Chairpersons*, San Francisco, CA: Jossey-Bass.

—— (2001) 'The Myth of the Dichotomy: Complementarity of Politics and Administration in the Past and Future of Public Administration', *Public Administration Review*, Vol. 61, No. 2: 176–183.

Sweeting, D. (2002) 'Leadership in Urban Governance: The Mayor of London', *Local Government Studies*, Vol. 28, No. 1: 3–20.

Sweeting, D., Hambleton, R., Huxham, C., Stewart, M. and Vangen, S. (2004) 'Leadership and Partnership in Urban Governance: Evidence from London, Bristol and Glasgow', in: M. Boddy and M. Parkinson (eds) *City Matters. Competitiveness, Cohesion and Urban Governance*, Bristol: Policy Press.

Taylor, M. (2003) *Public Policy in the Community*, Basingstoke: Palgrave.

Travers, T., Jones, G. and Burnham, J. (1997) *The Role of the Local Authority Chief Executive in Local Governance*, York: Joseph Rowntree Foundation.

Walsh, K. (1995) *Public Services and Market Mechanisms. Competition, Contracting and the New Public Management*, London: Macmillan.

Wegener, A. (1998) 'Kommunale verwaltungsrestrukturierung im internationalen vergleich', in: D. Grunow and H. Wollman (eds) *Lokale Verwaltungsreform in Aktion. Fortschritte und Fallstricke*, Basel, Boston, MA and Berlin: Birkhäuser Verlag: 337–353.

Wilson, D. (1998) 'From Local Government to Local Governance: Recasting British Local Democracy', *Democratisation*, Vol. 5, No.1: 90–115.

Wollman, H. (2003) 'Public Sector Reforms and Evaluation: Patterns and Trends in an International Perspective', in: H. Wollman (ed.) *Evaluating Public Sector Reforms*, Aldershot: Elgar.

Yates, D. (1977) *The Ungovernable City – the Politics of Urban Problems and Policy Making*, Cambridge, MA: MIT Press.

10 Legitimacy and community involvement in local governance

Jan Erling Klausen and David Sweeting

Introduction

In the current debate on collective government in Western societies, increased community involvement is frequently cited as a remedy for the perceived crisis of legitimation as well as effectiveness of political institutions. On the other hand, there is an increasing awareness of the normative problems relating to participatory mechanisms in 'governance' systems. While possibly strengthening the overall societal capacity for collective action, governance arrangements are often perceived as wanting in terms of democratic accountability and representativeness. It is argued that selective and unsystematic inclusion of organised actors, in combination with increasingly dispersed, fragmented and polycentric systems of decision making, are eroding the legitimation basis of collective institutions.

Arguments promoting the virtues of community involvement are made in the context of local government as well as on the transnational level. In the European Union, the Commission's White Paper on Governance argued that 'the quality, relevance and effectiveness of EU policies depend on ensuring wide participation throughout the policy chain [...] Improved participation is likely to create more confidence in the end result and in the institutions which deliver policies' (European Commission 2001: 10).

The concern about the wanting legitimacy of transnational institutions is reflected in the concern about decreasing voter turnout in local government elections. In many countries, the institutions of local government are under severe pressure stemming from popular indifference and in some cases outright distrust. In many cases, the remedy as well as the diagnosis is similar on the two levels. As noted by Rainer Schmalz-Bruns (2002: 41–42), direct citizen involvement can be seen as an obvious solution to the problem of 'democratic deficit' resulting from the weak and porous democratic legitimacy of a multi-level and network-driven political system on the transnational level. Hence the call for increased and improved participation in the White Paper, and correspondingly, the promotion of participation in local government in many countries. Farrell, for instance, describes the promotion of citizen participation in a number of local government services in the UK, as a means 'to enhance user involvement, promote democratic legitimacy and develop the responsiveness of organisations to one of their key stakeholders' (Farrell 2000: 31).

A substantial number of measures have been introduced with the aim of promoting community involvement. However, as several writers have noted, these measures differ substantially in terms of their normative standing. The question is not solely one of *how* to promote community involvement, or one of *who* should participate. There is also the *why*-question: why is it that increased community involvement is seen as desirable? What ends are such developments expected to serve? This question has generally been given two kinds of answers, based on procedural and functional premise respectively. In the first case, participation is required in order to secure the consent of the governed. In the latter case, participation is only seen as valuable to the extent that it contributes to instrumental goal-attainment. This distinction has been explicated as one between government *by* the people and government *for* the people (Scharpf 1999). A political system is legitimised either through the derivation of political choices from the authentic preferences of the members of a community by means of formal procedure, or by virtue of its capacity to adequately respond to emerging wants and needs. Fritz Scharpf has labelled these legitimising beliefs 'input-oriented' and 'output-oriented' (Scharpf 1999: 6). In this volume, Haus and Heinelt (in Chapter 2 of this book) add throughput-legitimation, where political systems can be legitimised by making the decision-making procedures transparent, and by making decision makers visible and accountable to local publics for those decisions. One important theme of this chapter will be the various ways in which these forms of legitimising beliefs interact. Input-legitimation will ultimately be inadequate in the face of poor accountability and inefficient policies; throughput-legitimation would be insufficient without public consent or effective policies; and the legitimacy bestowed by instrumental goal attainment cannot be sought completely in isolation from procedurally legitimated institutions and decisions.

As regards community involvement, we would argue that the answer to the *why*-question has substantial implications for the *how*- and *who*-questions. The choice of institutions of participation (*how*) and principle of inclusion (*who*) cannot be made without consideration of input-throughput-output dimensions, simply because not all kinds of participation can serve all ends. Consider for instance Farrell's observations about 'Parent governors' in schools in the UK: the system was found to be substantially weakened by parental perceptions that they failed to represent the other parents (Farrell 2000: 36). User boards and focus groups may promote the quality of public services, but they may not serve to alleviate legitimacy deficiencies stemming from unsatisfactory systems of accountability and authentic representation. On the other hand, dissatisfaction with public service provision may not be alleviated by the introduction of measures aiming to enhance effective representation. If these premises are accepted, it is clearly necessary to categorise institutions of participation and principles of inclusion according to the three principles of legitimation. This is the primary aim of the present chapter. We wish to arrive at a classification of various forms of participation and community involvement that takes the legitimacy implications into consideration.

Several questions must be addressed, however, before this end can be reached. First, a discussion of key terms locates concepts of community, citizen and participation in the context of government and governance. It is then necessary to situate the principles of legitimation within the context of democratic theory and institutional developments in local government. This task is undertaken in the third section. As initially noted, legitimacy concerns are currently being voiced especially in relation to the purported shift 'from government to governance' (John 2001). It can be argued that this shift corresponds closely to a change of focus concerning legitimacy, more specifically emphasising effectiveness and efficiency perhaps at the expense of representation and accountability. To address these issues, this section will elaborate some dimensions of the *why*-question, contrasting 'traditional' (procedural) democratic norms with emerging functional ones.

As already mentioned above, there is also the question about the relationships between input-, throughput-, and output-related grounds for legitimacy. Although the distinctions between *consent, accountability and utility* implicit in the kinds of legitimacy beliefs are real enough, it can be argued that the three are and should be interacting and complimentary, not mutually excluding. Wolf, for instance, has argued convincingly that a one-sided output-based legitimation strategy may actually be detrimental to effectiveness and efficiency (Wolf 2002). Related to this, is the debate about the relationship between *system capacity* and *effective representation*. In the current debate, the arguments made by Dahl (1967, 1989, 1994) to the effect that there is a zero-sum relationship between the two is called into question (Heinelt 2002). This leads to an explicit consideration about the ways effective representation may enhance system capacity, and correspondingly, what specific functions output-related forms of participation and community involvement are actually meant to serve. These questions will be addressed on pages 222–223.

As for the *how-* and *who*-questions, the choice of institutions and principles of inclusion, these will be dealt with in the fourth section. Procedural considerations may require full inclusion, however much participation is based on the representation of organised actors (selective inclusion). And whereas some procedures are informal (based on individual modes of mediation), for instance the workings of issue networks that are fundamentally horizontal in nature, other approaches entail institutional procedures of mediation. There is also the question of community involvement in different phases of the policy process. As argued by Haus and Heinelt earlier in this book (see Chapter 2), some of the normative problems associated with non-representative community involvement may be alleviated if 'voice' in participatory deliberation and joint policy implementation is combined with 'vote' in decisions taken in representative bodies.

Citizen and community participation

There is a tendency to use terms such as citizen participation and community involvement as though they were synonyms. However, while the terms are used interchangeably, the words 'citizen' and 'community' have different meanings, different connotations and different implications. 'Participation' also takes on different meanings when used in conjunction with the terms 'government' and 'governance'. This section discusses the differences between the uses of citizen and community, and the differences in the uses of the terms of participation and involvement in government and governance. These differences between these terms may often be slight, but are of significance as they enable a more precise usage of key terms that precedes a fuller discussion on various forms of public involvement in government and governance.

Community involvement is a general term that covers the participation of two basic sectors (see Haus and Heinelt, Chapter 2 of this volume):

- the involvement of the 'local public and its associations', comprising individual citizen participation, and the communities of civil society (e.g. neighbourhood associations, citizen groups, clubs), and
- the involvement of 'resourceful societal actors', organisations and institutions from the public and private sectors and their representative associations.

In relation to the first category, where community involvement can refer to individual citizen participation, an understanding of citizenship is important. Citizen and citizenship are explicitly political constructs, describing the nature of relationships that individuals have with the institutions of the state and civil society. In normative terms citizens can be seen as members of society who hold some notion of the common good, and the idea citizenship is tied up with that of democracy. Gyford emphasises that citizens are political creatures by arguing that 'the citizen debating public issues in the agora of ancient Greece could be seen as the historical symbol of political democracy [. . .] debates about public issues amongst the citizens lead to collective political decisions' (1991: 18). Citizens can be distinguished from customers, clients and consumers (Burns *et al.* 1994: 41–49; Gyford 1991: 16–20), but in many respects these roles are complementary and overlapping (Haus 2003). Largely drawing inspiration from the private sector, customers and consumers relate to organisations as purchasers who choose services and goods clients depend on, and are largely subservient to, professional expertise; citizens have an awareness that goes beyond their own sphere and are concerned to 'influence public decisions which affect the local quality of life' (Burns *et al.* 1994: 51), perhaps at the expense of their own individual interests.

Marshall's classic construction of citizenship saw citizens having legal, political and social rights (Marshall 1965). But as well as the acquisition of rights citizenship also implies duty. There are expectations placed upon 'active citizens' from the right (to lessen reliance on the state) and the left (to address social cohesion). In the context of 'third way' Blairite politics, citizens

> play an active role in the constitution of governance and society [to] offer a way forward in a context of growing social fragmentation, life opportunities, and expectations. Active citizens are defined [...] as democratic agents, empowering themselves through their challenges to the activities of institutions and organisations that shape their everyday lives.
>
> (Raco and Imrie 2000: 2188)

Citizenship is about the contribution, or the input, of the individual to the collective, and the relationships between the individual and their broader relations with society. Citizens are expected to be involved in public affairs and contribute to issues in the public arena. But citizenship also implies rights to participate in the welfare of society and is therefore also about output. Citizens have rights to receive common benefits available in society.

Where community involvement refers to involvement through local associations, community is a key concept. 'Community', instead of focussing on the individual (as with citizenship), has a group level focus. Community implies some sort of commonality and has integrative connotations. It expresses the existence of some common feature or interest. There can be communities of interest, based around some sort of common activity, communities based around identities of race and ethnicity and communities of place, where identity is shared and forged around some sort of attachment to some territorial unit, most often (but not exclusively) neighbourhood, town or city (Burns *et al.* 1994: 227). But while community might express commonality within groups, it can at the same time emphasise differences between groups (Brent 1997). One sort of community (e.g. place-based) can contain numerous other communities (e.g. identity-based) that jar against each other and hence 'community politics in any given area is fraught with divisions, tensions, and conflicts' (Raco 2000: 576).

Nevertheless, while community involvement has a group focus, the participation of that group would normally occur through individual representatives of community groups, or group leaders, rather than by involving of the whole group. Representation is therefore a feature of community involvement and how far community representatives are able to represent their community is a complex issue (Purdue *et al.* 2000). Additionally, people who might assume the role of public voice of a particular constituency or neighbourhood might not necessarily be the official representative of that community. People might participate as individual citizens, but because they are from a certain district, or a particular (minority) ethnic group, might be seen as representing that group, even though there has been no formal recognition from that community of such a role.

The idea of community is durable and underpins communitarian democracy and also (as with citizenship) links to the politics of the third way (Hoggett 1997: 13). Within the context of community, citizenship is one of a number of roles of individuals that helps bind community and generate a cohesive society. For example, according to Driver and Martell (2000: 151):

> individuals should not simply claim rights from the state but should also accept their individual responsibilities and duties as citizens, parents, and members of communities. A third way should promote the value of 'community' by supporting the structures and institutions of civil society – such as the family and voluntary organisations – which promote individual opportunity and which ground responsibility in meaningful social relationships.
>
> (Driver and Martell 2000: 151)

It would therefore be mistaken to wholly separate ideas of community from those of citizenship, as citizens are members of communities. But citizen tends to refer to individual activity, albeit within a wider societal context, whereas community refers to certain groups. This is mirrored by the fact that collective rights for groups are still considered at least problematic if not completely out of the question in a democratic polity whereas individual rights are taken for granted.

Community involvement also refers to the involvement of various agencies in the public sphere (the second of the above categories). While 'community' can refer to some sort of grouping of people it can also refer to groupings of organisations, and it is in this sense that community involvement also refers to 'resourceful societal actors'. It is possible to hear of the 'business community', for example. In academic literature Rhodes and Marsh popularised the idea of a 'policy community', a form of policy network where the various actors of governance are tightly grouped around a particular issue, or in a particular locality (Rhodes and

Marsh 1992). Here too, the actual participation is taken on by individuals within organisations. With reference to various organisations this can be seen as the involvement or participation of 'spokespersons' (Schmitter 2002: 53).

'Participation' and 'involvement' are broadly similar, and mean to take part, to join in, to be included. But the meaning of 'participation' changes in the context of use in settings of government and governance. Traditional political participation in government means: 'taking part in the processes of formulation, passage and implementation of public policies. It is concerned with action by citizens which is aimed at influencing decisions which are, in most cases, ultimately taken by public representatives and officials' (Parry *et al.* 1992: 16). While the above definition includes implementation, its primary concern is influencing the nature of policy that is decided upon by others.

Participation in government includes attempting to lobby and influence public representatives and officials, but excludes merely receiving public services. Examples of participation including writing to MPs and councillors, protesting, attending public meetings, involvement with pressure groups and political parties. It refers to individual citizen activities either directly with government or mediated by some citizen group – such as party or pressure group. Participation in government also includes voting in elections and in referenda.

Participation in governance, however, tends to refer to the involvement and interaction of the organisations and institutions which have responsibility for or are concerned with collective action in the public sphere. Horizontal relationships between actors or stakeholders in networks are characteristic of governance, and it is implied that those participating in governance are affected by the policy (Schmitter 2002: 56). Partnerships are a key feature of urban governance and are often the point at which a variety of organisational interests in a local area intersect (Stewart, this volume). Additionally, many 'third sector' organisations – voluntary and community organisations – have acquired responsibility in governance (Stoker 1998: 21). The relative importance of participants in governance arrangements can be uneven, and can favour those public and private agencies with financial and organisational resources at the expense of less well resourced voluntary and community interests.

Participation in governance links strongly to ideas concerning interactive decision making, where:

> citizens, users, interest groups and public and private organisations that have a stake in a decision are involved in its preparation. It is aimed at creating support for policy proposals, improving the quality of decisions by mobilising external knowledge and expertise, and enhancing the democratic legitimacy of decisions.
>
> (Klijn and Koppenjan 2000: 368)

Participation in governance takes place within the context of a shared responsibility between numerous organisations for the provision of mixes of services and programmes. It implies that participants have a direct interest in the decision or issue at stake, it may have some responsibility concerning the execution of the policy. In contrast to traditional participation in government, participation in governance tends to refer to the interaction of a number of collective actors. Individual participation in governance is likely to occur via some institutional setting, such as through some community or voluntary organisation.

Therefore, 'citizen participation' (or involvement) refers to individual actions, whereas 'community participation' (or involvement) refers to a more group level activity. Citizen participation is a subset of the involvement of the local public and its associations, which also includes the involvement of the organisations of civil society; whereas community participation can refer to both the involvement of the local public and the involvement of resourceful societal actors in government and governance.

The *whys* of participation – legitimacy and local governance

Governance, like government, needs to demonstrate legitimacy to be acceptable in modern society. As argued by Haus and Heinelt (see Chapter 2), legitimacy refers to the acceptance and support of a political system by those who are bound by its decisions, and legitimation to the ways in which a political system generates that acceptance and support. Input-, throughput- and output-legitimation all refer to ways in which a political system can be legitimated. Input-legitimation occurs by following correct procedures and demonstrating the consent of the governed. Throughput-legitimation occurs through being accountable and transparent. Output-legitimation occurs through instrumental goal attainment, where governance systems are geared functionally towards task accomplishment. Traditionally elected local governments have been defended as having strong input-legitimation, but local governance, as it brings together many organisations in bargaining and negotiating arenas appears to be more geared to task accomplishment, and therefore would be based on output-legitimation.

Community involvement can be justified in relation to input-, throughput- and output-legitimation. Input-based legitimacy reveals the value of widespread participation in governance, demonstrating the need for popular consent and self-determination, where 'democratic' values are strong. Legitimation occurs through elections. John Stewart argued:

> a local authority is justified by the fact of local election. The councillors are elected to be the representatives of its citizens. In the election the citizens choose councillors to speak and act on their behalf – that is the starting point for local democracy.
>
> (Stewart 1991: 27)

Citizen participation beyond elections gives further channels for the citizenry to express their preferences, and theory relating to participatory democracy contains elements relating to input-legitimation. Pateman (1970: 22–29) reviewing the work of Rousseau, Mill and Cole, points to three reasons why widespread participation is desirable – it educates participants, it gives citizens control and it generates community identity. Democratic government, guided by the inputs of community involvement, generates just policies, as it would not be possible to agree upon activities that are inequitable. Moreover, citizen participation sustains and supports the participatory system, as 'the very qualities that are required of individual citizens are those that the process of participation itself develops and fosters' (Pateman 1970: 25). Citizen participation thus helps educate people in the art of involvement.

Throughput-legitimation can occur through community involvement as it can help make stakeholders more informed, make institutions more transparent and make decision makers more accountable. Freedom of information is widely seen as a basic hallmark of democracy, and in order to participate in any sense or way stakeholders need information. This is one of the reasons why in many states there are particular rules regarding access to information. At the local level in order to be, for example, members of partnerships, or to sit on customer panels, participants will need to acquire information regarding the functioning of certain local activities. In order to scrutinise the activities of decision makers, participants need to know, for example, who made the decisions, why those decisions were made or what alternatives there might have been. This helps to make institutions more transparent, and allows oversight of local decision makers. Moreover, it will also make leaders and decision makers more accountable.

As well as the benefits of citizen participation in relation to input- and throughput-based legitimation, citizen participation can contribute to output-oriented legitimation. Community involvement helps secure widespread consent, and this in turn will help the execution of policies and the fulfilment of goals. Those involved in the preparation of and deliberation about policies are more likely to be compliant when those policies come to be put into effect, especially if they are among those who are impacted and affected. This justification is one that emerged from both older and more recent debates. Pateman argued participation 'aids the acceptance of collective decisions' (1970: 43). Similarly Wolf argues that 'models of inclusion such as public debates, involvement of those affected, or involvement of experts are justified functionally on the grounds that they help enhance problem-solving and acceptance, or help facilitate implementation' (2002: 41). This participation can also help policy makers make more informed, and therefore more effective decisions, as representatives and professionals make decisions that are based on public knowledge as well as professional and political expertise.

Participation can also make local authorities and other organisations more responsive. Against the background of the growth of contracting in local governance, Bucek and Smith argue that citizen participation in local government can be geared towards the 'redefinition of standards' in the contract culture (2000: 9). In relation to other bodies that deliver services, traditional private sector approaches to participation (hot-lines, surveys etc.) can be combined with traditional public sector approaches (advisory boards, consultation) in order to reveal citizen preferences. In this way both input- and output-legitimation are strengthened; there is more citizen participation, and service providers are able to act on the preferences of citizens and therefore be more effective service providers.

The *whos* and *hows*

Who should participate? The question of inclusion

Starting off with the *whos*, the question of inclusion is basically a choice between participation by all or participation by some. More specifically, it is a question about participation *rights*, because 'all' rarely can be expected to participate. In democratic theory, the justification of full inclusion is related to the principle of democratic equality. In his discussion of this principle, Robert Dahl has defined 'the strong principle of political equality' as the assumption that 'all members of the association are adequately qualified to participate on an equal footing with the others in the process of governing the association' (Dahl 1989: 31). Arguments supporting this view include liberal ideas about the *intrinsic equality* of human beings,[1] considerations about self-determination and moral autonomy, human development and protection of personal interests. If these arguments (which are by nature fundamentally axiomatic) are accepted, clearly any model of selective inclusion has to be explicitly justified. Hence the debate about principles of exclusion, focussing on the ways in which some members of a political system can be excluded from the franchise without affecting the democratic quality of the political system.[2]

In representative political systems, the strong principle of political equality primarily applies to the existence of free and fair elections. In other words, citizen's equality is seen to be taken care of by the presence of elected representatives. The representative logic is meant to assure that someone can be held accountable for decisions. Representatives who fail to act in accordance with the public interest may not be re-elected. Also, elections are supposed to bring political decisions roughly in line with public opinion, because candidates normally are elected on the basis of some sort of a political platform.

Representative systems also accommodate for various forms of participation apart from voting, however. Single citizens as well as organised interests are allowed to make attempts to influence decisions throughout the different phases of the policy process. Available channels for participation of this kind include petitions, demonstrations, lobbying and so forth. These channels can be said to maintain the principle of citizen's equality through the representative logic, to the extent that they are open and accessible to all members of the political system, *and* on the condition that they do not entail decision making. The former condition is a direct application of the strong principle of political equality. The latter prescribes hegemony on part of the elected bodies when collective decisions are to be made. If this condition is violated, the elected bodies can not be made fully accountable for political decisions – thus jeopardising input- as well as throughput-oriented legitimation. Also, the system of representation is supposed to bring political decisions in accordance with public opinion through formal procedure. If representative government bodies do not possess hegemony, political decisions may become unduly biased. Some interests may gain more weight than others, again contradicting the strong principle of political equality.

This quick draft of some essential features of traditional input-based legitimation indicates that normative problems relating to inclusion may arise in situations where a) inclusion is selective, *and* b) elected bodies do not possess hegemonic decision-making powers. When observed empirically, conditions like these demarcate the boundaries of the sphere of representative *government*, in the traditional sense. Because public government in non-totalitarian societies is not supposed to be all-encompassing, this is in itself unproblematic. According to liberal principles, state power *should* be limited. However, not least in complex modern societies, political aims will not exclusively relate to matters within the state's sovereign jurisdiction. As a consequence, the state will have to make attempts to achieve collective action even in situations where elected bodies do not possess hegemonic decision-making powers. Clearly, this will in many cases put the strong principle of political equality in jeopardy. Voters may find that some interests have been given primacy in decisions, even though these interests do not constitute the majority of the electorate. Resourceful groups may get the upper hand, thus violating the principle of equality in line with Stein Rokkan's famous contention to the effect that '*Votes count, but resources decide*' (Rokkan 1966).

Clearly, by moving outside the context of representative hegemony, elected government runs the risk of endangering its own basis of (procedural) legitimation. In principle, one may ask why elected governments would want to do this. In practice, the answer is that there is not much of a choice. A frequently voiced contention is that modern societies have become too complex and fragmented to allow for the centralised, hierarchical control associated with representative hegemony. In a much-quoted article, Robert Dahl (1994) has made the case that collective action in modern societies necessitates horizontal coordination between public and private actors, in order to achieve system capacity (governability), however at the direct expense of effective representation. This is the gist of the *governance* perspective on collective action: representative institutions cannot unilaterally solve problems by means of hegemonic power, because these problems can only be solved by pooling the resources of private and public actors. These resources can in many cases not be solicited by use of the state's coercive powers, and so the need for horizontal coordination arises. Schmitter has argued, in line with this, that 'governance only emerges as an attractive alternative when there are manifest *state failures* and/or *market failures*. It is almost never the initially most preferred way of dealing with problems or resolving conflicts' (Schmitter 2002: 54, emphasis in original). Representative government will primarily want to deal with policy challenges through the use of hierarchical power legitimated by democratic procedure, and will only deviate from this strategy when dictated by necessity. Such necessity arises only because 'system capacity' – the (perceived) ability to deal with policy challenges – is a necessary part of the legitimation basis for representative institutions. In other words, legitimation must partially be derived from the ability to deliver *output*, not just from concurrence with procedural norms regarding *input*.

If the line of reasoning so far is accepted, it has been demonstrated that the 'shift to governance' runs the risk of violating the strong principle of political equality as expressed by the system of representation, because governance involves collective decision making outside the boundaries of hegemonic decision-making powers in the hands of representative institutions. If the principle of full inclusion is not violated, however, it could in principle be argued that governance arrangements[3] may constitute an alternative system of representation. If traditional representation cannot accommodate the strong principle of political equality, full and equal access to decisions may instead be guaranteed in the form of all-inclusive governance arrangements. Because all members of a political system clearly cannot be involved in arguing and bargaining simultaneously, however, this would by necessity involve a shift away from the territorial system of representation. Some alternative principle of inclusion would have to be established. One potentially viable approach to this problem is offered by Phillipe Schmitter, who has proposed a typology of seven grounds for legitimate claims to participation in governance arrangements (Schmitter 2002: 62–63). Persons or organisations can make such claims to the extent that they are 'holders' of certain qualities or resources needed to solve a problem or a conflict. These are:

1   *rights* derived from citizenship;
2. *spatial location* (all those living within a defined territory);
3   *knowledge*, as with expertise or any other uniquely held information or skill;
4   *share*, as related to ownership;

5 *stake*, being materially or spiritually affected;
6 *interest*, participation in the sense of being a spokesperson for some constituency; and
7 *status*, the allocation of special participation rights on virtue of being recognised by accountable authorities as a representative for some interest.

As acknowledged by Schmitter, *rights holders* would have a pre-eminent status in traditional input-oriented systems. The other grounds for legitimate claims to participation in governance arrangements may constitute the basis of alternative principles of inclusion to the territorial principle.

The somewhat problematic aspect of Schmitter's argument is that he does not clarify the status of the legitimacy claims. Because it cannot be assumed that the legitimacy of these seven types of claims of participation rights is actually acknowledged by real-life governments, the composition of any governance arrangement (the totality of actors involved) must at least partially depend on additional principles of selection. One would for instance expect local and temporal contingencies, such as personal relationships, to play a significant part. This means that the holders' perspective cannot adequately explain *empirical* findings concerning inclusion. Alternatively, one might assume that Schmitter's typology is a *normative* model: (local) governments *should* institute procedures for securing the participation rights of all holders. If so, it is unclear whether this prescription is based on efficiency considerations or on principle. Regardless, the justification is left unelaborated.

One potentially fruitful interpretation is the assumption that actors may be able to help enhance problem solving and acceptance, or help facilitate implementation (the output-oriented reasons for participation) if and only if they belong to one of the seven categories of holders. This would amount to something approaching a theory of effective governance, because it would provide the criteria for excluding participants who cannot make useful contributions.

As noted by Wolf, it is perhaps necessary to stop conceiving of democracy as synonymous with the territorial principle of representation (Wolf 2002). This notwithstanding, the potential for establishing some form of alternative system of procedural (input) legitimation based on functional representation (supplementing the principle of territorial representation) is in the short term probably not a viable solution to the potential legitimation problems associated with current governance arrangements. A less radical approach is suggested by Heinelt and Haus (in Chapter 2 of this book). One may differentiate between the phases of the policy process in terms of 'modes' of governing. The representative logic might be retained in the decision-making phase, whereas arrangements entailing selective inclusion and horizontal coordination are consigned to other phases of the process. With Fritz Scharpf (1999: 20), policy networks may describe informal patterns of interaction *preceding* or *accompanying* formal decisions taken in formally legitimised modes of interaction. Extensive participation ('voice') in problem definition and implementation may be accompanied by procedural equality ('vote') in the decision-making phase.

The obvious attraction of this proposition is its potential for retaining the public–private sector cooperation essential to governance arrangements, yet not at the expense of input-oriented legitimation. We will not pursue this line of reasoning much further in this context; however we want to take note of one issue which remains to be resolved. It could be argued that the term *governance* essentially denotes a system of decision making, not solely consultation. As noted by Schmitter, governance is associated with 'A shared responsibility for resource allocation and conflict resolution' (Schmitter 2002: 55). The above mentioned notion about allocating voice and vote to certain phases of the policy process could be conceived of as underplaying the essential characteristics of the governance concept. The non-governmental actors involved may not be contented with being consulted in advance of decisions, or with being included in implementation. Private actors may demand a chair at the decision-making table, so to speak, if they are expected to make substantial contributions out of their own resources.

A solution to this problem may be found by recourse to a less one-dimensional conception of decision making. Considerations about procedural legitimacy may apply in different ways to different kinds of decisions made in politico-administrative systems. One could conceive of a specific domain of cooperative decision making in which there is room for negotiation and compromise *within restrictions defined by over-arching political decisions*. Elected representatives (and civil servants) could enter into horizontal, cooperative decision making with private actors with a 'mandate' in the form of preceding, procedurally legitimated decisions concerning more general policy aims. For instance, if a city council decides that the city should try to attract high-technology industries in order to promote economic competitiveness, this 'strategic' decision could be followed by a phase of decision making of a more horizontal nature, in which public government bodies (politicians and officers) make consensus-based agreements with private actors. This could leave room for arguing and bargaining in governance arrangements without infringing too much on input-oriented grounds for legitimation.

In such an arrangement, we would argue that the conditions for input-oriented legitimation would *not* be violated even in the face of selective inclusion and lack of hegemony on the part of elected bodies participating in the governance arrangement. The elected participants (the politicians) would act in accordance with procedurally legitimated goals, and they would retain power over the resources they themselves put on the bargaining table. They would only commit these resources in order to secure the implementation of preceding, over-arching decisions. As for the non-governmental parties to the governance arrangement, they could only be expected to commit their own resources to the extent that they are satisfied with the outcome of the bargaining process. All in all, this is to say that governance arrangements will only be effective if agreements can be reached. Like state and market, governance may fail (Jessop 2002).

How to participate?

Democratic theory has a lot to say about the justification for participation and the question of inclusion. Regarding the specific forms of participation, the *how*-question, it is possible to relate some general dimensions to various conceptions of democracy.

One key distinction in democratic theory is that between *aggregative* and *deliberative* collective decision making (Cohen and Sabel 1997). These principles represent alternative strategies for safeguarding the strong principle of political equality.[4] The gist of aggregative decision making is that people are treated as equals if their interests are given equal weight. Hence the principle of 'one man, one vote'. Deliberative decision making, on the other hand, entails that decisions proceed 'on the basis of free public reasoning among equals; interests unsupported by considerations that convince others carry no weight' (Cohen and Sabel 1997: 320). This distinction corresponds to that between the *voluntaristic* and the *epistemic* principles of democratic legitimacy (Schmalz-Bruns 2002: 64). The first principle states that everybody should have the equal chance to decisively bring to bear his preferences, whereas the second is based on the idea that '*people as autonomous persons are best represented in their faculty of demanding and giving reasons to each other*' (Habermas 1998: 165, quoted from Schmalz-Bruns 2002: 63). The aggregative/voluntaristic principle is at the heart of liberal and pluralistic conceptions of democracy, in the sense that it is recognised that people's interests and opinions will often be diverging and conflicting. Liberal institutions are in different ways designed to allow collective action even in the face of diverging interests, for instance by means of voting. If fundamental rights and freedoms are guaranteed in the constitution, people will have morally sound reasons to accept decisions even when they go against their own interests. This is the liberal principle of legitimacy.[5] The deliberative/epistemic principle, on the other hand, takes departure in the assumption that consensus can be reached through free and unrestrained discourse. Democratic institutions need to secure the preconditions for this kind of discourse. Because all relevant points of view should be represented in the discourse, this model can in general be said to put higher demands on the level of participation in society than, say, the liberal-representative model.[6]

As noted, deliberative decision making is geared towards consensus whereas aggregative decision making is rooted in the need to make decisions even in the face of irreconcilable differences of interest and opinions. Regarding the forms of community involvement on the local level, this distinction has several implications. Some forms of participation clearly fall within the confines of the voluntaristic perspective, because 1) they aim to influence decisions that are to be made in representative bodies, and 2) they are carried out with the intention of furthering one particular interest or viewpoint. Petitions, rallies and various lobbying activities are cases in point. As for voting in local government elections and local referenda, these are even clearer examples of 'aggregative' political behaviour. These forms of participation are designed so as to give each voice an equal say (one person, one vote), but they do not in themselves involve deliberation or consensus seeking. On the other hand, there are also many forms of community involvement with distinctly epistemic or deliberative features. Public hearings, public debates arranged by local governments or non-governmental organisations, as well as debates in the local media, *preceding* decisions in representative bodies, are clear signs of '*free public reasoning among equals*', in the words of Cohen and Sabel (1997: 320). Furthermore, cooperative schemes on the local level, involving representatives from public, private and civil sector actors (notably, initiatives concerning social inclusion and urban regeneration) have in many cases been found to be in line with the assumptions of consensus-seeking, deliberative decision making. This is the defining trait of for instance the model of 'directly-deliberative polyarchy' promoted by Cohen and Sabel (1997).

Following this, we would contend that the distinction between aggregative and deliberative participation should be regarded as fundamentally important to the development of a conceptualisation or typology of participation. In the context of input-oriented legitimation, aggregative decision making (decisions made by vote in representative bodies or democratic assemblies) should be preceded by deliberation. In the context of horizontal decision making, often associated with output-oriented legitimation, decisions have to be made on the basis of consensus through deliberation.

Furthermore, a distinction between various forms of participation may usefully refer to the phases of the policy process. For simplicity, we would suggest a distinction between three phases: initiation, decision and implementation. The initiation phase would include agenda-setting and deliberation in advance of decisions, whereas implementation would be the phase succeeding formal decisions. We regard this distinction between phases as critical if the normative considerations about democratic equality and procedural legitimation are to be sustained. As noted, we support the notion by Heinelt and Haus earlier in this volume of distinguishing between 'voice' and 'vote' in different phases of the policy process. This argument implies that decisions should be taken in representative bodies or by means of referenda ('vote') whereas the exercise of 'voice' has broader applications in the preceding and subsequent phases. We have, however, suggested that there could be room for horizontal decision making within the context of over-arching decisions made in representative bodies, without putting input-oriented in jeopardy.

We would suggest a *tentative typology of participation* based on 1) the different functions of participation and 2) the phases of the policy process. The typology would include:

- *Participation in the initiation phase*: aggregative forms of participation would include the organisation of petitions, rallies and *ad hoc* pressure groups aiming to promote a specific interest or point of view. To the extent that these and related forms of participation involves public debate, not just one-sided agitation, the aggregative forms would take on a deliberative quality.
- *Participation in decision making*: decision making through local referenda is the direct mode, whereas voting for representatives can be considered an indirect form of participation in aggregative decision making. Participation in deliberative decision making takes place in the horizontal context of public–private relations. Governance arrangements, interactive governance, neighbourhood councils and so forth would be cases in point.
- *Participation in implementation*: because the implementation of political decisions in the context of traditional government primarily is the domain of public administration, there is little room for participation in implementation. Exceptions would include non-governmental organisations taking on tasks decided upon by public government, either out of idealistic purposes or in exchange for (financial) support. Outsourcing of public works to private contractors should not be considered a form of participation as such. On the other hand, in the deliberative/horizontal domain, extensive private participation in implementation is often called for. The involvement of local NGOs, businesses and other civil sector actors in measures pertaining to urban regeneration or economic competitiveness are relevant examples.

Conclusions

This chapter has discussed the contribution that community involvement can make to input-, throughput- and output-based means of legitimation in local governance. The typology of participation in the policy processes, presented at the end of the chapter, is based on the distinction between deliberative and aggregative forms of democracy on one dimension, and between different stages of the policy process (initiation, decision and implementation) on the other. It therefore offers two basic criteria upon which to categorise forms of participation in governance. With reference to democratic theory, the chapter has also discussed the normative bases of the various forms of involvement, and how they can contribute to legitimising governance. We would point out that there are more caveats to bear in mind when discussing forms of participation – for example the differences in emphasis between citizen and community participation, and participation in government and governance. However, the deliberative/aggregative distinction is one that chimes well with the alternative forms of community involvement in governance and captures different methods of involvement in policy making that may occur in various settings, or perhaps in the same setting at different times or in different policy arenas.

Notes

1 This principle is basic in the democratic model which has been termed protective democracy (Held 1996; Schmalz-Bruns 2002). The idea of intrinsic equality is elaborated by John Locke in his *Second Treatise of Government*, and is found in the opening phrases of the American Declaration of Independence: 'We hold these truths to be self-evident, that all men are created equal, that they are endowed by their Creator with certain unalienable Rights, that among these are Life, Liberty and the pursuit of Happiness [...]'.

2 As noted by Hyland (1995: 77), non-nationals, children and the certified insane are among those denied franchise in modern-day Western democracies. Hyland is highly critical about various justifications for this apparent breach of the strong principle of equality. Robert Dahl also recognises these problems (Dahl 1989: 129).

3 This concept is borrowed from Schmitter (2002: 56).

4 As previously stated, this principle has been defined by Robert Dahl as the assumption that 'all members of the association are adequately qualified to participate on an equal footing with the others in the process of governing the association' (Dahl 1989: 31).

5 This principle has been stated as follows: 'Our exercise of political power is proper and hence justifiable only when it is exercised in accordance with a constitution the essentials of which all citizens may reasonably be expected to endorse in the light of principles and ideals acceptable to them as reasonable and rational' (Rawls 1993: 217).

6 The republican tradition of political thought is associated with these ideas. Following David Held (1996), one may distinguish between protective and developmental republicanism, depending largely on the perspective of participation. In protective republicanism, participation is necessary to protect citizen's objectives and interests, whereas the developmental model puts stress on 'the intrinsic value of participation for the enhancement of decision-making and the development of the citizenry' (Held 1996: 45). In liberal democratic thought, the distinction between protective and developmental models has been a focal point in the debate about the functions of participation. Whereas for instance writers like J. S. Mill and Carole Pateman have put emphasis on the 'enlightening' and 'empowering' aspects of participation, others have emphasised the instrumental value of participation. The latter position was taken to the extreme by writers in the school of competitive elitism, most notably Joseph Schumpeter, who relegated participation to the act of choosing representatives. This distinction can be related to the distinction between input- and output-oriented grounds for legitimacy. In the output-oriented perspective, participation is only valuable and desirable to the

extent that it contributes to problem solving, accept and implementation (Wolf 2002). This implies that the developmental perspective is not given weight. Input-oriented systems, however, would easily accommodate the developmental perspective as well as the protective.

References

Brent, J. (1997) 'Community Without Unity', in: P. Hoggett (ed.) *Contested Communities*, Bristol: Policy Press.

Bucek, B. and Smith, J. (2000) 'New Approaches to Local Democracy: Direct Democracy, Participation and the Third Sector', *Environment and Planning C: Government and Policy*, Vol. 18: 3–16.

Burns, D., Hambleton, R. and Hoggett, P. (1994) *The Politics of Decentralisation*, Basingstoke: Macmillan.

Cohen, J. and Sabel, C. (1997) 'Directly-Deliberative Polyarchy', *European Law Journal*, Vol. 3, No. 4: 313–342.

Dahl, R. A. (1967) 'The City in the Future of Democracy', *The American Political Science Review*, Vol. 61, No. 4.

—— (1989) *Democracy and Its Critics*, New Haven, CT: Yale University Press.

—— (1994) 'A Democratic Dilemma: System Effectiveness Versus Citizen Participation', *Political Science Quarterly*, Vol. 109, No. 1: 23–34.

Driver, S. and Martell, L. (2000) 'Left, Right, and the Third Way', *Policy and Politics*, Vol. 28, No. 2: 147–161.

European Commission (2001) *European Governance. A White Paper*. COM, Brussels.

Farrell, C. M. (2000) 'Citizen Participation in Governance', *Public Money and Management*, Vol. 20, No. 1: 31–37.

Grote, J. R. and Gbikpi, B. (eds) (2002) *Participatory Governance*, Opladen: Leske + Budrich.

Gyford, J. (1991) *Citizens, Consumers and Councils*, Basingstoke: Macmillan.

Habermas, J. (1998) 'Die postnationale Konstellation und die Zukunft der Demokratie, in: J. Habermas, *Die postnationale Konstellation Politische Essays*, Frankfurt: Suhrkamp: 91–169.

Haus, M. (2003) 'Towards a Postparliamentary Democracy in Germany? Theoretical Considerations and Empirical Observations on Local Democracy', in: S. A. H. Denters, O. van Heffen, J. Huisman and P.-J. Klok (eds) *The Rise of Interactive Governance and Quasi-Market*, Dordrecht: Kluwer: 213–238.

Heinelt, H. (2002) 'Civic perspectives on a Democratic Transformation of the EU', in: J. R. Grote and B. Gbikpi (eds) (2002): 97–120.

Held, D. (1996) *Models of Democracy* (2nd edn), Cambridge: Polity press.

Hoggett, P. (1997) 'Contested Communities', in: P. Hoggett (ed.) *Contested Communities*, Bristol: Policy Press.

Hyland, J. L. (1995) *Democratic Theory. The Philosophical Foundations*, Manchester: Manchester University Press.

Jessop, B. (2002) 'Governance and Metagovernance. On Reflexivity, Requisite Variety, and Requisite Irony', in: H. Heinelt, P. Getimis, G. Kafkalas, R. Smith and E. Swyngedouw (eds) *Participatory Governance in Multilevel Context. Theoretical Debate and the Empirical Arena*, Opladen: Leske + Budrich: 33–58.

John, P. (2001) *Local Governance in Western Europe*, London: Sage.

Klijn, E. H. and Koppenjan, J. F. M. (2000) 'Politicians and Interactive Decision

Making: Institutional Spoilsports or Playmaker?', *Public Administration*, Vol. 78: 365–387.

Marshall, T. H. (1965) *Class, Citizenship, and Social Development*, New York: Anchor.

Parry, G., Moyser, G. and Day, N. (1992) *Political Participation and Democracy in Britain*, Cambridge: Cambridge University Press.

Pateman, C. (1970) *Participation and Democratic Theory*, Cambridge: Cambridge University Press.

Purdue, D., Razzaque, K., Hambleton, R. and Stewart, M. (2000) *Community Leadership in Area Regeneration*, York: Joseph Rowntree Foundation.

Raco, M. (2000) 'Assessing Community Participation in Local Economic Development – Lessons for the New Urban Policy', *Political Geography*, Vol. 19: 573–599.

Raco, M. and Imrie, R. (2000) 'Governmentality and Rights and Responsibilities in Urban Policy', *Environment and Planning A*, Vol. 32: 2187–2204.

Rawls, J. (1993) *Political Liberalism*, New York: Columbia University Press.

Rhodes, R. and Marsh, D. (1992) *Policy Networks in British Government*, Oxford: Clarendon Press.

Rokkan, S. (1966) 'Norway: Numerical Democracy and Corporate Pluralism', in: R. A. Dahl (ed.) *Political Opposition in Western Democracies*, New Haven, CT: Yale University Press: 70–115.

Scharpf, F. (1999) *Governing in Europe.* Oxford: Oxford University Press.

Schmalz-Bruns, R. (2002) 'The Normative Desirability of Participatory Governance', in: H. Heinelt, P. Getimis, G. Kafkalas, R. Smith and E. Swyngedouw (eds) *Participatory Governance in Multilevel Context. Theoretical Debate and the Empirical Arena*, Opladen: Verlag Leske + Budrich: 59–74.

Schmitter, P. (2002) 'Participation in Governance Arrangements', in: J. R. Grote and B. Gbikpi (eds) (2002): 51–69.

Stewart, J. (1991) 'The Councillor as Elected Representative', in: J. Stewart and C. Game (eds) *Local Democracy – Representation and Elections*, Part 2, The Blagrave Papers No. 1, London: Local Government Management Board.

Stoker, G. (1998) 'Governance as Theory: Five Propositions', *International Social Science Journal*, No. 155: 17–38.

Wolf, K. D. (2002) 'Contextualizing Normative Standards for Legitimate Governance Beyond the State', in: J. R. Grote and B. Gbikpi (eds) *Participatory Governance*, Opladen: Leske + Budrich: 35–50.

11 Participation and leadership in planning theory and practices

Alessandro Balducci and Claudio Calvaresi

In this chapter, we try to explore the concepts of participation and leadership – as well as possible complementarities between the two – in the theory of spatial planning.

The concept of participation, rooted as it is in the anarchist (i.e. anti-hierarchical and non-state-centred) school of thought that nurtured an important part of the planning movement, has occupied a crucial place throughout the history of planning. Although the fundamental role of participation in the construction of the discipline has long been denied, some of its key features such as community involvement in planning processes still form the basic content of many current planning practices (see pages 234–236).

In contrast, leadership is not a usual concept in planning theory, because spatial planning is traditionally linked with a strong idea of formal authority (planning rules and zoning ordinances are 'enforced by law'). It is only recently, after the emergence of new approaches (strategic planning, consensus building in group processes, 'argumentative turn'), which emphasise the interactive nature of planning activities, that leadership has become more popular in planning literature (pages 236–240).

We hypothesise that it is now possible to speak about the complementarity of urban leadership and community involvement by considering the effectiveness of planning vis-à-vis the emerging demands on urban policies (pages 240–243).

Participation in planning has now entirely lost its ideological character. Today it is a tool for producing decisions that are really tailored to the needs of the citizens. It involves and mobilises actors, recognises and resolves conflicts, promotes cooperation, negotiation and innovation and fosters social learning (pages 243–245). From this perspective, leadership and participation occupy a common ground where the planner too comes into play (pages 245–249).

The origins of participation in planning

As Peter Hall argued in his book on the history of planning theories (Hall 1988), the call for participation in spatial planning goes back to the anarchist roots of thinking about planning and runs through Patrick Geddes' teachings and the early garden city movement.

During his long stay in India (Ferraro 1998), Geddes observed how royal engineers, obsessed with sanitation in cities, tried to introduce housing and urban models tailored for Western cities into India, which were completely inappropriate for the life styles of Indian people:[1] Geddes defined this approach as 'Haussmanising' (after Haussmann, the planner of 'modern' Paris), and noted that not only did it fail to consider the real needs of the inhabitants and follow different criteria from those of local people, but it also produced inefficient results and wasted resources. Ahead of his time, many of his criticisms of traditional spatial planning were to become accepted thinking after the Second World War.

The issue raised was the gap separating 'professional social inquiry' (Lindblom and Cohen 1979) and ordinary knowledge. It was precisely the same issue that gave birth to the community architecture movement led by John Turner as early as the 1950s. Supporters of this movement were of the opinion that the huge gap that separates the professional who designs a house, a school or a hospital from those who have to live in those spaces, creates the risk that the needs of the users will be completely misunderstood. They argue that the underlying reasons and causes of the separation between 'expert' and 'user' must be reconsidered: why and when, as inhabitants, did we lose our knowledge of how to build a house? Why do we take it for granted that we do not have the skills required to design our own living spaces? Are the arguments that justified this separation still valid?

We should also consider that John Turner worked in Lima's *barriadas*. It is precisely where resources are really scarce that the defects of a self-centred approach become more evident.

A further issue is public services, in the field of social housing for example. Housing policies modelled on industrialised countries have failed when employed in developing countries and this has forced planners to explore other paths based on a recognition of cultural and societal values and not just on the problems of the so-called *bidonvilles*. But, there again the same problems of adequacy and effectiveness are also relevant in Western countries, since the crisis of traditional forms of public service delivery has become evident and the continuous quantitative expansion of welfare policies has become unsustainable.

Economic unsustainability and the ineffective treatment of social problems are in fact the causes of the crisis in public sector intervention. It is the crisis of a model that Antonio Tosi (Tosi 1984) has described as the 'administrative theory of needs', a bureaucratic form of intervention that produces a standardised treatment for each type of social need. This model fails to interpret the diversity and the specific characteristics of pluralistic societies. It acts by matching types of population or categories of needs with types of services or public amenities: children with schools, health with hospitals, urban sociability with new squares, etc.

Obviously we are no longer talking only about architecture or spatial planning, but about the actual principles underlying the provision of services, and the need (or ability) to involve citizens in these systems in order to make intervention more effective.

There is an explicit proximity between these two activities (i.e. spatial planning and service provision). Participatory planning means going beyond the merely physical aspects and seems to develop greater potential when it is applied to the entire process of making choices.

The participation experiences that shaped the field of urban planning in Europe and the United States during the 1960s and 1970s are different from the Geddes and community architecture models discussed above. 'Advocacy planning' and cases of 'institutionalised participation' in the planning process in Europe posed the question for the first time of how to open up the decision-making process of spatial planning to traditionally excluded actors (Davidoff 1965).

The arguments on which those experiences were based were essentially ethical and political, and only indirectly based on effectiveness. The actors were urban movements rather than the inhabitants themselves. The emphasis was on the antagonistic nature of the viewpoint that these movements were able to bring into the planning process, and this has become more and more ideological over the years in the US as well as in Europe.

Although those experiences constituted a fundamental moment in the evolution of planning culture, they had serious limitations as far as practical outcomes were concerned. If the reintroduction of participatory approaches in planning processes has encountered some difficulties in recent years, it is probably the result of a general distrust of community involvement in planning, an approach widely seen as a mere expression of conflict or, at the other extreme, as manipulation of consent.

The challenged legitimacy of spatial planning and the search for new sources of legitimation

Spatial planning is basically the administrative regulation of land use. It is a tool that local authorities use to determine rights and obligations concerning urban functions and uses (by means of zoning) as well as to govern future development (urban general plans shape the cities of tomorrow).

They follow a logic where local plans conform to higher level plans and where individual actions conform with zoning rules and to the dictates of the general plan. In this sense, spatial planning is strictly connected to a formal and hierarchical vision of authority: its rules and ordinances are 'enforced by law'. The legitimacy of planning depends on two basic conditions.[2] One is that it relies on its own scientific canons. According to a purely rationalistic approach, a planning process starts by determining general goals, is followed by the formulation of the possible courses of action and assessment of these and ends with the selection of the best alternative and the implementation of the plan. The process has three characteristics:

1   it is comprehensive, because it takes into account all the possible alternatives;
2   it is progressive, because it goes from the general to the particular;
3   it is cyclical, because the plan and its implementation are just a temporary final step that has to be reconsidered to cope with new demands and problems.[3]

The other condition is that it depends on the authority of the state. If the main functions of urban planning are to control and manage the development of cities, to avoid market failures, to coordinate the plurality of private interests and to promote equity and well-being, then they depend on the legitimacy of the state to guarantee the pursuit of the 'public interest' in the organisation of space:[4] this view of spatial planning was hegemonic at least until the late sixties, when planning was attacked from different directions.

The first criticism concerned the cognitive and practical limits of planning. These limits are best explained using some of the concepts developed by Charles Lindblom, probably the scholar who formulated the most convincing arguments against the 'rational-comprehensive method' in public policies. One criticism is that it is impossible to take into account the full set of possible variables involved in planning decisions and this makes it impossible to select the best alternative. What results is people practising the 'art of muddling through'. Another criticism is that in a pluralistic society, a planner is just one of the various actors involved in a decision-making process who is forced to deal with other legitimate (and often conflicting) preferences and goals. In this situation, a planner has to employ a 'partisan mutual adjustment' model rather than evoke some kind of superior authority.

The second criticism concerned the legitimacy and the effectiveness of planning. Several empirical planning policy case studies which analysed the actual behaviour of actors, showed that all definitions of common interest are unstable and that it is impossible to determine what it really means (Meyerson and Banfield 1955) – but also that outputs of city planning processes can be very different (Altshuler 1965). In the years that followed, other case studies demonstrated the failures and disasters of planning beyond any doubt (Pressman and Wildavsky 1973; Hall 1980).

In that period, planning theory tried to formulate credible answers to these critics, by exploring the epistemological, political and practical dimensions of planning. In the following, we will briefly outline some of the main contributions concerning these dimensions.[5]

On the epistemological side, planning theory tried to escape from a conventional view of the role of information in planning. Within this conventional approach, experts acquire information to gain more knowledge of the phenomena to be planned (survey before planning), or in response to questions from decision makers, or to solve problems that these decision makers have identified (Innes 1998). The conventional view of information and the myth of scientific canons of professional inquiry were rejected as planners began to accept a lay vision of knowledge. Judith Innes in her book *Knowledge and Public Policy* (Innes 1990) argued that: i) knowledge is not produced only by experts, but non-experts also have knowledge to contribute; ii) the process of informing policy is an interactive process, where the division of labour between technician and politician is not rigidly defined; iii) first we must know what kind of policy we want and then we can gather information and create indicators.[6]

So 'usable knowledge' is a mix of expert and ordinary knowledge. The relevant information is socially constructed in the community where it is used and must promote a process of social learning.[7] A 'new epistemology of practice', as Schön called his approach (Schön 1983), began to emerge. By constructing problems the planner helps actors to generate new frames and to establish a 'back-talk' conversation with the problem situation. The important knowledge is that which is based on reflection in action, produced by a strategy of continuous shifting between problems and solutions.

Another important contribution to this topic comes from Lindblom's definition of strategic planning, without any direct reference to spatial planning.[8] He defines strategic planning as follows:

> A method that treats the competence to plan as a scarce resource that must be husbanded, carefully allocated, not overcommitted. Because planning is both costly and limited in what it can accomplish, planners are seen as needing a strategy for guiding their planning, [...] which means planning that picks its assignments with discrimination, that employs a variety of devices to simplify its intellectual demands, that makes much of interaction and adapts analysis to interaction as a substitute for an analysis, and that departs from logical and scientific canons because they are rules for achieving a level of intellectual mastery that planners cannot achieve when faced with actual complex social phenomena. [...] We call [this] method strategic planning, thus emphasizing that it requires discrimination or selection among tasks to which the intellect is to be assigned, as well as a calculated interplay between thought and social interaction.
>
> (Lindblom 1975)

Therefore, strategic planning is for Lindblom, a substitute for analytical problem solving; it plans the participation of planners in interactive processes; it introduces systematic alterations in interaction patterns; it makes use of the intelligence with which individuals pursue their own preferences.

Planning also discovered (or disclosed) its political core. The planning theorist that best and most radically expressed this position was Melvin Webber: 'Planning is unavoidably and inherently a political activity [...]. In a democratic society the interplay of partisan groups effectively determines not only what is wanted, but, therefore, what is right' (Webber 1969: 291–292).

Webber presented his 'permissive planning' model, an approach that literally permits individuals to achieve their own purposes, devises incentives which enable people rather than imposing regulatory constraints, helps to reach decisions in acceptable ways and ensures that all voices are heard. Permissive planning is a 'subset of politics, its central function being to improve the process of public debate and public decision'. It is 'an integral aspect of governing, rather than a separate function of government' (Webber 1978: 156, 158).

Finally, planners became more concerned about the issue of a plan's effectiveness. In a well-known article, Karen Christensen (1985) pointed out that much of the ineffectiveness of planning was the result of a simplistic view of planning practice. She referred to a famous matrix of public policy analysis, see Figure 11.1 (Thompson and Tuden 1959).

Christensen applied this matrix to planning problems and observed that very different kinds of planning actions are required according to whether there is agreement or disagreement on planning goals and to whether technologies are known or unknown. While there is usually a premature assumption of consensus on goals and a premature assumption of knowledge of technologies, most planning problems are characterised by uncertainty in one or both the dimensions considered (Rittel and Webber 1973).

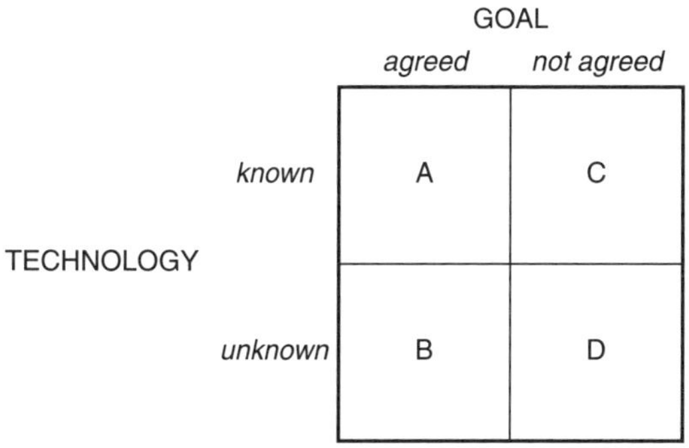

Figure 11.1 Prototype conditions of planning problems.

When there is consensus over goals and knowledge of the appropriate technologies (A), planning action can assume a standardised programming form, the typical approach of technical rationality. However, in all the other combinations of the two factors in the matrix, planning action is called upon to perform in a very different way. So in situations dominated by uncertainty over technologies (B), planning action must involve experimentation of new technologies. In situations dominated by conflicts over goals (C), planning action must involve negotiation between actors. Finally in situations dominated by uncertainty over both dimensions (D), planning action must involve reframing and redefinition of the problem to be solved.

What we wish to stress here with this image, is that in all the situations to which planning is applied, it must involve strong interaction with other actors, with stakeholders of all kinds from interest groups to individual citizens. Strategies that favour experimentation, mediation or problem redefinition require the design of interaction processes and the participation of interested parties that may lead to new technologies, new agreements, new problem definitions.

As we have seen, the efforts of planning theorists to redefine the epistemological, political and practical dimensions of planning underlie a series of issues, which can be briefly summarised as follows:

a   planning is an interactive practice that has to deal with problems such as consensus building, promoting cooperation, dealing with conflict, fostering social learning, mobilising actors, etc.;
b   planning has dismissed the original basis of its legitimacy (pursuit of the public interest, the rational-comprehensive method) and must acquire legitimation on the grounds of the ability to produce efficient and effective decisions;
c   planning – as Webber made clear – is an aspect of governing, rather than a separate function of government;
d   planning has to cope with situations in which the capacity to innovate and negotiate are required.

In our view, these issues seem to be linked with the concept of leadership, which we define as a purposeful activity, designed to mobilise actors and to generate innovation outside the routine processes (see Haus and Heinelt in this book).

New demands for participation and leadership in spatial planning

Early in 1971 Donald Schön wrote in his influential book *Beyond the Stable State* (Schön 1971) of the 'loss of a stable state' as a specific feature of contemporary society, in contrast to the alternation of long stable periods with periods of rapid and intense change in the past. From this perspective Schön invited us to reflect on the need to rethink forms of public intervention that were basically designed to function in a stable and slowly changing society. A quick look at the past tells us that new information technologies are in the process of changing the entire world economy in just a few years, while the so-called post-industrial era lasted 25 years and the industrial age before that about a century.

Political systems, power structures, the use of capital and population trends themselves are all highly unstable. The great axioms of traditional politics no longer function, but fall quickly into empty rhetoric; political leaders rely more and more upon volatile opinions to interpret fast changes in society and these provide a very weak basis to legitimate decision making. It is all too evident that the inability to produce credible tools to orient urban policies is also a result of this rapid change and of the inadequacy of the attitudes and paradigms employed by those responsible for taking public decisions.

A look at recent years quickly shows that the list of problems that local governments are required to deal with has become longer and longer. This widening of the urban policy field is at the same time both the cause and effect of societal and political fragmentation processes, instability and acceleration of change.

New demands on government all concern the complex issue of support for local economic development, a problem which until very recently was dealt with as a national and regional sectoral policy or at local level by the simple allocation of land for use. De-industrialisation processes and the fragmentation of the economy have given local governments a series of difficult tasks in the area of economic leadership: guaranteeing territorial competitiveness by means of urban marketing policies and attracting infrastructure investment; coordinating economic development processes through a series of policies designed to keep economies flexible and varied; organising training programmes to provide a rapidly changing labour market with new skills. All this goes far beyond the traditional land-use support of the past.

There is a new demand in the field of land use changes for leadership, for people to lead complex redevelopment projects in parts of cities that have lost their former function such as factories, schools, hospitals, railways, military barracks and so on. The demand here is twofold, to build and maintain consensus around development schemes and to guarantee the public sector action which is essential if schemes are to be feasible.

While the atomisation of urban society accentuates the threat of Nimby syndromes, it is also all too evident that the implementation of major urban private sector projects depends on huge public sector investment (universities, congress centres, museums, theatres, etc.) that must be guaranteed both financially and politically, conditions that are extremely difficult to meet and forecast.

There are also other new demands to improve the quality of the environment, after the functional era of the past where the only things that mattered in housing, transport and workplaces were the numbers. There are also demands for the care of public spaces and for the quality of the environment in town centres as well as on the outskirts and these come not only from residents, but also from businesspeople who are starting to consider the quality of the environment as an important factor in the location of new businesses over and above the traditional question of mere access.

New demands are arising from the growing interest in leisure and culture due among other things to the crisis of traditional methods of socialisation and these are related to demands for changes in urban timetables and for a wider range of choice for citizens.

A new category of demands of growing importance has arisen from the problems of social exclusion and poverty that have worsened due to the weakening of primary assistance networks. Problems include access to housing and services for workers who become permanently unemployed in middle age, for single-parent families in economic difficulty, for the elderly and for the huge numbers of immigrants.

Also new, and strongly emphasised in the media in recent years, is the demand for law and order policies, rooted in processes by which individuals and families become isolated with the erosion of sociability and a sense of insecurity.

All these are demands for new policies in which the spatial dimension is either completely absent or is linked to management type decisions.

One last area of new demands made on local government is that of the need to compete for European Union or national government funds. Transfer of these funds is becoming less automatic and more competitive with funding going to integrated projects which are also able to attract private sector funds. It is a demand that selects local administrations on their ability to grasp opportunities rapidly as they arise and to abandon traditional and bureaucratic attitudes in favour of business practices and skills in complex project management. This type of demand again tends to discard the logic of a general plan.

General planning is therefore still called upon to offer an overall vision of the future of a city and an area but without any pretence of general control. It must aim at orienting and mobilising action, not by making any abstract definitions of what is in the common interest, but by bringing the actors together to participate in the actual process of defining orientations so that they are bound by agreement on specific priorities and areas of common interest. From this point of view, the overcrowding of decision-making arenas constitutes a resource rather than an obstacle and positive consensus building around future development projects is performed with the knowledge that the consensus is always ephemeral and it is a continuous activity precisely because of this.

From this viewpoint, it is important to encourage the experimentation of contexts that allow public discussion and debate of missions, priorities and tasks to be accomplished in a specific geographical area. These new contexts must address the problems of how to direct a group of public, private and third sector actors using the tools of representation, argument and persuasion (Majone 1989; Forester 1999), once the ineffectiveness of imposing a line of action by law has been recognised.

The new participatory approaches

The new participatory approaches try to cope with the problem of re-constructing and recognising an area of common concern in a fragmented and rapidly changing society. They are based on community architecture experiences and on a non-technocratic and reductive conception of urban planning. They entertain a more complex relationship and a greater dis-continuity with the more ideological and institutionalised forms of political participation of the 1970s. The formulation of these approaches is strongly pragmatic, based on a lay and pragmatic vision of planning and on what is realistically obtainable in a participatory process. The main feature is the full use of all the analytical and design capabilities possessed by the inhabitants in their daily lives. To make them feasible, participatory processes are usually organised in a series of stages running from the redefinition of the problems to the identification of the possible solutions.

The underlying philosophy and the characteristics of these participatory approaches can be summarised in a few basic points.

Participatory planning is a challenge to the profession as such, conceived of in terms of the gap that separates the expert from the ordinary people, according to the paradigms of technical rationality (Schön 1983, see above). It is a way of mobilising various kinds of actors and skills, a process of 'social probing' that emphasises the value of 'ordinary knowledge', rather than ignoring the contribution from ordinary people because it was considered as impaired (Lindblom 1990).

Participation is an antidote to the self-centred systems of service provision. It is a tool that can be used to deepen the relationship between the supply and demand of goods and services in a way that is not merely quantitative.

Citizen participation is allowed for in the first stage of a policy process (problem definition). In this case, not only does the degree of citizen involvement grow, but the 'quality' of citizen involvement also improves. It is not a matter of involving a larger number of people, but of involving the 'relevant' actors. There may in fact happen to be a larger number of people involved at the later stages of a policy process, for example in a referendum on a certain decision. However, there may be only a few people involved in the first stage of a policy process, but they are the stakeholders in that policy (the inhabitants of a neighbourhood to be rehabilitated, the users of a renovated building that will host new businesses). They are the 'relevant' actors because they possess strategic resources to make that policy possible and to make that policy effective and socially legitimate.[9]

They are mainly intellectual and informational resources because, first, the knowledge citizens possess is deep and local, different from technical and political knowledge. It is knowledge that does not usually enter into the process of preparing plans, projects and policy decisions. Second, citizens possess important design resources which make it possible to widen the field of opportunities considered, if these interact with the skills of other political and professional actors.

Participation seems an appropriate strategy when replication of standardised models is impossible and innovation must be fostered to create 'design contexts' in which all the kinds of knowledge can interact to generate new ideas and new solutions. In this sense, participation is a methodology that is more efficient than traditional methodologies in simultaneously mobilising all the cognitive resources available and stimulating interaction between all the stakeholders to solve a complex problem. Participation also seems appropriate for promoting negotiations, when there are conflicts between actors, over interests or problem definition. By anticipating these conflicts and making them explicit, it makes it possible to deal with them in a public arena and avoids the risk that they will arise in or after the implementation stage. It also encourages agreement between the actors.

Furthermore, participation is a strategy that is consistent with an integrated approach to the different dimensions of complex projects, plans and policies: physical and organisational dimensions, feasibility aspects, management problems, compatibility of different kinds of goals (general and specific). It gets close to the needs of the final recipients of policies and plan. It is not a matter of finding the right answer to a given problem, but of interpreting the problems and processes, of highlighting the available resources, facilitating the collective process of deliberation and discovering the appropriate solution.

Finally, participation is a specific technical means of building plans and policies, and also a process that fuels the self-reliance of (local) actors and helps to eliminate the practice of merely delegating power or just making claims. It produces broader involvement in the actual solution of problems and develops a sense of ownership of the plan on the side of the participants which in turn creates favourable conditions for its implementation. The communication channels set up between the various actors involved will probably remain in place as permanent (social) capital for future initiatives.

There is therefore a double sense and a double use of participation: as a means of building more effective policies because it allows a better probing of choices and as a means of reconstructing social links and of counteracting the process of fragmentation.

A final point must be stressed with regard to the strengths and weaknesses of participatory approaches. Their major strength is the consensus that is produced over a plan and this is expressed by all the actors involved, a sort of 'common heritage' consisting of knowledge, trust and communication channels, an important resource for coping with implementation problems. Their weakness is the fragility of the result: an informal planning tool that can be set aside without any problems at any moment. This weakness requires a commitment to find a number of different ways to formulate and implement a community's plans. It is, however, quite clear that this kind of approach leads inevitably to a rethinking of the entire way in which public administrations work.

New approaches to planning and the complementarity of leadership and participation

In recent years, new approaches to planning which emphasise the interactive nature of planning practices have been developed.[10] These approaches seem to be relevant to our discussion because they entail a common concern with the role of participation, the effectiveness of planning processes and the exercise of effective leadership.

At the beginning of the 1990s, Judith Innes and the California Policy Seminar Team (a research group at the Institute of Urban and Regional Development of Berkeley University) were engaged in studying cases of 'growth management' programmes (programmes developed at all levels of government to guide the location, density, timing and character of spatial growth) in California as well as in other states (Innes *et al.* 1994). They discovered that many of these programmes were conducted using *'consensus building' strategies* (long-term, face-to-face group processes which incorporate key stakeholders, including representatives of public agencies, interest groups and local governments) in order to coordinate consensually the different policies involved in a growth management programme. The growth management programmes that used consensus-building strategies – the researchers concluded – were the most successful in reaching their goals.

The interesting findings of this research concerned not only the effectiveness of the consensus building approach, but also its consequences and outcomes, and the opportunities it opened up for planning activity.

The researchers emphasised that, besides the direct results of the processes, there were by-products of this approach that had been defined as the production of 'intellectual, social and political capital'.

> Social capital, in the form of trust, norms of behaviour, and networks of communication [...]; intellectual capital, in the form of agreed upon facts, shared problem definitions, and mutual understandings [...]; political capital, in the form of alliances and agreements on

proposals [...]. These can be thought of as capital because they represent value that grows as it is used.

(Innes *et al.* 1994: ix–x)

They also contended that consensual group processes were playing a growing role in planning practice and that consensus building was appropriate for dealing with complex, multiparty, multi-issue problems, and was an important factor in redefining forms of public intervention.[11]

The so-called '*argumentative turn*' (Fischer and Forester 1993) is an attempt to redefine the nature of planning practices. It emphasises the growing attention to the role of arguing in a planner's work. This approach has a descriptive as well as a normative content. Two aspects are important. The first aspect is that it recognises the intrinsic communicative dimension of planning activity, its rhetorical function, the narrative structure of planning documents, the use of persuasion and of storytelling in group processes, the role of a planner as an 'attention shaper'. The second aspect is that this approach calls for stronger participatory forms of planning practice based on 'inclusionary argumentation', and able to cope with the problems of power relations.[12] But what kinds of skills are needed to promote 'inclusionary argumentation'? A crucial skill – according to Forester – is the capacity to listen. Listening by planners 'can work to create a sense of mutuality in place of the suspicion of a vociferous collection of individuals' (Forester 1989: 111). By listening and posing questions, planners 'probe for deeper interests, for still undisclosed but relevant information, for new ideas about possible strategies, agreements or project outcomes' (Forester 1989: 109). A crucial element, however, is the possibility of using conflicts strategically. A controversial issue can force actors to change the way they interpret it. A planner can move towards the resolution of policy disputes by reframing the problem and helping actors to reflect on what they are doing (Schön and Rein 1994).

Such a move can provide real potential for change, for expanding an opportunity, but it needs leaders to be activated. 'Such activators need not necessarily be in formal leadership positions. They may arise in all kinds of institutional settings and relationships, and are merely those with the capacity to see and articulate to others a strategic possibility' (Healey 1996, with reference to Bryson and Crosby 1992).

At the end of our brief excursus around the attempts of planning theory to redefine the nature, role and effectiveness of spatial planning, we come back to the problem of its legitimacy. It seems that today, it can no longer rely on the authority of the state or on scientific methods. Instead, it has to rely upon a call for an effective combination of new styles of planning (strategic, argumentative, participatory, inclusionary) and the exercise of leadership.

A crucial final question concerns planners themselves. Are planners, according to planning theory, the real leaders of group processes, able to build consensus, to organise participation and cooperation, to mobilise actors, to mediate conflicts, to foster social learning and to promote innovation?

If we look at some definitions of a planner's activity, we suspect that the answer is affirmative:

> Planners may position themselves in a neutral space between regulators and regulated, functioning as mediators who convene interested parties, helping them to understand one another's position, to identify common interests, or to fashion an acceptable compromise.
>
> (Schön 1982: 351)

> Planners would accordingly be more in the thick of things rather than removed from the actions that their planning under the old model was intended to guide [...]. In this entrepreneurial role planners must be publicly accountable.
>
> (Friedmann 1993: 482, 484)

> In a competitive political system [...] a planner must be a political mobilizer and develop support for his plans. In a fragmented system, the planner must become a broker–negotiator, often acting as a liaison among contending power blocks in his community.
>
> (Rabinowitz 1989: 87)

> Both organizing and mediated negotiation work require planners to exercise political judgement and skill – to be able to listen sensitively and critically, to speak cogently and persuasively, and to encourage and mobilize action.
>
> (Forester 1989: 103)

Paradoxically, after decades devoted to the demolition of false myths and to building a 'weak', post-rationalistic view of planning, planning theory seems to propose a strong, comfortable and reassuring view of planners as leaders. After having discovered (or finally admitted) the political nature of planning, planning theory has nevertheless failed to solve the dilemma of the relationship between planning and politics. To transfer authority from planning to the planner would in reality seem a contradictory and inadequate solution. It is contradictory because the planning technician is given the task of legitimating the practice of a discipline that is finding it difficult to legitimate itself in its own theory. It is inadequate because one of the characteristics of a leader is that of being accountable, but this is precisely the weakness of planners. Their accountability is very low because there is no accepted theory of how to assess the effectiveness of urban planning. In other words, how can professionals be considered accountable if we do not know how to measure the effectiveness of what they produce? There are two possible types of answer to this dilemma.

The first is an answer that seeks to highlight the technical role of planners. This answer coincides with the positions of Luigi Mazza in Italy (Mazza 1997) and in some ways with that of Dutch authors (Faludi and Van der Valk 1994). It tends to state that there is a difference between planning and politics by recognising a specific field for the former (that of zoning and regulating land use) and the formulation of urban development policies and strategies for the latter. Planning may provide the input for the construction of policies and strategies with its own technical tools (designs and plans) but the responsibility for making choices (of a political nature) lies with local political leaders for which planners provide a consultancy service. The legitimacy of planners relies on their technical expertise and their accountability has to be assessed on the capacity to produce technical answers to political problems.

The clarity in stating the responsibilities of planning and politics and placing planning activity back at the service of politicians is precisely the weak point of this position, because it returns to a vision in which urban planning is the exclusive responsibility of the institutions and of local politicians and not also, as appears increasingly more obvious, a field in which other actors (private and third sector) are mobilised and active and in which the roles played by planners are more political (mobilisation, consultation, support, supervision in processes, etc.).

The second answer sees the political character of planning in the interactive nature of planning activities where a number of different actors participate and professional and lay practices combine. Consequently, it would be inappropriate to imagine that planning activity is a professional prerogative only, as all the approaches (strategic planning, the consensus building approach and the argumentative turn, etc.) that emphasise the political role of planners tend to do. These approaches paradoxically end up by depoliticising the interaction that occurs in planning processes, because – as Pierluigi Crosta claims (Crosta 1998) – they acknowledge the central importance of interaction to the extent that it reinforces the professional perspective so that the planner is no longer isolated from politics and society but is an activist, socially interactive, a leader of participatory processes. In the final analysis, in these approaches, the people subject to planning are persuaded to participate in the process by the planners, whereby the strategy is to enrich the role and the efficiency of the planners themselves, which would in turn improve the overall effectiveness of the planning process, according to a purely professional perspective. Basically what these planning approaches share with traditional planning theories is trust in the role of the experts. This reproduces the idea of a 'scientifically guided society' which is different – again using Lindblom's terms (Lindblom 1990) – from the perspective of a 'self-guiding society'.

The position expressed by Crosta helps us to understand that the true distinction then is between a perspective that sees the complementarity between leadership and participation as something which strengthens customary models of public action (both for planning as a service to politicians and where planning becomes a political activity through the politicisation of the planner) and between one which sees participation as a means of mobilising society where one of the aims is to build the capacity to guide planning processes, or in other words to build forms of leadership. The question is whether planners should work to strengthen the position of the person fulfilling the leadership function (whether it is a local politician or the actual planner) or they should encourage forms of leadership to grow in the local community. This second possibility redefines the problem of the accountability of the planner, according to a perspective that sees his or her activity as dedicated to produce and reproduce social webs and common goods.

Notes

1 Geddes, in his city reports, wrote that 'the engineer's approach led to absurdities such as provision of water-closets that cost twice as much as the value of the houses', and that 'their road widenings and clearances were mostly unnecessary'. 'The existing roads and lanes are the past products of practical life, its movement and experience, they only need improvement' (quoted in Hall 1988: 245).
2 Donald Schön argued that

> through the mid-sixties, centralist planning proceeded in this mode. Its operations were based on two main assumptions: There is a working consensus about the content of public interest, sufficient for the setting of planning goals and objectives; and there is a system of knowledge adequate for the conduct of central planning.
>
> (Schön 1982: 353)

3 We find this explanation of the planning process in the manuals of the 1960s (Chapin 1965; McLoughlin 1968).
4 According to Innes, there is a division of labour between policy makers and planners, according to which the former set the goals, frame the problems and ask the questions, and the latter answer questions and identify the best solutions to achieve the goals (Innes 1996).
5 Melvin Webber, with his usual clarity, synthesised very well these dimensions:

> Some of us are being increasingly disenchanted by any conception of planning that accords it the capacity of authoritative expertise. We are becoming convinced that a science of planning is impossible, that social engineering is intolerable, and that the concentration of goal-setting in any sort of planning agency, however benign, is politically unacceptable.
>
> (Webber 1978: 156)

6 In another contribution, she points out that planners have learned to rely more on qualitative, interpretative inquiry than on logical deductive analysis (Innes 1995).
7 Friedmann states that 'the definition of the problem may result from linking expert with experiential knowledge in a process of mutual learning' (Friedmann 1993: 484).

8 The notion of strategic planning is one of the most ambiguous in planning literature. It means many different things. It applies e.g. both to structure plans, a development plan introduced in Britain by the Town and Country Planning Act in 1968, and to corporate plans, a planning model imported from the management literature for private firms to the public domain.

9 As Friedmann states:

> Transactive planning seeks to draw potentially affected populations into the planning process from the very beginning, when problems still need defining. It is a participatory style with its own characteristics.
>
> (Friedmann 1993: 484)

10 These new interpretations of planning activity, that have been described as a 'new paradigm', see 'planning as an interactive, communicative activity and depicts planners as deeply embedded in the fabric of community, politics and public decision-making' (Innes 1995).

11 As Friedmann states:

> Planning has ceased to be a matter to be decided by government and corporate interests without participation of what in political jargon are called stakeholders. Today, most planning issues bring fragments of 'organized civil society' to the negotiating table. Planning has, in essence, become political, a negotiable process.
>
> (Friedmann 1994: 378)

12   'Despite the fact that planners have little influence on the structure of ownership and power in this society, they can influence the conditions that render citizens able (or unable) to participate, act, and organize effectively regarding issues that affect their lives.

> (Forester 1989: 28)

References

Altshuler, A. (1965) *The City Planning Process*, Ithaca, NY: Cornell University Press.

Bryson, J. and Crosby, B. (1992) *Leadership for the Common Good*, San Francisco, CA: Jossey-Bass.

Chapin, F. S. (1965) *Urban Land Use Planning*, Urbana, IL: University of Illinois Press.

Christensen, K. (1985) 'Coping with Uncertainty in Planning', *Journal of the American Planning Association*, Vol. 51, No. 1: 63–73.

Crosta, P. L. (1998) *Politiche. Quale conoscenza per l'azione territoriale*, Milano: Franco Angeli.

Davidoff, P. (1965) 'Advocacy and Pluralism in Planning', *Journal of the American Institute of Planners*, Vol. 31, No. 4: 331–338.

Faludi, A. and Van der Valk, A. (1994) *Rule and Order. Dutch Planning Doctrine in the Twentieth Century*, Dordrecht: Kluwer.

Ferraro, G. (1998) *Rieducazione alla speranza: Patrick Geddes Planner in India, 1914–1924*, Milano: Jaca Book.

Fischer, R. and Forester, J. (eds) (1993) *The Argumentative Turn in Policy Analysis and Planning*, Durham: Duke University Press.

Forester, J. (1989) *Planning in the Face of Power*, Berkeley, CA: University of California Press.

—— (1999) *The Deliberative Practitioner: Encouraging Participatory Planning Processes*, Cambridge, MA: The MIT Press.

Friedmann, J. (1993) 'Toward a Non-Euclidean Mode of Planning', *Journal of the American Planning Association*, Vol. 59, No. 4: 482–485.

—— (1994) 'The Utility of Non-Euclidean Planning', *Journal of the American Planning Association*, Vol. 60, No. 3: 377–379.

Hall, P. (1980) *Great Planning Disasters*, London: Penguin Books.

—— (1988) *Cities of Tomorrow*, Oxford: Blackwell.

Healey, P. (1996) 'The Communicative Turn in Planning Theory and Its Implications for Spatial Strategy Formation', *Environment and Planning B*, Vol. 23, No. 2: 217–234.

Innes, J. (1990) *Knowledge and Public Policy*, New Brunswick: Transaction Books.

—— (1995) 'Planning Theory's Emerging Paradigm: Communicative Action and Interactive Practice', *Journal of Planning Education and Research*, Vol. 14, No. 3: 183–189.

—— (1996) 'Planning Through Consensus Building: A New View of the Comprehensive Planning Ideal', *Journal of the American Planning Association*, Vol. 62, No. 4: 460–472.

—— (1998) 'Information in Communicative Planning', *Journal of the American Planning Association*, Vol. 64, No. 1: 52–63.

Innes, J., Gruber, J., Neuman, M. and Thompson, R. (1994) *Coordinating Growth and Environmental Management Through Consensus Building*, Berkeley, CA: California Policy Seminar Report.

Lindblom, Ch. (1975) 'The Sociology of Planning: Thought and Social Interaction', in: M. Bornstein, (ed.) *Economic Planning, East and West*, Cambridge: Ballinger Publishing: 23–60.

—— (1990) *Inquiry and Change*, New Haven, CT: Yale University Press.

Lindblom, Ch. and Cohen, D. (1979) *Usable Knowledge*, New Haven, CT: Yale University Press.

Majone, G. (1989) *Evidence, Argument and Persuasion in the Policy Process*, New Haven, CT: Yale University Press.

Mazza, L. (1997) *Trasformazioni del piano*, Milano: Angeli.

McLoughlin, J. B. (1968) *Urban and Regional Planning: A Systems Approach*, London: Faber & Faber.

Meyerson, M. and Banfield, E. (1955) *Politics, Planning and the Public Interest*, New York: Free Press.

Pressman, J. and Wildavsky, A. (1973) *Implementation*, Berkeley, CA: University of California Press.

Rabinowitz, F. (1989) 'The Role of Negotiation in Planning, Management, and Policy Analysis', *Journal of Planning Education and Research*, Vol. 8, No. 2: 87–95.

Rittel, H. and Webber, M. M. (1973) 'Dilemmas in a General Theory of Planning', *Policy Sciences*, Vol. 4: 155–169.

Schön, D. (1971) *Beyond the Stable State*, New York: Norton.

—— (1982) 'Some of What a Planner Knows', *Journal of the American Planning Association*, Vol. 48, No. 3: 351–364.

—— (1983) *The Reflective Practitioner*, New York: Basic Books.

Schön, D. and Rein, M. (1994) *Frame Reflection. Towards the Resolution of Intractable Policy Controversies*, New York: Basic Books.

Thompson, J. D. and Tuden, A. (1959) 'Strategies, Structures and Processes of Organizational Decision', in: J. D. Thompson and J. Woodward (eds)

Comparative Studies in Administration, Pittsburgh, PA: University of Pittsburgh Press: 197–216.

Tosi, A. (1984) 'Piano e bisogni: due tradizioni di analisi', *Archivio di studi urbani e regionali*, No. 21: 29–54.

Webber, M. (1969) 'Planning in an Environment of Change: II Permissive Planning', *Town Planning Review*, Vol. 39, No. 4: 277–295.

—— (1978) 'A Difference Paradigm for Planning', in: R. Burchell and G. Sternlieb (eds) *Planning Theory in the 1980s*, New Brunswick: Rutgers University Press: 151–162.

Index